CHRIST

The Alpha and Omega

Cover: Stamatis Skliris, *Christ – the Alpha and Omega,*
egg tempera on wooden board, Athens 2007

Artwork of Fr. Stamatis Skliris. Specially painted for Bishop Athanasius's book and inspired by the representation of Christ's Resurrection in Monastery Kurbinovo (Prespa), 12th century.

Christ is ascending in "doxa" (the circle around Him) and receiving into His "doxa" inorganic creation as represented by the Mount of Olives, visible creation as represented by animals, and invisible creation as Seraphims; impersonal creation is inhypostasized in His own Person.

Historically speaking animal world was first included in Christ's "doxa" by the artists of Kurbinovo frescoes (12th century). It is from them that Panselin has borrowed the idea of including the two prophets, Elijah and Moses, in his own version of "doxa" of the Transfiguration of Christ.

CHRIST
The Alpha and Omega

Bishop Athanasius Yevtich

Edited by the St. Herman of Alaska Monastery

WESTERN AMERICAN DIOCESE
2007

Published by the
Western American Diocese of the Serbian Orthodox Church

Edited by the
St. Herman of Alaska Monastery

Contemporary Christian Thought Series, number 1

First Edition.

Prepress & printing
Interklima-grafika, Vrnjacka Banja

Address all correspondence to:
Serbian Orthodox Diocese of Western America
1621 West Garvey Avenue
Alhambra, California 91803
E-mail: info@westsrbdio.org ∗ Website: http://www.westsrbdio.org

Publishers Cataloging-in-Publication

Jevtic, Atanasije, 1938–
    Christ, the Alpha and Omega / Bishop Athanasius Yevtich.–1st ed.
    255 p. ; 23 cm.
    ISBN-13: 978-0-9719505-2-8
    ISBN-10: 0-9719505-2-0
    Includes bibliographical references and index.
    1. Jesus Christ–Person and offices. 2. Orthodox Eastern Church–Doctrines. I. Title.
BT203 .J48 2007
232–dc22 0705   2007929243

Contents

Ἀπαρχὴ Χριστός, μεσότης καὶ τελειότης· ἐν πᾶσι γὰρ ὁ ἐν τοῖς πρώτοις, ἔν τε τοῖς μέσοις καὶ τελευταίοις ὡς ἐν τοῖς πρώτοις ἐστίν· τὰ πάντα καὶ ἐν πᾶσι Χριστός

Christ is the beginning, the middle, and the end. He Who is in the first is in all, and as He is in the first so He is in the middle and the end as well—Christ is all and in all.

St. Symeon the New Theologian (*Chapters* 3.1).

Part I

1

O Gentle Light

O Gentle Light of the holy glory of the immortal, heavenly, holy, blessed Father, O Jesus Christ!

Having come to the setting of the sun, having beheld the evening light, we praise the Father, the Son, and the Holy Spirit God.

Meet it is for Thee at all times to be hymned with venerable voices, O Son of God, Giver of Life. Wherefore, the world doth glorify Thee.

This God-inspired hymn, "O Gentle Light" (Φῶς Ἱλαρόν, *Svete Tikhiy*), which we sing today at Vespers[1] and which our Church sings at every evening service, is a sacred evening hymn of the early Christian Church of the East. St. Basil the Great, the Archbishop of Caesarea and of this whole Cappadocian plateau (the central southeastern part of Asia Minor), calls this hymn the "early evening thanksgiving" (ἐπιλύχνιος εὐχαριστία). He also cites this hymn of the early Christians in his renowned work *On the Holy Spirit* (chapter 29), where he wrote about the Holy Tradition of the early Christian Church of the East, which clearly

---

[1] This article is an expanded version of a homily given at the Vespers service following the feast of the holy Apostles Peter and Paul (June 29, 1988) in a half-collapsed ancient Christian church which had been cut into volcanic rock in Cappadocia (Asia Minor), situated in a gorge called Balcanic (or Volcanic) close to the city of Ortahisar in present-day Turkey. This homily was given to Greek and Serbian students during their joint pilgrimage to the martyrdom sites of the early Christians in Greek Orthodox Cappadocia, Pontus, and the seven Ionian Churches of the Apocalypse. Martyrdom for Christ in these areas has not ceased even to this day. First published in Greek (in a book of the same title: Φῶς Ἱλαρόν [O Gentle Light], Athens, 1991) and now in Serbian, this article based on the homily is dedicated to our Greek brethren—our traveling companions through the kingdom of this world toward the Heavenly Kingdom of Christ, of Truth, of Justice, of Light, and of Freedom—but most of all to our brother in Christ, Emanuel Saris, our inspiring guide in Cappadocia, Pontus, and Ionia, and presently our benefactor and co-struggler in Zahumlje and Hercegovina.

testifies to a God-given faith in the Divinity of the Holy Spirit. St. Basil mentions that this same hymn was sung by one of the early martyrs for Christ who was from these regions of Cappadocia and Syria. According to an ancient tradition, which is mentioned by St. Basil, this hymn is attributed to the holy Hieromartyr Athenogenes, who, with his disciples, was martyred for Christ during the reign of Diocletian (at the beginning of the fourth century) on July 16, in the Armenian city of Sebaste not far from Cappadocia. St. Athenogenes was held in high esteem in Cappadocia, and his image is frequently found painted on icons in Cappadocian churches and carved in stone, as we have observed. The traces of martyrdom for Christ, which continues to this day, are evident from these churches, too.

I shall continue to cite St. Basil, who came from this region and later became the archbishop of the living Church of Christ here. In one place he declares that he himself does not know who is "the father of these words of evening thankfulness" to God. He goes on to mention a hymn of the well-known martyr, St. Athenogenes. This hymn was an evening hymn as well, which St. Athenogenes had sung to God in the presence of his disciples as a departure (ἐξιτήριον) from this life and world—"rushing through fire toward the end (τελείωσιν)," namely, going voluntarily to fiery martyrdom for Christ, to perfection (τελείωσιν) in Christ.

In any case, whoever the author of the hymn "O Gentle Light" may be, it is quite certain that it is an early Christian hymn from the second—or, at the latest, third—century in the life of the Eastern Orthodox Church (the papyrus Oxyrhynchos 178b from the third century points indirectly to this hymn). St. Basil himself says that this hymn was passed on to the early Christians "from our fathers," and it is well known that their fathers and forefathers were the Christian martyrs in the greatly persecuted Cappadocia and Pontus. Regarding the same subject, the holy Cappadocian Father adds the following: "Our fathers considered it wise not to await the gentle evening light in silence (τὴν χάριν τοῦ ἑσπερινοῦ φωτός—the agreeable nature and the beauty of the sunset), but, as soon as it appeared, they started giving thanks to God" for the peaceful and gentle light of the sunset. During St. Basil's time the Christian people of Cappadocia and all over the East chanted this hymn every evening: "All the people sang out the ancient tone," that is, they all sang this early evening hymn together to the glory of the *gentle light,* or, more exactly, to the glory of the Creator of the light: God the Father, Christ the Son of God, and God the Holy Spirit, as our hymn declares and as we shall see further.

∴

In its content and inspiration, the evening hymn "O Gentle Light" is an explicit poetic expression of the spirit of early Eastern Orthodox Christendom. It was sung to glorify God in the evening, at the setting of the sun, at the hour when a pleasant and gentle light spreads over our mother earth as the day comes to an end and the nightfall is announced, and, following the night, a new day dawns. A quiet joy, a melancholy but equally optimistic early Christian experience of light, and of the visible world and life in general as a great gift of God to us in Jesus Christ, the Son of God, is characteristic of this hymn. In this hymn, the world is experienced as a magnificent creation of God, full of light, through which the presence and action of God is tangibly felt. One should emphasize here that the first Christians, and we, too, following in their footsteps and together with them, experience the whole world—and its visible light in particular—in a directly physical way, with our senses, which pertain to the soul as well as the body. At the same time we experience this light anagogically—or, to be more exact, mystagogically—as a means of raising and leading man from this world to the Trinitarian God, from the visible universe to the invisible, spiritual Kingdom of Heaven.

Hence, the beginning of the hymn proceeds from nature, from the physical light of the early evening, which showed that the first Christians were observant, and that they beheld the beauty of the visible nature around them—for nature, like mankind, is the work of God the Creator. Such a view was shared by the Hebrews in the Bible and was also shared by the ancient Greeks.[2]

---

[2] It is certain that the Old Testament Hebrews, the Greeks, the Romans, and other nations of the East had a religious tradition to pray and chant thanksgiving to God for the evening and morning light, which is given by God. St. Hippolytus of Rome (*Apostolic Traditions* 25), St. Clement of Alexandria (*Protrepticus* 11: "Rejoice, O Light ..."), St. John Chrysostom, and others illustrate how the Hebrews sang evening

The first Christians experienced nature as a poem (ποίημα)—the *creation* of the Living and True God (as Bishop Njegosh stated: "God is occupied with creative poetry"). Thus, Christians have always seen in nature, as well as through nature, God the Creator of nature, Who is the greatest Poet, and hence they have glorified Him for all the splendors of nature.[3] Of course, they glorified God for light in particular, which has always been and still is to this day one of the most attractive mysteries of our visible world. After all, nature is ultimately light. It was seen as such by the early Christians, and after them by the Orthodox hesychasts; and it is viewed similarly by modern science. Macrophysics and microphysics point everything to light and reduce everything to light, just as the first words of the Bible say: "And God said, Let there be light: and there was light. And God saw the light, that it was good" (Gen. 1:3–4).

This is why, from its opening words, our hymn "O Gentle Light" draws one's attention to light, which is the finest, most beautiful, and deepest element of the visible nature around us. This sacred hymn in particular emphasizes the gentle and quiet light of the setting sun, which always leaves a slightly mystical impression, and has an even greater mystagogical effect, for its gentle rays indicate, reveal and also conceal the Otherworldly and the New Dawning.

Our hymn, therefore, undoubtedly has a cosmological feature, and this feature is biblical and Orthodox. In this regard, the biblical and Church experience of the world in the Old and New Testaments is closely related to human experience in antiquity.

However, there is a fundamental difference between the two with regard to their view of nature, that is, between the early Christians and

songs of thanksgiving. This Old Testament tradition, together with New Testament and early Christian tradition and liturgical practice, have their origin in the divine revelation of the Bible, and they continue in the life of the Orthodox Church and of Orthodox peoples, especially during the era of hesychasm. They continue to this day, for today the hymn "O Gentle Light" is sung at every Vespers service in the Orthodox Church. One such prayer was found in the chronicles of the Church of St. Nicholas in Lelic near Valjevo by an old soldier from the Thessalonica front, Dragica Radosav-ljevich (see the journal *Vidoslov,* vol. 2 [1994], pp. 54–56).

[3] After all, one of the early Christian writers of the Orthodox East says: "According to the early Christians, the Wisdom of God is called God's Nature and Providence" (St. Methodius of Olympus, *On the Resurrection* 2.9).

the subsequent generations of true Christians on the one hand, and the people from the classical period of history and the current Western civilization on the other. Man from both the classical and modern ages admires nature; however, he frequently worships and deifies it, particularly the light of the sun and the radiance of the stars. It is good, therefore, to be familiar with the pagan cult "Invincible Sun" (*solus invictus*).[4] Christians rejected every form of "physiolatry" and idolatry, i.e., the worship of nature, for they confessed, recognized, and liturgically revered the Living and True God only, Who has revealed and announced the Holy Only Begotten Son of God—the God-Man Jesus Christ (cf. John 1:14, 18). This radical, early Christian rejection of every other cult except the worship of the Living and True God frequently led to one's own martyrdom. This, however, did not prevent the Christians from holding nature in high regard as the work of God, and observing and revering everything in nature, and light in particular, as the breadth of God's Providence, as the place of the presence and work of the Living God, the Omnipresent One. After all, these Christians considered the world to be their home—the "House of God"—and as such they did not want to renounce it, or to leave the world in the hands of the devil or of any pseudo-gods on this earth or under the heavens. Hence, instead of the *"cosmolatry"* of the classical Greek and Roman periods or of more recent times—i.e., the cosmic or pantheistic mystique of pseudo-religions—the first Christians possessed a healthy, Orthodox *cosmology*, a correct cosmology because they considered the world and the entire universe as the work of God in Christ—the Logos and Savior of the whole cosmos.

The Bible is the inspirational source of the hymn "O Gentle Light," which contains biblical elements that are both poetic and theological,

---

[4] Some ethnologists and Marxists—Western-educated "specialists of religion" who do not know the real traditions or the national Church life of Orthodox peoples—nowadays talk about this and other similar "pagan remnants." They state, for example, that Christmas was established (December 25) as a "feast of the sun cult," even though Christmas is actually a Christian national-Church celebration of Christ God as the true "Sun of Truth"—the "East from on High," as we sing in the Christmas troparion. If they were only modestly knowledgeable about the divine services of the Orthodox Church, our partially educated ones would not speak in such an ignorant way.

such as the Psalms and the prophetic biblical hymns. The hymn begins with the vision and the experience of the gentle, pleasant, quiet light prior to the setting of the sun, which is the handiwork of the Creator of the world and of light. However, no matter how beautiful and pleasant that early evening light is, the thoughts and the heart of the early Christian are led immediately further and deeper than that: to the True Light of the world that is Christ (cf. John 1:4–9, 8:12). The early Christian poet's starting point was, therefore, the natural phenomenon—how beautiful, quiet and gentle the evening light of the setting sun glows! In this, he immediately perceived the image of the divine reality and of the personification of Christian Truth: how Christ, the Son of God, comes and shines in the world as the Gentle Light, as the "holy glory of the immortal, heavenly, holy, blessed Father."

The anagogical parallel is evident in our hymn: on the one hand there is a quiet, gentle and natural light spread over the western horizon, which shows us the beauty, the almost sanctified glory of the setting sun and evokes pleasant and grateful feelings; on the other hand, a strong Christian nostalgia is present—or, more precisely, the original, first love for Christ, the original eschatological faith and hope in Christ, which makes up the interior Christian fullness (πληροφορία πολλή), i.e., the active realization of the living and manifest *presence* and testimony of the Holy Spirit in the heart (cf. I Cor. 1:6; Heb. 6:11, 10:22), which leads one from an inferior beauty and limited sensual experience to the higher Reality. The Holy Spirit leads one to the experience of infinite Beauty, which has a divine content: the meeting with Jesus Christ, Whose Name—so dear to the early Christians, who eagerly met death for His sake (cf. Acts 5:41, 15:26)— is repeated in this hymn in each of its three stanzas.

Our poet glorifies this Name at the end of the first stanza and returns to it in each of the subsequent stanzas, each time with a new aspect and a new content. This allusion to Jesus Christ, the Son of God, in every stanza demonstrates that our hymn, besides its cosmological aspect, undoubtedly has an economic (i.e., pertaining to the household) and soteriological aspect, too. This is because the hymn includes Christ's *providential salvation* of the world and of mankind in its glorification and in its praises of God the Creator. In no way does it renounce or revoke the existing world, created by God; rather, it indicates that it is actually through Christ that the world is transfigured, enlivened, and given eternal meaning. We will see later that the soteriological experience of our poet is actually his point of departure in his cosmological perception of the world and in his glorification of God, the Giver of Light.[5]

According to this early Christian poet, this natural, gentle, evening light merely reminds us Christians of Christ, the Son of God and Savior, as the true, eternal and uncreated Gentle Light of the holy heavenly glory of the immortal God the Father (and not just simply of this visible and fragile sun). Our poet then characterizes God the Father with other attributes (which may not necessarily stem from the sight of the sunset): Heavenly, Holy, and Blessed. With these epithets, clearly derived from the Bible, our poet—together with the first Christians and with us, the unworthy contemporary Christians—demonstrates love, or infinite reverence, and gratitude to the Father of LIGHTS (ὁ Πατὴρ τῶν ΦΩΤΩΝ—in the plural, from the Epistle of St. James 1:17), for all that He is and for all that He has given to us: for light and holiness, love and blessedness, our being and life; for His act of creating and His Providence; for all the other natural and supernatural gifts and good things; and above all for the blessed Kingdom of Heaven. We give even greater thanks to the Heavenly Father for an incomparably greater and much more significant gift to the created world and mankind: His Only Begotten Son, Jesus Christ, the Giver of Life and the Savior, Who is the *Light*, that is, the *Splendor* and the *Radiance* of the eternal Glory, Sanctity and Blessedness of the Father (cf. Heb. 1:3, 5:1; I Tim. 6:16; John 12:46). We may freely declare that, for our early Christian poet, beginning

---

[5] This Christological (or Christ-like, as St. Nikolai of Zhicha and Fr. Justin Popovich of Chelije used to say) approach that the early Christians had to the world, and which present-day Orthodox Christians have to the world, has consequences that carry over into all the other areas of life and behavior of Orthodox Christian individuals and peoples, inasmuch as these have remained faithful to the living tradition and experience of the Orthodox Church. For example, in Orthodoxy even today, along with the early Christian Faith there exists a living, liturgical-ascetic (Eucharistic and hesychastic) ecological practice, that is, a correct and salvific attitude toward the human environment for the sake of both man and nature. This is because, in Orthodoxy, ecology (οἰκολογία) is basically connected with the divine Economy (Θεία Οἰκονομία) of the salvation of man and the world. This subject demands more attention; we only mention it briefly here.

with the very first stanza of his poem, theology determines cosmology and not vice versa, as we shall see further on.

In the first stanza we are also able to detect a hesychastic vision of the created world and of the divine, uncreated world; a vision which, undoubtedly, is the fruit of biblical, hesychastic practice and experience.[6] Specifically, the visible light is the "glory" of our sun. The sun reveals itself to us through the radiance of its light and we become partakers of it, that is to say, of its light. This illustration and experience of the material world leads us to a genuine, grace-filled Christian experience. Christ is the Divine Light and the Glory of the Father, and, as such, He reveals to us the Heavenly Father in His Glory, Light and Sanctity, and makes us partakers of these bright, deifying and divine attributes, of divine energy or grace (cf. II Cor. 4:6; II Peter 1:3–4).

To avoid being impersonal and indefinite, the poet hurries to complete the first stanza with the Name most beloved to all Christians, and above all to Orthodox hesychasts: Jesus Christ (the prayer "Lord Jesus Christ, Son of God ..." was the unceasing prayer of the heart of all the holy hesychasts). Without Jesus Christ, the incarnate Savior and God-man, everything we have already mentioned—the gentle evening light, the glory of the blessed Heavenly Father, and all the heavens and the earth, all the heavenly and divine worlds—would be void of meaning and significance for mankind. All of that would be distant, inaccessible, and unapproachable.

It is interesting to note that our poet first mentions the name "Jesus Christ" in the opening stanza, and only later mentions the name "Son of God." Although they are actually synonyms, we are almost certain that the poet expressed himself this way because his point of departure was not cosmology, not even theology, but rather *soteriology*. The poet, being a Christian, starts with the Gospel, the New Testament,

---

[6] The late Russian and Serbian Byzantologist Georgi Ostrogorsky was not the only one to point out (in his early work in 1931: "Svetogorski isihasti i njihovi protivnici" [Hesychasts of the Holy Mountain and their opponents]) that hesychasm was already deeply rooted in the early Christianity of the East. St. Gregory Palamas, a great theologian and leader of the hesychasts in the fourteenth century, also clearly demonstrated that Orthodox hesychasm originates from the Bible and from the early Christian faith and experience of the Church, that is to say, from divine revelation itself. Hesychastic theology is just the faithful interpretation of the biblical revelation.

and with the early Christian knowledge and experience of *salvation* in Christ, the real and personal testing and taste of the grace of *salvation* and of *new life* with God in Christ through the action of the Holy Spirit in the Church and in the hearts of the faithful. It is from this soteriological knowledge and experience that he recognizes the Divine *Gentle Light* of the Eternal Sun of Truth. This recognition occurs not only through the gentle light of the evening, but also through the historical Jesus Christ. In Jesus Christ he recognizes the Son of God, as he will address Him in the subsequent stanzas. The early Christians observed and measured everything around themselves—the morning and evening light, day and night, life and death, nature and meta-nature, time and eternity—according to the new vision they had acquired after experiencing in their hearts and beings the grace-filled knowledge of the glory of Christ the Savior, which is given as a gift of God, the Holy Spirit, Who reveals Christ as Lord and God to us (cf. I Cor. 12:3; Gal. 4:6, etc.). Hence, we may express in Orthodox theological language that not only cosmology, but also theology (actually Christology in this case) has *soteriology* as its point of departure. This is completely in the spirit of early Christianity and of any authentic Christian experience. This is also an additional reason and proof that our hymn is the work of a martyr from early Christianity. This is exactly the way it was, the way it has been, and the way it remains to this day: the experience of the Christian martyrs of early Christianity and the experience of the Gospel of the Church. Christians are foremost the disciples and the followers of Jesus Christ, the Son of God, the Lord Savior, Who revealed the Holy Trinity to us. The poet continues to sing about the Holy Trinity in the second stanza.

Our poet, along with the early Christians, first cites Jesus Christ from the Gospels: the historic, New Testament Jesus Christ (first stanza). Next, he cites the Holy Divine Trinity: the Father, the Son of God, and the Holy Spirit (second stanza). At the end of the hymn, he declares the Son of God, the Giver of Life and the Savior (third stanza), Who is the same Jesus Christ as in the first stanza and the same Son as in the second stanza. The order of the stanzas is a soteriological order derived from grace-filled experience, and not a theoretical, or even a theological order. The experience of *salvation* through grace and the *taste of a new life*—in communion with Christ—is the key to the order and to the author's approach to our hymn, "O Gentle Light."

The second stanza (which certain scholars of early Christian poetry consider to be a refrain sung by the people, whereas the chanter sang the first and the third stanzas; however, this is just an assumption without any reliable evidence)[7] demonstrates how our poet grasped Jesus Christ within the *Triadic* context, because the *Christology* (i.e., the Faith and science of Christ) of the early Church, as well as of the entire contemporary Orthodox world, has always been understood only as part of the complete and correct (orthodox) *Triadology* (i.e., the Faith and science of the Holy Trinity), and it is not separate, since Christ as the Son of God is never separated from God the Father and the Holy Spirit, not even when incarnated. This is why our poet connects the eternal *Divine Light* with Christ in the first stanza, and why he later connects this same Light with the Holy Trinity in the second stanza: "Having beheld the evening light, we praise *the Father, the Son, and the Holy Spirit God.*"

We can also say that the early Christian poet takes this evening light of the setting sun as a motive to glorify the Holy Trinity. The early Christians, and the Holy Church Fathers (e.g., St. Gregory the Theologian) following their example, considered the sun as the created icon of the Triune God, the sun's *sphere* signifying God the Father, the sun's *light* signifying the Son of God, and the sun's *warmth* signifying the Holy Spirit. We can also conclude that, in the setting of the evening light, our poet perceives the announcement of the dawning of the following day, and he anticipates the full revelation and manifestation of God as the eternal *Triune Light* from an *eschatological perspective* (cf. I Tim. 6:14; I John 1:5–7).

In this manner, the first Christians considered all of physical nature as a guide, departing as we have said from the natural light, from the created sunlight as the natural *mystagogy*, toward the glorification of God the Creator, Who, for Christians, is the Triune God, and not just a Creator-God (as, for example, in the abstract, sterile monotheism of Islam). For biblical, New Testament, Orthodox Christians, the True and Living God is more than just the Creator of all of creation. He is

---

[7] Prof. P. Chrestou, Πατρολογία (Patrology), vol. 2 (Thessalonica, 1978), p. 82.

the Triune God, the God Who is an eternal *Communion of Persons* (κοινωνία προσώπων). Hence, as He creates the world He invites us all into personal communion with Himself: a communion with the love of God the Father, with the grace of the Son, and with the Holy Spirit (cf. II Cor. 13:14).

This has already been noted in the first stanza, where, in the gentle light of the evening, the poet perceives Christ, Who announces the eternal light of the Divine Glory of the Father. The eternal relationship between the Son and the Father—that is, the relationship between two Hypostases of the Holy Trinity—is thus glorified. The poet then goes on to complete his hymn of thanksgiving (εὐχαριστήριος εὐχαριστία) to the Holy Trinity by naming also *"God the Holy Spirit."* According to St. Athanasius and the Cappadocian Holy Fathers, the Holy Spirit completes the perfection of the Holy Trinity, for only *"in the Holy Trinity is there perfection"* (ἐν τῇ Τριάδι ἡ τελείωσίς ἐστιν).[8]

In the third stanza of our hymn—a hymn which, as we mentioned above, took as its starting point the gentle light of the setting sun in the evening hours in its glorification of Christ and, through Him, of the Holy Trinity—the poet now enlarges his hymnody and doxology of Christ to include "at all times to be hymned," saying to Christ: "Meet it is for Thee at all times to be hymned!"

The poet, along with the first Christians, began offering hymns to God in the evening (the world was first created in the evening: "And the evening and the morning were the first day"—Gen. 1:5). However, since Christ and the Holy Trinity is for Christians the Creator of all times and of every hour, as He is of every creature and of the entire world, so too it is natural for Christians to emphasize that it is meet to serve, glorify, and hymn God in the evening hymn also, as it is at every hour of the day and night, every day and at all times—"now and ever and unto the ages of ages," as we are accustomed to say at every thanksgiving and glorification of the Living and True God in the Orthodox Church. The entire life of a true and pious Christian is a lifelong and unceasing glorification and hymnody to God, the Lover of mankind.

8 St. Athanasius the Great, *Letters to Serapion*; St. Basil the Great, *On the Holy Spirit*.

19

In the third stanza, the poet adds an indispensable ethical and moral element, which is a prerequisite for our full participation in our regular service and glorification of God. It is the need to glorify Christ and the Holy Trinity worthily, with "holy" or "venerable voices" (φωναῖς ὁσίαις).⁹

This means that we should glorify Christ the Savior and the Holy Trinity with a *pure* heart and a venerable (holy, God-pleasing) soul, so that out of such a heart and soul a pure, dedicated and blessed voice fit for glorification and thanksgiving can emerge. The Psalms say the same thing: "Chant unto the Lord, O you saints of His, and give thanks at the remembrance of His holiness" (29:4). The Proverbs (22:11) also confirm this: "The Lord loves holy (ὁσίας) hearts" (Septuagint). Again, in the Book of Wisdom (6:10), it is said: "For those who keep the holy precepts hallowed shall be found holy..." (οἱ φυλάξαντες ὁσίως τὰ ὅσια, ὁσιωθήσονται—those who in all holiness guard that which is holy, will themselves become holy, i.e., God-pleasing).

These words point to the fullness of our Christian position before God and toward God. This position is a theological, Christian-religious, and also ethical-moral position. In addition, it is a position of virtue, worthy of God Whom we glorify, and worthy of us, as of those who glorify and hymn God. Hence, after cosmology, Christology and Triadology, this third stanza emphasizes the ethical aspect of our Christian Faith, of our Christian being and existence, and of our Christian life and manner of glorification. In other words, Christians cannot just profess faith in Christ and the Holy Trinity divorced from a truly dedicated and blessed holy life: a holy life as is appropriate for a Christian before our Holy God. For our poem also asserts that the Spirit of God, the Holy Spirit, does not dwell in unclean souls, as is written in the Holy Scriptures (cf. Wisdom 1:4–5). This is why God calls us to salvation and to holiness, which in Christianity is one and the same thing (cf. I Peter 1:15–16).

Thus, our hymn "O Gentle Light" holds and expresses the completeness, universal fullness, and wisdom of Christian faith and life (in accor-

---

⁹ In the contemporary printed Greek Horologion (Ὡρολόγιον), φωναῖς αἰσίαις (joyful voices) is written; however, in ancient Greek manuscripts from which the Slavonic has been translated, it is written: φωναῖς ὁσίαις (venerable, holy voices). Prof. P. Chrestou confirms this in his *Πατρολογία*, vol. 2, p. 82.

dance with the rule of ancient Christendom: *lex orandi—lex credendi— lex vivendi* = rule of prayer—rule of faith—rule of life). True Christian life comes from true faith in Christ, and that faith comes from the revelation of the Personal Triune God and from the works of the Savior Jesus Christ, the Son of God and the Son of Man, through the power of the Holy Spirit.

It is exactly because of this that our poet continues the hymn, calling upon the Name: "Son of God, Giver of life!" This expression requires further explanation. We have observed in the first stanza that the poet addresses this most precious Name: Jesus Christ! The Name of Christ relates first of all to the divine Economy of salvation (θεία οἰκονομία); however, in the context of this first stanza, *"O Gentle Light of the holy glory of the immortal, heavenly, holy blessed Father,"* the divine attributes of Christ, together with His divine nature, are made evident. This divine majesty of Christ is expressed by the poet in the second stanza with the Name *Son* (*"We praise the Father, the Son, and the Holy Spirit God"*), and is expressed in fullness with the theological Name for Christ, *"Son of God,"* in the third stanza.

Along with this divine Name of Christ—*Son of God*—our early Christian poet now adds a key economic and *soteriological* feature of Christ: *"Giver of Life."* This does not refer to biological life only, which Christ as the Son of God and as Co-Creator with the Father and the Spirit gives to us, but primarily to the *new life in Christ*, a regenerated, renewed, new life of grace of the *new creature in Christ* (καινὴ κτίσις—II Cor. 5:17; Gal. 6:15; cf. Rom. 6:4). Of course, the first kind of life—namely, physical, biological life—given by Christ the Creator is included within the experience of this *new* and salvific, eternal life in Christ, the God-man and Savior. This is in fact what we meant at the beginning, when we asserted that the poet of the hymn "O Gentle Light" proceeded primarily from the daily Christian experience of a new life and salvation in Christ. The poet proceeds from *soteriology,* and from there he observes the world, nature, our human existence, the natural light of the evening sun, etc., with this new light (*"new eyes,"* according to the Orthodox hesychasts).

Our poet deliberately interchanges the names of Christ—economic (i.e., soteriological), cosmological, and theological names—as is done in many texts by the Apostles in the New Testament, by the Holy Fathers of the first centuries of Christendom, and also by the holy hymnographers of the early and later centuries of the history of the Orthodox Church. In this manner, our poet—a rare, profound and discerning Orthodox theologian—bears witness to the ancient Eastern Church's understanding of the essential Christological and soteriological truths of our Faith: that there exists a reciprocity of the attributes (ἀντίδοσις ἰδιωμάτων) of the divine and human natures of Jesus Christ, the Son of God and the Son of Man, the God-man and Savior.

The early Christian hymn "O Gentle Light" unites, hymns and glorifies all of Christ's attributes: the *Light*—the Logos, Wisdom, and Glory of God; *Jesus Christ*—the Messiah and the Savior; *Son of God*—One Hypostasis of the Holy Trinity. We repeat, however, that the poet experiences, expresses and hymns this by proceeding from the purely Christian, soteriological experience of *salvation* and of the *new life* in Christ, as his Lord, Savior, Giver of Life, Creator, and Giver of Light. God's original creation and human life, our existence on this earth and in history, have their full, immortal meaning and their eternal content only in the light of our redemption and regeneration, in the renewal of our human nature and existence through grace, in our *new life* in Christ. This is why the poet adds, "Wherefore, the world doth glorify Thee." He turns to Christ, the Son of God, once again, at the end of this wondrous evangelical hymn. With this, he wants to say that the world glorifies Christ as its Lord and Savior, as its Creator, and as the Giver of light and life in this physical existence, and even more so in that grace-filled, regenerated, renewed, divine and supernatural existence and life. That life is a holy, bright, blessed and immortal Life, and corresponds to those characteristics which Christians receive from Christ, and which He eternally possesses from the Heavenly Father. This is our newly established being and life in the Holy Spirit, in the Holy and Light-generating, Life-giving Trinity, in the Kingdom of the Father, Son, and Holy Spirit—God.[10]

---

[10] In the expression of the second stanza: "Father, Son and Holy Spirit *God*" (θεόν), the word God relates primarily to the Holy Spirit, as St. Basil the Great (*On the Holy Spirit,* chapter 29) clearly demonstrates. This is why a comma should not precede the word God (as it stands erroneously in our printed Slavonic Horologion). Poetically, however, one may also understand that the word God relates to the aforementioned Father and Son together with the Holy Spirit, namely, the entire Holy Trinity.

The beautiful hymn "O Gentle Light," sung as the first Christian evening thanksgiving to Christ, is truly a perfect liturgical song, which contains the seeds of all the basic elements of the unique, new, Christian, and universal vision of the world and man, of time and life. We are sure that its author, who was most likely one of the proto-martyrs who suffered for Christ the Lord, did not premeditate its content, but rather *sang* this song spontaneously, employing with inspiration all the cosmological, soteriological, and theological elements that we have written about. He simply "let his heart" praise and glorify the Living God in the way in which he, together with his Church, *experienced* and *knew* Him. The words of the Holy Apostle are especially appropriate here: "For prophecy never came by the will of man, but holy men of God spoke as they were moved by the Holy Spirit" (II Peter 1:21).

This short but an all-encompassing song about the Gentle Light is a poem full of light—exalting and glorifying light—which begins with glorification of the Heavenly Father through Christ in the Holy Spirit, and ends with the same glorification of God the Father in the Life-giving Son and the Life-bearing Holy Spirit, encompassing the whole world and everything that is given by God—including, most importantly, light.

In the center of our song are *man* and the human race, since Christ came into the world *for us men and our salvation*, revealing the Light-bearing Father and giving us the Holy Spirit (and Light); and through His incarnation He became our *Life* and *Light*—Unwaning and Unsetting.

In Him and with Him "your life is hidden with Christ in God" (Col. 3:3); and with Him and in Him we become "children of light" (I Thes. 5:5).

For, Φῶς Χριστοῦ φαίνει πᾶσι! — the Light of Christ enlightens all!

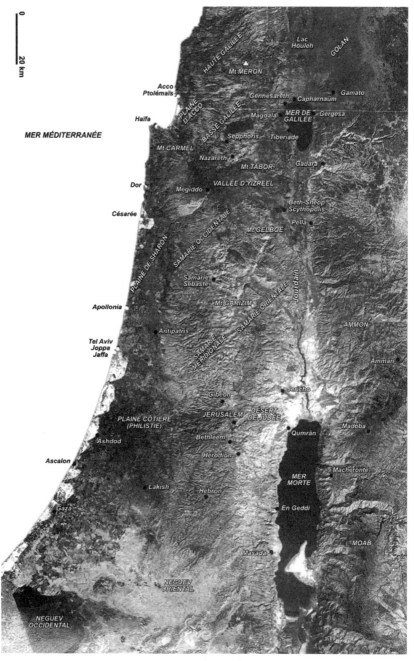

The Holy Land
(satellite view)

2
The Holy Fathers and the Holy Scriptures
Belgrade, 1990[1]

As I read the poems of John Milton, the great English poet from the seventeenth century, particularly his poems inspired by the Bible, *Paradise Lost* and *Paradise Regained,*[2] I thought about how the Holy Fathers of the ancient Eastern Orthodox Church were completely different from him in their vision and understanding of the Holy Scriptures. This applies not only to the Old Testament but to the New Testament as well—to Holy Scripture in its entirety.[3]

It is well known that, in *Paradise Lost,* Milton intended to poetically portray man's entire destiny within the framework of the biblical teaching on man's creation and his fall from and loss of Paradise, including man's sin against his Creator and God's relationship to fallen man, which is mentioned in many different passages of the Bible. In his second poem, *Paradise Regained,* Milton, according to his understanding, extolled what the Bible says about the way man regained Paradise (according to Milton it was through Christ's endurance of the temptations in the desert only!).

After reading these two otherwise magnificent poems of the great English poet—who later undoubtedly influenced our Njegosh (*Rays of the Microcosm*)[4]—in spite of all the enthusiasm for Milton's poetry, the Orthodox reader is left with the impression that Milton basically saw

---

[1] A lecture held at the Kolarac Peoples' University in Belgrade, 1990.

[2] Both poems of John Milton (1608–1674) have just recently been translated into our [Serbian] language, in two volumes, in the translation by Darko Bolfan and adaptation by Dušan Kosanović, ed. "Filip Višnjić," Belgrade, 1989.

[3] Fr. Georges Florovsky wrote on the topic *The Church Fathers and the Old Testament* in *The Student World*, vol. 32, no. 4 (1939), 281–88, reissued in *Collected Works*, vol. 1 (Belmont, Mass., 1987).

[4] See our paper *Njegosh and Patristics*, "Teološki Pogled," 1–2/1989.

and understood the Bible as a "holy book," i.e., just a *religious* book. We shall attempt to briefly explain the difference between Milton's and the Holy Fathers' approaches to the Bible.

As a Protestant, and a Calvinist at that, Milton was predominantly occupied with the Old Testament (an approach to the Bible which is frequently pursued by many Europeans and by Serbian intellectuals). In his treatment of the entire Holy Scriptures and in his very detailed interpretation of them, there is missing an essential prophetic-apostolic component in the vision and understanding of the Bible, which we find in the Holy Fathers: the Bible is divine, but it is also a human, historic-eschatological book, or, more precisely, a *divine-human* document and testimony. Milton is mostly concerned with God's creation of the world and of man. He insists mainly on the first act of creation and on the creatures; in Milton's view, God is first of all the *Creator*. Hence, he sees the Son of God primarily as the revelation of the perfection of the creative power and glory of God the Creator, a perfect work: God's *creature*, the greatest and most perfect creature, for the Son, too, is the personification of God's wisdom, power, and omnipotence. (Milton was obviously an Arian in his convictions; to this day the Arian heresy has not been completely overcome in a vast number of Protestants.)[5] He does not even consider the possibility of seeing in the very Son of God—in Christ—the center, meaning, and fullness of the whole content of the Bible, the fullness of God's revelation recorded in it. This, however, is exactly the way the Holy Scriptures have been seen and understood by the Fathers of the ancient Church and by Orthodox theologians up to today.

The Church Fathers regarded the entire Holy Scriptures and the divine revelation to which they bore witness as a document and testimony wholly turned toward the glory of the *coming Messiah*—the Christ. Consequently, however paradoxical it might sound, the Bible is above all a book about the Messiah and not primarily a "book about God." Of course, in the (Old Testament) Bible, the Messiah is God, but the emphasis is on the God of protology—God the Creator, the Almighty,

---

[5] See Fr. Justin (Popovich), "Od Arijevog do modernog evropskog arijanizma" (From Arius to Modern European Arianism), *Hrišćanski Život* (Christian Life), no. 5, 1925.

the Righteous, the Judge, etc. God's "creative work," however, is not central as a goal in itself because God's creatures have the role of proving and testifying to His power and perfection. The Bible is primarily a book about the Messiah, about the Lord's Anointed One and about His future all-encompassing Mystery, in which all of the destiny of the created world and man is perceived. Thus, the Bible is completely inclined toward eschatology. For the Church Fathers, the Bible is a book about Christ in Whom all of the divine *oikonomia* is combined and fulfilled, from the creation of the world to life eternal and the Kingdom of Heaven. The Messiah, Jesus Christ, is—as the Son of God and as the Son of Man—the God-man, the Alpha and the Omega of the entire Holy Scriptures. He is the culmination and the central knot of the Bible, the final *revelation* of God, of the world and of man—that is to say, the whole purpose of creation and of history. As a written document of this revelation, the Bible cannot be exhaustive.

However, for Milton the Bible remains primarily a *religious* text, a collection of religious and metaphysical truths, a special system of divine philosophy and less of a sacred history of God's working and leading mankind and the chosen people to Christ—"the schoolmaster to bring us to Christ," as the Apostle Paul says in Galatians 3:24. Hence, if we continue to perceive the Bible merely as a religious text that describes God's creative power and glory as revealed in His creatures, then we are constantly turned toward the *past*, toward that which already exists, toward eternal inertness with no prospect of a movement or orientation toward that which is still to come—toward the *Future*, toward the *"Last Days"* of the Messiah and His Kingdom, about which the Bible says so much. It is equally dangerous, or at best one-sided, for us to consider the Holy Scriptures only as a book dealing with the past, with that which has been completed, which has already happened, because this outlook would be a static perception of the Bible, and of the Living God of the Bible.

In contrast to this Calvinistic, fundamentalist view of the Bible as a book of eternal verdicts—of *predeterminations*, of final pronounced judgments from the past, or merely of things that have been established in the past without possible *future* changes or a *new oikonomia* (divine *arrangements* in God's *household*)—the Holy Fathers possess a *dynamic*, *eschatological* and messianic understanding of the Holy Scriptures as the *Words of God* regarding God's Anointed One and His people. The Apostles John and Paul share this patristic view of the Bible, since the center of their prophecies and evangelical messages is the Only Begotten Logos, the Incarnate Son of God, and the Church as His *Body*. Father Georges Florovsky has already observed that the Holy Fathers of the Eastern Church perceived the announcement and prefiguration (προτύπωσις) of the Incarnation of the Hypostatic Logos of God—the personified *Word of God*, Christ the Savior—in the very *words* and *events* of the Bible. Moreover, St. Maximus the Confessor, like St. Gregory of Nyssa, perceived in the very creation of the world and of man the announcement of the Incarnation and the beginning of the building of the Church.[6]

Hence, for the Holy Fathers, the Bible is first of all Christ-centered, pertaining to Christ, and therefore it is a messianic and eschatological book. This means that Holy Scripture is a *Church* book, not a "cosmic" book, that is, a book that interprets the "mysteries of the world" in a cosmic, philosophical, or religious manner. The Bible is not a religious or "theological" book in the sense of a broad theological speculation, of a theological system of truths about God, the world, and man. However, this is exactly the way Milton and many Protestants look at the Bible. In such a view, the Bible becomes just another book in a series of religious books or "sacred" religious texts, such as the books of Islam and other world religions. The Bible is not the *Koran*, or the *Talmud*, or even merely the Hebrew *Torah*. Here one needs only to remember Christ's words in Luke 24:44: "All things must be fulfilled, which were written in the *law* of Moses, and in the *prophets*, and in the *psalms*, concerning Me"—that is, concerning the Messiah.

In his poem *Paradise Lost*, Milton views the Bible primarily as a religious, philosophical, and metaphysical story about man and his destiny; and in that destiny there is little space for the personality of the Messiah, Christ the Savior. Our Serbian poet, Bishop Njegosh, in his poem *Rays of the Microcosm*, which is to some extent similar to John Milton's poem mentioned earlier, partially succumbed to the influence of Milton and other philosophers and poets who similarly viewed and

---

[6] St. Maximus the Confessor, *To Thalassius* 60 (PG 90:620–25); St. Gregory of Nyssa (PG 44:1049).

interpreted the fate of man and mankind predominantly in a theological-cosmological manner. However, in the last part of *Rays of the Microcosm,* Njegosh, an Orthodox bishop and a man with Church experience through which he observed both the Bible and its pronouncements about man, made a radical turn toward the eschatological Messiah, Christ Incarnate and Resurrected, Who in terms of Milton's logic regarding justice, unexpectedly enters into human history and saves man personally through Himself, thus changing man's established fate, which until then was harsh and inescapable because of sin.[7]

However, a much better explanation of the fate of mankind, one that is also far more faithful to the Bible than Milton's work, is found in the sacred poetry of St. Ephraim the Syrian, the great Church poet of the fourth century. While Milton sees Paradise and man's destiny somewhere in the *past,* St. Ephraim sees man's Paradise, even the one described in the very first pages of the Bible, in the *future.* In his poem *Paradise Regained,* Milton perceives the regaining of Paradise only in the religious and moral battle of Christ against Satan that takes place in the desert during Christ's temptations. He does not notice that Paradise, both in the Bible and for the Holy Fathers, is actually Christ Himself: a fact which was seen and extolled by St. Ephraim the Syrian. In his *Hymns on Paradise,* St. Ephraim talks about man's *lamentation of Paradise;* however, when this holy Church Father sees nostalgia in the repentant grief for Paradise, it is a nostalgia that looks not back at the past but to the future. In St. Ephraim's writings, the eschatological premonition as well as the foretaste of Paradise—of Christ—prevails. According to St. Ephraim, Paradise is found in the very anthropological and cosmological—or, more precisely, in the Christ-like—structure of the world; it is the center and culmination of all that was created, of the spiritual and material cosmos created by God for man; and it is Christ, the Messiah, Who is the *Tree of Life,* the Temple, and God's Church for men, the Garden or the Land of the Living. This is the all-encompassing *"Mystery of Christ"* of which the Apostle Paul and St. Maximus the Confessor spoke.[8] Thus, in the Holy Fathers' vision and experience of Paradise, the beginning and the end of

---

[7] See more about this in the article mentioned in footnote 3.

[8] Romans 16:25; Eph. 3:3, 9; Col. 1:27, 4:3; St. Maximus the Confessor, *To Thalassius* 60 (PG 90:620–25).

the Bible coincide, the Book about the Creation and the Book about the Revelation, and in the center of the one and the other is the Tree of Life—Christ, the Creator and the Savior of man, the Incarnate and the Resurrected Glory of man and of all God's creation.

Milton does not simply proceed onwards from the very first pages of the Bible, from the creation of man and from his fateful fall in Paradise, but instead he essentially remains there, with an outlook of predetermination (Calvinists believe in God's absolute predetermination, in the *predestination* of man, in a fate of mankind that has already been predetermined), where the destruction and salvation of each man is virtually independent of the Person of Jesus Christ the Savior, of His Body and of His action as the God-man, of His philanthropic Providence as the immortal Eucharistic communion of man in the Holy Spirit, which is Paradise and the Kingdom of God. We may freely say that Milton almost completely sidesteps Christ in his theology and anthropology. Milton does not have a biblical, patristic, or true Church Christology and soteriology. This is because, in our opinion, Milton neither had nor was able to sense the living Church-liturgical experience and the life in Christ, and therefore the Holy Scriptures remained somewhat remote, accessible only at the level of a holy, universally religious book and as a theological text. It appears, therefore, as if Milton was left with reading the Bible merely as a holy book of the Old Testament Synagogue, and not as a sacred *liturgical* book of the New Testament Church.

The Holy Fathers' approach to the Bible stands in stark contrast to Milton's approach. The former approach is characterized, for example, by what St. Ignatius the God-bearer said to the Jews of his time (the end of first century). When the Jews were disputing Christ as the Messiah in his presence, because, allegedly, the *"archives"* (i.e., the Old Testament texts of the Bible) did not bear witness to Him, St. Ignatius answered them without any reservations: "For me the *archives* [i.e., the biblical documentations] are Jesus Christ, His Cross, death, and Resurrection, and faith in Him and through Him constitute the sacred (inviolable) archive... However, this is the Prophecy and the Gospel: the *Coming* (Παρουσία) of the Savior, our Lord Jesus Christ, His Passion and Resurrection—the synthesis and perfection of immortality."[9]

---

[9]   St. Ignatius of Antioch, Letter to the Philadelphians 8–9.

When reading Milton and the Holy Fathers concurrently, it becomes obvious that for this renowned Protestant theologian and poet, the Bible is by itself and unto itself a "religious text." For the Holy Fathers, however, the Bible is primarily a *Church* document, and consequently a testament and witness of the *"community of Israel"*—both the old and the new one (cf. Eph. 2:12)—i.e., the Church that God leads as His people through the history of salvation to the future Kingdom. Hence, the Holy Fathers consider the Bible understandable only within the Church. The Church is the sole guarantor of the correct and comprehensive understanding of the Holy Scriptures. She is the normal and natural atmosphere, the pulsation of life which the Holy Scriptures breathe, and in which they exist as a living document of the divine *Testament* and *union*, as the *Prophecy*, as the *Gospel*, and the *Good News* that bears witness to the living relationship and reciprocal actions between God and His people, between the living God and man. The Holy Scriptures primarily originated as the text of a living community and have remained as a testimonial book of the union and community of God and man in the Church, that is, the Body of Christ, the eschatological union of man with God in the Holy Spirit. The convergent and universal Person of this union is the Messiah—Christ.

Although the Old Testament originated "before Christ," the Holy Fathers consider that it still testifies to and speaks directly about Christ the Messiah. Therefore, whoever does not recognize the Messiah in Christ, the Anointed One of the Lord, actually betrays the Old Testament, fails to comprehend it; a veil remains on his face, as the Apostle Paul says (cf. II Cor. 3:15–16). That is why St. Paul understood and interpreted the entire Old Testament *Christologically*, as Christ-centered. According to the Protestant understanding, Paul interpreted the Old Testament in a "self-willed" way, i.e., not as a Jew but as a Christian. (That is why the Jews who have remained steadfast to Moses do not accept that Moses testified of Christ; hence they have also never tolerated Paul). However, St. Paul's interpretation and vision of the Old Testament, in his epistles to the Romans and to the Hebrews in particular, represent the lawful, Christological and *Christ-centered* understanding of the entire Bible, of all the events described therein, in the spirit of the divine revelation. Paul sees the *Incarnate* Christ through-

31

out the whole Old Testament, i.e., that which St. Maximus the Confessor would later express in the same words, in St. Paul's words: the entire Old Testament is a shadow of the New one (cf. Col. 2:17; Heb. 8:5 and 10:1). The New Testament is the icon of eschatological reality, and *truth* is "the state of the awakening reality," that is, the *Kingdom of Heaven*.[10] This perception pertaining to St. Paul points to the *dynamic motion* into the future, in the messianic direction of the whole sacred history described in the Bible, so that the entire Old Testament actually aspires toward the New, and the New Testament gravitates toward the eschatological Kingdom of God.

Earlier, St. Gregory the Theologian had expressed the same thought as St. Maximus—about the dynamic motion of the Old Testament toward the New and the gravitation of both toward the eschatological Kingdom of God—in his renowned *Theological Orations*. In this work, he says that the Old Testament clearly preached the Father, along with the Son less clearly, and the New Testament revealed the Son openly and only announced the Holy Spirit, and, from there the period of the Holy Spirit and a clearer experience of Him commence.[11] Regarding this interpretation of the holy Theologian about the dynamic movement toward the eschatology of sacred history recorded in the Bible, one should observe that the *Holy Spirit* Himself is, in fact, the key to the correct and complete interpretation of the Holy Scriptures, for the Holy Scriptures originated as a *prophecy* by the Spirit (cf. II Peter 1:21), and it is possible only in the Spirit, the Comforter, to acquire a full understanding of the words, the truth, the facts, and the mysteries of God which were spoken of and described in the Bible (John 16:13, 14:26). In addition to this point, one must emphasize that these, however, are merely records of the Lord's *testimonies*, messages, and prophecies of the Holy Spirit; they are accounts in human language of the wondrous deeds and actions of God. One must always keep in mind that in all of God's words and deeds there is always something that

---

[10] St. Maximus the Confessor, *Scholia on St. Dionysius the Areopagite: On the Ecclesial Hierarchy* 3.32 (PG 4:137).

[11] *Fifth Theological Oration* (*Oration* 31) 26. Somewhat earlier, St. Gregory also spoke of "three earthquakes," which likewise signify the dynamic direction of the entire biblical history toward the *eschaton*.

clearly surpasses all the limitations of history and all the possible ways of description, which are limited by human words, expressions, and images. This is why the Apostle Paul says: "O the depth of the riches both of the wisdom and knowledge of God! How unsearchable are His judgments, and His ways past finding out! For who has known the mind of the Lord? Or who has been His counselor?" (Rom. 11:33–34).

After all, a long time before the other Holy Fathers, St. John the Theologian, the Seer of the Mysteries of the Revelation, said the same: "And the Spirit and the bride [*the Church*] say, 'Come!' ... Even so, come, Lord Jesus!" (Rev. 22:17, 20), showing that historically *live persons* such as the Prophets and the Apostles spoke and bore witness, even as the Church does today as the eschatological community of the people of God. This eschatological community manifests itself in a most tangible way in its liturgical assembly; therefore, one must observe, as the Holy Fathers did, that Holy Scripture is above all a *liturgical* book for a *liturgical* (i.e., eschatological) community.

For this reason, we Orthodox listen to and best understand the Holy Scriptures in the context of the Holy Eucharist (*Liturgy*), that is, within the framework of the *living Church* (*eschatological*) community that gathers for Liturgy and for union in the Messiah—in the God-man Christ—through the grace of the Holy Spirit, to the glory of God the Father. All the works and mysteries (*mystagogies*) that are carried out in the Liturgy explain to us in action the same things that the words of Holy Scripture tell us.[12] Thus, even a simple person, an ordinary Christian, can comprehend the full meaning of the Holy Scriptures, and this is not just given to the educated "men of letters" (nowadays, the biblical scholars), whom Christ rightfully criticized during His time on earth because they had blocked and alienated the simple-hearted people from the true meaning of the Holy Scriptures. This is why St. Gregory the Theologian said fittingly that Holy Scripture is "a river across which a lamb can swim but in which an elephant drowns."

---

[12] This is why St. Irenaeus of Lyons said: "Our belief (*comprehension*) is in agreement with the Eucharist, and the Eucharist confirms our belief" (*Against Heresies* 4.18.5). St. Dionysius the Areopagite, St. Maximus the Confessor, St. Nicholas Cabasilas, and other Fathers who interpret the Liturgy make similar statements.

To better demonstrate how the Holy Fathers viewed the Holy Scriptures, we will cite a passage from the works of St. Maximus the Confessor: "The mystery of the Incarnation of the Logos (Christ) contains the meaning (τὴν δύναμιν—the dynamic power and meaning) of all the riddles and types (figures) in Holy Scripture, as well as the knowledge of created things sensible and intelligible. And he who comes to perceive the mystery of the Cross and Burial (of Christ) perceives the reasons (τοὺς λόγους—principles, meanings) of the abovementioned. But he who is initiated into the ineffable meaning of the Resurrection perceives the purpose for which God first established everything."[13]

This passage by St. Maximus, opulent in its biblical and theological content, requires much more discussion in order to cover the accurate view of the Holy Scriptures by the Holy Fathers. It will be mentioned here, however, that such a view of the Holy Scriptures—one that is closely tied to the "Mystery of Christ" (and this is the essence of the *messianic mystery*)—clearly displays the messianic dynamics, the eschatological motion of everything in the Bible toward the Kingdom of God: from the creation of the world, through the Old Testament to the New Testament and the Resurrection, i.e., to the *eschaton*. St. Maximus clearly demonstrates that the Incarnation of Christ—that is, Christ as the Messiah and God-man—is the key to understanding all that is in the Holy Scriptures, and all that is in God's entire creation. Without Christ, everything in the Bible and in all of creation remains as a "riddle" and "shadow" of an inaccessible and incomprehensible reality. This is the reason the Apostle Paul talks about the observance of the Spirit and not of the "letter" (*the literal*) in the Bible, for the letter kills but the Spirit alone gives life (cf. II Cor. 3:6). Therefore, only in the mystery of the Messiah-Christ does one find the spirit and meaning of the Bible, and understand all that is written in the Bible. We understand Holy Scripture as the word, the image (*picture*), the symbol, and the history and description of events that always refer to the Messiah, to the messianic times, to the messianic people, to the messianic eschatological Kingdom. History merely begins here on earth. St. Maximus says the same about the whole creation of the cosmos, and about God's entire

---

[13] *Two Hundred Texts on Theology and the Incarnate Dispensation of the Son of God* 1.66 (PG 90:1108).

creation. According to St. Maximus, everything, ontologically and historically, aspires toward Christ; everything leads to Christ.

We will add one more thought to this central one of St. Maximus: the beginning of building a house does not establish the final building plan and the conclusion thereof, but, vice versa: it is the *end* that actually sets the *beginning*, i.e., the final goal and the designation of the edifice is decisive for both the beginning and the construction of the house. When we apply this to the *divine oikonomia* of the creation and salvation of the world, says St. Maximus, then it is the *Omega* (the End) Who determines the *Alpha* (the Beginning), and not vice versa, although *Alpha* is at the beginning and *Omega* is at the end. This means that Christ, the Messiah, is the key to and the measure of everything. Since Christ is God's Alpha and God's Omega of the world and of the entire divine system of the world and mankind (cf. Rev. 1:4, 8; 22:13), He as God-man is the key to understanding the entire sacred biblical history and eschatology. This is the primary *dynamic* characteristic of the Holy Scriptures: a messianic, Christological, and eschatological direction of the Scriptures. This is the biblical dynamism that St. Maximus pointed out, a dynamism that actually has a Theophany-like, a liturgical, and a Christological spirit, as well as character and content (see the complete *Mystagogy* of St. Maximus).

Such an approach to the Holy Scriptures by the Holy Fathers of the Eastern Church and of Orthodoxy up to today in no way disparages the significance and importance of the very words and events in the Holy Scriptures; rather it merely puts them in their normal, living Church context, placing them in the very being of the Church organism, as the living Body of the Incarnate Word—God's Logos—Who is the content, the purpose, the words, and the events of the Holy Scriptures. The Holy Scriptures understood in this manner, then, as the living word of God, are not separate from the hypostatic Word of God, and so the actual biblical, prophetic, and apostolic words and messages *liturgize* (i.e., *function*) as a description of personal, messianic and divine acts, and provide facts about God and God's people. "That which was from the beginning, which we have heard, which we have seen with our eyes, which we have looked at and our hands have touched—this we proclaim concerning the Word of life" (I John 1:1), says the Apostle John.

This understanding is similar with regard to Orthodox icons. In the Orthodox Church and in the Liturgy, holy icons are not merely pictures and works of art, but are above all dogmatic testimonies. They are liturgical documents of the living faith and of the experience of the Church of all the saints in communion with the only Holy One, Jesus Christ, as the first and as the prototype of God-like man and of all God's children. The prophets and the apostles, the martyrs and the saints, the choirs of angels and archangels, the Theotokos (as, for example, in the icon "More Spacious than the Heavens"), and among them and in the midst of them Christ as the Land of the Living, as the Only Begotten Son of God among His brothers and the children of the Heavenly Father, illumined and made God-like through the grace of the Life-giving Spirit—such is an Orthodox church with icons and frescoes. However, their full meaning and function are obtained only in the Holy Liturgy that is celebrated in the church and joins the heavenly and earthly community of saints. In such an atmosphere and environment, within the *womb* of the Church, which is alive and gives birth (*rebirth*) to living people for the eternal Kingdom of God,[14] the Holy Scriptures function and are comprehended properly and correctly as the living Word of the Living God to His people, assembled around Christ, incorporated into His divine-human Body, into the heavenly and earthly Church of the Living God, the pillar and foundation of Truth (cf. I Tim. 3:15–16).

The mistake of the Jews, especially during Christ's time on earth, and of Milton, too, consisted of their separating and isolating the Holy Scriptures from Christ as the Messiah and Son of God; and thus they lost the correct notion and understanding of the Holy Scriptures, of their true and abundant knowledge and power. "You are in error because you do not know the Scriptures or the power of God," the Savior said (Mark 12:24) to the Hebrew Pharisees and Scribes, and to all the Talmud scholars (biblical scholars of every orientation, interpreters of the Word of God without Christ, the Logos). Islam's failure to see this, and Islam's misfortune, is even greater because of the regression it made

---

[14] See the *Symposium* (*Banquet*) of St. Methodius of Olympus, and our text "Pravoslavna vera i život" (Orthodox faith and life) in the book *Traganje za Hristom* (Searching for Christ) (Belgrade, 1989).

after Christ by ostensibly returning back to Abraham, actually to Esau and to Hagar, to the earthly Mount of Sinai in Arabia, which the Apostle Paul spoke of prophetically and with great discernment (in the third and fourth chapters of his Epistle to the Galatians).

As we thus experience Holy Scripture as the living Word of God in the living context of the Church, we Orthodox sense it as do the Holy Fathers, as the "Spirit Who gives life," as the "words of eternal life," as "spirit and life" (John 6:63, 68), and as what Christ spoke of in His famous sermon in Capernaum, when He called Himself the "Bread of Life" (John 6), for in Him are both the *Word* and the *Bread*—that is, the *Holy Scriptures* and the *Liturgy*—inseparable because both the one and the other are the work of the Holy Spirit. After all, the holy Apostles too, as well as the holy Prophets before them, wrote the Holy Scriptures inspired and enlivened by the Holy Spirit (cf. II Peter 1:21). Later on, the same Holy Spirit led and guided (cf. John 16:13) the Apostles of the New Testament and the holy Church Fathers in the correct and complete understanding of the Holy Scriptures of the Old and New Testaments, since the writers and interpreters of the Holy Scriptures lived a life in one and the same atmosphere as all of God's people—the Church of Sinai and of Zion, that is, the Church of the New Testament and the eschatological Church. The Apostle Paul also testifies to us Christians that, without the Holy Spirit, we are not able to pray as we should. The Holy Spirit teaches, inspires, and guides us, and what is more He Himself prays in us "with groans that words cannot express" (Rom. 8:26). Likewise, we cannot understand or explain the Holy Scriptures on our own, without the "Life-creating Holy Spirit to guide and illumine us," as St. Symeon the New Theologian says.[15]

In conclusion, we will add something that is very significant in the patristic approach to the Bible. Frankly speaking, the Holy Scriptures have one intrinsic "weakness." According to the Holy Fathers, this inherently "weak" spot is not merely due to the limitation and to the inability of human language to encapsulate and express divine Truth and the reality of the *eschaton;* this "weakness" is also due to the Bible's dependency on the future, on the fullness of God's revelation which God

---

[15] *Ethical Sermons* 9.

has kept for Himself only and for His Kingdom. This is what St. Paul says of himself not only as an Apostle but as a man, too: "But we have this treasure in earthen vessels, that the excellence of the power may be of God and not of us" (II Cor. 4:7). This applies even more so to the text of the Holy Scriptures, since it is a book which can in no wise replace the Person of the Living God and one's living relationship with Him. That is why St. John Chrysostom can calmly say, particularly in the introduction to his interpretation of the Gospel according to St. Matthew, that the Holy Scriptures have been given to mankind as an act of God's condescension toward our weakness, and that the men and women of God who have the Spirit of God are not even in need of the Scriptures.[16]

Holy Scripture, as the divine word and book given to us human beings, is in its entirety dependent "on the hope in Christ" (Rom 8:24; Col. 1:5, 27, etc.). Thus, in relation to all other texts and books of this world, this text carries us onto another level altogether. I would go so far as to say that Holy Scripture takes us to an *insecure security*, which is not comparable to insecurities or securities of this world and time. After all, the Holy Fathers spoke about the "weakness of the Godhead (God Who has the Power)" (θεαρχικὴ ἀσθένεια)[17] of Christ the Lord Himself, as the Savior; that is, they emphasized not so much His omnipotence (as Milton did when he spoke about God) as His "wounds" and His "infirmities," which are salvific for us and by which we are saved and are healed (Isaiah 53). The "weakness" of Holy Scripture is likewise evident when one has drawn near to Scripture and has become acquainted with it, for one is not forcefully being imposed upon, not even by the virtue of Scripture's Truth and eternal Justice; that is, a person is not forced to accept it, which is, however, often the case with many logical truths and axioms of this world. In spirit and character, the Holy Scriptures resemble the "gentle breeze" in the Prophecy of Elijah, or the "breath of life" in the Prophecy of Ezekiel that revived the dead and the dry bones of Israel. This is the humble and modest, awe-inspiring and fear-inspiring attitude of the Bible toward us, as well as ours toward the holy Word of God. This is that "fear of God," which according to the Bible is the "be-

---

[16] Regarding this refer to our work "Sveti Sava kao prosvetitelj" (St. Sava as enlightener), in *Glasnik SPC,* 1980, vol. 2.

[17] St. Dionysius the Areopagite and St. John Damascene.

ginning of wisdom" of both man and God (Prov. 1:7): and, the Wisdom of God, according to the Bible, is Christ (cf. I Cor. 1:24). Our Orthodox faithful possess exactly this kind of awe-inspiring respect toward the Holy Scriptures, especially toward the Gospels, but without creating a cult around them. Our pious people listen to and learn the Holy Scriptures primarily from the Holy Liturgy as part of the church services. That is why the best patristic commentaries on the Holy Scriptures are liturgical *sermons*, spoken to a live church community, to the people of God, to whom even today God speaks with His Spirit through the prophets. This is the source of all church hymnography, of all the songs and hymns of our church services, which constitute an excellent, practical, and poetically inspired interpretation of the Holy Scriptures. (It is characteristic that the great Fathers, the interpreters of the Bible, were actually more often than not great liturgists and hymnographers of the Orthodox Church).

In addition, it must be said that the patristic approach to the Holy Scriptures was never confined to allegorical or literal interpretations, but included something more than both, and that is typological, mystagogical, and *liturgical* interpretations, of which the *Epistles* of St. Ignatius of Antioch, the works of St. Ireneaus of Lyons, the *Theological* and the *Festal* works of St. Gregory the Theologian, the work of St. Basil the Great *On the Holy Spirit*, St. John Chrysostom's *Sermons*, the *Interpretation of John's Gospel* by St. Cyril of Alexandria, the *Mystagogy* by St. Maximus, the *Catechism* of St. Symeon the New Theologian, among others, constitute the best examples. Of course, all this in no way belittles or marginalizes the need for modern biblical sciences: archeology, history, philology and other sciences helpful to biblical hermeneutics. However, the sum of all of this can show only "the binding covers of the Holy Scriptures," as Fr. Justin Popovich, one of the greatest contemporary neo-patristic interpreters of the Holy Scriptures, sometimes said,[18] unless the central link of the Holy Scriptures with Christ and His Body—the Church—is fully understood.

For the Holy Fathers, the interpretation of the Holy Scriptures is first of all the initiation into and revelation of the *Great Mystery of*

---

[18] See, in numerous volumes, his *Tumačenje Jevandjelja i Poslanica* (Commentary on the Gospels and Epistles).

Christ, which is spoken of particularly by the Apostle Paul and by St. Maximus the Confessor. The Liturgy in our Church is the presence and actualization of this Mystery. In other words, up to today the Orthodox approach to the Holy Scriptures and their interpretation by the Holy Fathers is the approach to the living Gospel of Christ—or, to be even more exact and faithful to the Holy Fathers, it is the approach to the living Christ the God-man, Who is the First and Last, the personal and all-encompassing Gospel of the Lord.

For what is the Gospel? According to the words of St. Maximus the Confessor, repeated literally also by St. Gregory Palamas: "This is the Gospel of the Lord, God's message to mankind through the Incarnate Son, Who rewards those who believe in Him: the uncreated deification."[19] Thus, the Holy Scriptures are, in their entirety, the *Gospel of Christ,* inseparable from the very Incarnation of God's Logos, the Messiah and the God-man Christ, Who is always in His Body and with His Body. This Body is the Church, the community of God the Word, and of the rational children of God, Christ's brothers.

[19]   *To Thalassius* and PG 150.

3

Christ—The Land of the Living

(*The Synodikon of Orthodoxy*)[1]

When you come to Constantinople, the ancient metropolis of the Orthodox Byzantine Empire, from where we Serbs were also christened, you will find many churches and monasteries, among which are the churches of Hagia Sophia and St. Irene, and also the Monastery of *Chora*, which means "Land." This monastery is named Chora because it is dedicated to Christ—the Land of the Living. Naturally, under the Turks it is now a museum; it used to be a Muslim mosque for many centuries. There is a minaret even today, but the Christian soul, the Orthodox architecture, mosaics, and icon and fresco paintings of this monastery—of this Orthodox church of the Monastery of Chora, the Land of the Living—have remained.

At the entrance of the monastery, above the door, is a large mosaic image of Christ down to the mid-torso. Dating from the beginning of the fourteenth century, when Theodore Metochites (a friend of King Milutin of Serbia and a facilitator of the king's marriage to Simonida) was building this monastery, this icon is named Christ, ἡ Χώρα τῶν ζώντων—the Land of the Living. When you enter the narthex you are welcomed by beautiful mosaics. To the right, in the chapel for the reposed (the mausoleum chapel), you see a magnificent fresco of the Resurrection from the thirteenth century. When you enter the temple itself (the nave) you are welcomed by a beautiful mosaic of the Theotokos holding Christ in her arms. This icon is called the Theotokos, ἡ Χώρα τοῦ Ἀχωρήτου—"the Placement of the One that cannot be placed," i.e., "the Land that placed the One Who is the Land of all the Living"—Christ.

[1] A talk given for a television broadcast of Republika Srpska, on Saturday, November 4, 1995.

Thus, in this monastery we see the entire Assembly of Orthodoxy, the Synodikon of Orthodoxy. This is the core of our Orthodox Faith, and that is why we wish to speak about it. The central point of our Faith is Christ as the Land of the Living, as the Living Space, which God was well pleased to give us in order that we may live eternally in Him, with Him, around Him, before Him, together with Him, and with one another.

In our times, humanity faces many problems, including greater and greater ecological problems, which threaten human living space. Thus, this topic of Christ as the Land of the Living is very pertinent for today.

Christ is the real Living Space of all people. Christ is God Who incarnated and became man; Christ is the God-man. God made this world in such a way as to become a community in His Son, an assembly of the children and the whole family of God, and of everything that is in the House of God. For this reason, the whole world was made to be the Land of the Living. God did not create death; He did not create anyone for death, but for life, and thus He also created a living space. For this reason He created the universe or cosmos (*vselenny* in Slavonic, κόσμος, τὸ σύμπαν in Greek). The time of human life, which is directed toward eternity, is appointed for living, working, and communing with others in this living space.

When we say that Christ is the Land of the Living, and when we speak of the Assembly of Orthodoxy, we remind ourselves of the core of our Faith: that our God is the Holy Trinity, the Eternal Assembly, the Space for all of us. Our God is an Assembly, since He is the Holy Trinity. It is not without reason that the Bible (cf. Gen. 1:26; Is. 9:6) says that God, in His Pre-eternal Counsel or Assembly, took counsel and made an agreement to create the world, and initiated the creation and further direction of the world, the salvation and celebration of the world, and the world's immortalization and externalization—that is, its eternal life—in His Beloved Son, in Whom He laid the foundation of humanity. Thus, it was by Christ and for Christ that all things were created (cf. Col. 1:16).

When we say "Christ," we consider the fact that in our Orthodox faith He is the incarnate God and that we already are in Him and with Him. Christ is not only the Second Divine Person of the Holy Trinity, the Son of God and Eternal God, but He is at the same time the Son of Man. He is One of us, the First among us. He is amidst us, and as the God-man He gathers us together in Himself. He collects us; He makes us part of the Assembly; He introduces all existing creation, directed toward eternal life, to the Land of the Living. These are the essential truths of our Faith. This is the ontological summation of the Orthodox Faith. Our Faith is not only that God exists and that He is almighty, and that He is the Creator of the world, and that He rules the world and gives rewards or punishments. The essence of our Faith is the Holy Trinity, as the Eternal Community, as the Eternal Assembly of Three Eternal Divine Persons in a communion (κοινωνία) of divine nature, being, essence, life, love, blessedness, and immortality. This is the Eternal Land of the Living, for which all of us people long, consciously or unconsciously. Even when we stray and go off the path, our nostalgia for this Land draws us there. We are often not aware of it; we often act against it. Of course, we should freely take part in this Land, since man was created according to the image of the Holy Trinity. Man was also made as a small assembly, an assembly in himself and an assembly with all people, all beings and all things created, an assembly with "all the saints," as the Holy Apostle Paul says (cf. Eph. 3:18). Man is a small, living and walking assembly, and he wants to live in an assembly, in community and togetherness.

Thus, man is a being of communion, of togetherness, of convocation. However, he is crucified between his individuality, particularity, or distinctiveness on the one hand, and his basic, essential side or dimension on the other: to be in togetherness with everyone, to live a life of participation and togetherness with the Other and the others. For this reason God attached us to Himself as to a Fountain and Heart, and He also attached us to the world around us. We should not wonder about this latter fact, though materialists and atheists misrepresent it. Man is a part of the mineral, vegetable and animal worlds, for he was placed by God in the heart of the world, and the meaning and center of the world lies in man. Since man is a synthesis of everything spiritual and material, in him the entire world is supposed to be led into the Land of the Living, into Christ. Christ became man for this purpose, and as the God-man He fulfilled this purpose and is fulfilling it.

43

God not only took the first step in creating man, but He also came and was incarnated; He became man like us, lived our life, lived within man's nature and environment, and "settled himself" into human nature for all eternity, into the human being, human life, human community. This is indeed Christ's Church, and the Land of the Living is Christ's Church, the real, true, genuine, authentic Church; and for this reason it is called the Catholic (καθολική, *sobornaya*), Orthodox Church. The character of the Church as orthodox and catholic is not merely some confessional feature. As a matter of fact, it is ontological and essential. We speak of the Church as such just as we speak of a man as a living being, not to set him apart from other beings, but to express his life, dynamics, movement, work, and love. When we say that the Church is catholic and orthodox, this is not what is today being implied by some individuals who use the term "orthodox": e.g., the "orthodox" Jew who killed Yitzhak Rabin, leader and liberator of the Jewish people; an "orthodox" Marxist; an "orthodox" Islamic Fundamentalist; and so on. This is a misuse of the word, and unfortunately all words are liable to be misused. Orthodoxy, by contrast, is the real glory and truth of the Church of Christ the God-man, which is the Land of the Living.

Man is invited to live, to take part in life, to be alive, giving life to the whole of nature around him, which we call dead nature (i.e., still life) but which is actually not dead (still). Man revives, informs, and gives life to nature. He disseminates life around him, not simply by the prolongation of the species, as mere biology (particularly in its atheistic and anti-theistic forms) has grown accustomed to emphasizing, but rather by sharing with the other, by communion with others. And love and life, when shared with others, is multiplied. This is the way God has made and arranged things. This is from where joy wells up, from where immortality wells up. Evil and sin, which came into the world through man, are a separation from this partaking of and togetherness with God the Life-giver and the Land of the Living.

For this reason, when man secludes himself, when he becomes "independent," when he "individualizes," when he becomes selfish, when he comes to be "all on his own," as the great Dostoyevsky says, he encloses and confines himself into "his own solitude." In so doing, he does not actualize himself. On the contrary, he is destroyed, he obstructs and confines himself, he mortifies himself—and this is real death. Unfortunately, it can be eternal death, if he cuts off his relationship with God, his partaking of God, and his love for God and others, if he does not participate in the Land of the Living, in the Communion of the Living, in God, in Whom everything has its being. And since this God is Christ, Who is God and man, so in man, too, everything has its being. This is the "togetherness" of Orthodoxy and the basis of our Faith.

It is not that we, the young Orthodox faithful and theologians, the teachers of the Gospel and Orthodox theology, are so wise in our times. We simply remind others of what is the genuine, authentic Gospel of our Faith. We do not retreat into some conservatism. This is impossible to do, even if we wanted to. It would be a sham, a counterfeit and a failure, if we were to want to go backward. We say that our nostalgia for the Land of the Living is a future nostalgia, an eschatological nostalgia directed forward. It is not like the ancient Hellenic or Indian nostalgia, or any other nostalgia, which is entirely directed backward. Nostalgia means sorrow, pain for one's place of birth, for one's fatherland, for one's origin. But "our citizenship is in heaven," and our life is in heaven, as says the Holy Apostle Paul (Col. 3:1–4; Phil. 3:20). This is why we are nostalgic toward the future, toward eschatology, toward the fullness that actually attracts us to itself—naturally to the measure that we are open to it, participate in it and partake of it.

Orthodoxy is eschatological, and this means faith, life, reality, and the fullness of the future. The past and *paradosis* (tradition) are not diminished by this, and this is why our nation is a *zhizneoradostny* (having joy for life) nation, as Dostoyevsky used to say. The Orthodox man is always full of life, keen on life, but sometimes "over-full" with this present life, because he yearns for the greater, fuller, and eternal life. It would be too narrow-minded, selfish, small, and fainthearted to be satisfied only with this little and fleeting life, and then to talk like Scheherazade from *One Thousand and One Nights,* to linger and to deceive ourselves that this is all there is. This has been done by many utopians, many people from false religions, from idolatrous and newer ideologies, and this is done more or less by all totalitarians—and a man who is apart from God is very liable to totalitarianism. This is the abolishment of togetherness, openness, love, true improvement, progress, and

45

the yearning to come with all people and all God's creation to our Eternal Home, which is called the Land of the Living.

Orthodoxy, for this reason, has a permanent mission in the world. It is never totalitarian, and because of this it sometimes may seem unsuccessful. Some might expect it to be "efficient," to possess force, organization, administration, and effectiveness. This is not good, and Orthodoxy is not supposed to express itself in such a way. (Naturally, this does not mean that we should be idle and not work.) The West has imposed upon the present world such an "effectiveness," productiveness, successfulness, utilitarianism, and thus totalitarianism, and requests this from us also. For this reason the West mocks and cannot put up with Orthodoxy.

We sow, plow, dig, and tend the eternal life which God has sown in us, and which He has tended and watered, and we are required to make an effort, but success is in the hands of God. This makes us serene, temperate, and sober. It makes us not defeatists but workers, although it does not make us activists who transform their activity into "action for action's sake," *"l'art pour l'art,"* "success for success' sake"; it makes us more than that—partakers of life which is love. You cannot say that love is concluded or completed, that you have "finished the job" once you have come to love someone. On the contrary, you have just started your work. Life is love, life is freedom, life is joy, life is the future, life is togetherness in the Land of the Living, in the One Who is the Eternal Spring of life, the Eternal Synodikon of life, the Eternal Fullness of life: Christ—the Land of the Living.

This theme about the Land of the Living is well known in the Scriptures, in the Old Testament. The Psalmist David says: "I believe that I shall see the good things of the Lord in the Land of the Living" (Ps. 26:15). The Edenic Paradise at the beginning of the world used to be the land of the living, but just as a sketch, as a possibility, as a beginning, as a challenge and a chance for man. Man was placed into it; he did not lack anything. However, Paradise should have become his through creative participation and joint effort with God, through cohabitation and joint life, and not through seizure and some mechanical means of acquiring eternal life, as it came through the fruit offered by the devil: "If you want to become as God!" (cf. Gen. 3:5). Hence, man tried to become like God by some shorter and mechanical way, without participation, freedom, love, and togetherness. Then God, when He had chosen from fallen, estranged and irreconcilable mankind one man who trusted Him, the Forefather Abraham, and when He had taken him into the promised land, He promised that this land (geographically, present-day Palestine, Israel) was going to be the land of life, the land to live in, the land where "milk and honey" flow, that is, joy, happiness, and well-being. This was the promised land, and even when it was given it was not yet completely given, but assigned to man.

There is a paradox and dialectic in this, that God kept on promising the land to the Israelites. He promised it to Abraham even when he did not yet have a son: He promised that his posterity would inherit that land. And when Abraham received his son Isaac, God told him to sacrifice that son! Again paradoxical! Even when God gave the Jews this land, they would lose it and long for it again; they were in slavery several times and then returned. There is symbolism here, but biblical symbolism, which means something real, since in the Bible a "symbol" genuinely participates in what it symbolizes. The Jewish people always used to fight for this land; they used to have it and then lose it; and they used to long for it. When they were in slavery in Babylon, they sang that beautiful Psalm: "By the rivers of Babylon, there we sat down; and we wept.... If I forget thee, O Jerusalem, let my right hand be forgotten" (Ps. 136:1, 5 LXX). Jerusalem is a symbol of the Holy Land; and the Holy Land—Palestine—is a symbol of the Land of the Living in the heavens.

Our Serbian Orthodox people, and Greeks and Russians, too, love their fatherlands very much—not because they are nationalists or chauvinists, but because they are biblically hungry and thirsty for the Land of the Living. There is a paradox in this, also—that this country has been given to us as a fatherland, but it was also assigned to us, so that by it and with it we would reach the Land of the Living, the Heavenly Kingdom. The Heavenly Kingdom is another expression for the Land of the Living, the Kingdom of God, the Kingdom of eternal life, Paradise and heaven. These are all synonyms, names which denote the same reality: "The things which God has prepared for those who love him," as says the Apostle Paul (I Cor. 2:9). This is the Land of the Living, this is what we are straining toward.

The Land of the Living, however, is not comprised only of heaven and only of eschatology (the last things). The Land of the Living is eternity, but for us it has its beginning in the creation of the world and man, in the creation of our country, our motherland if you will, our living space here, our natural land of the living created by God in the beginning, in which we started to live God's life in God's world. This is why our fatherland is also important, and love for our fatherland is important, since it too is supposed to reach the Heavenly Kingdom. Of course, there are people who are without their fatherland—stateless people. There are many of these people nowadays, and we Serbs are among them. We became stateless persons in our ethnic homelands; we were left without our fatherland. Actually, we were driven away, refugees like Abraham, like the biblical nation; and we are a biblical nation. We have our fatherland and it is being blessed by us—or, unfortunately, condemned by us—in every place where we live, where we walk, where we work, where we love, where we suffer, where we rejoice. A child loves every place, but most of all he loves his mother and his birthplace. By this the value of one's country and fatherland is confirmed, and it too is supposed to enter into eternity. We are not *acosmoi* (ἄκοσμοι), i.e., without the world and against the world, but we are also not confined to the world, and we do not accept being imprisoned in the world, chained in this world, notwithstanding that it is our universe, our cosmos with all its galaxies. We want to elevate this world to God's endless world, the world of God's love, God's eternal life.

For this reason the Land of the Living sanctifies, enlightens and fulfills the meaning of our life and activity, our cosmos, our *chorochronos* (χωροχρόνος—space-time), and this is why the Orthodox used to fight so hard for their fatherlands.

It is interesting and characteristic that the Orthodox hesychasts in the Balkans—Greeks, Serbs, Bulgarians, as well as Russians and Romanians—used to fight bitterly and even used to be the initiators of battles and rebellions for the liberation of their people and their fatherland. Most importantly these were spiritual rebellions, and secondarily they were patriotic ones for the sake of liberation. Above all, Orthodox Christians fought them for the inward preservation of the freedom of their people, their soul, religion, consciousness, character. Nowadays, we Serbs are doing this also, as an Orthodox nation along with other Orthodox nations which are our fellow-sufferers, which come through for us and help us. We fight for the preservation of this inward freedom, for the preservation of our faith and soul, for Christ—our Land of the Living—and not for gaining territories, lands or states, or worldly dimensions and organizations, which are totalitarian, as we have already said.

There is a concrete place on earth where the Land of the Living is ✳ being experienced, through the connection between earth and heaven, between this land of the living and that eternal one. This place is of two natures, like Christ is of two natures, man and God, God and man—the God-man. This place is the holy temple, the Church. Therefore, we should speak about the temple, about what is going on in it, how it is a symbol of the entire world, and how the Church is experienced in the Liturgy, in the Holy Mysteries, in communion, in partaking, in togetherness, in anticipation, in the eschatological foretaste, pre-joy, and pre-life of the Land of the Living—just as childhood is pre-joy and pre-life, although it is already real and full life.

In particular, we should speak about the Holy Liturgy as the Land of the Living, as the Assembly of all living things which were created by the God of Love and Life. And before speaking and talking it is necessary to participate, to take part, to communicate. For the Holy Liturgy is the eternal, blessed Kingdom of the Holy Trinity, the grace of our Lord Jesus Christ, the love of God the Father, and the communion of the Holy Spirit, together with all of us.

Our eternal life in the eternal Kingdom of God, in Christ as the Land of the Living, will be an eternal and unceasing Divine Liturgy—the Eucharist. "A New Heaven and New Earth ... the Holy City, New Jerusalem.... The Lord God Almighty and the Lamb ... [and] the Bride, the Lamb's Wife ... [and] the Tree of Life.... And the Spirit and the Bride say: 'Come!'... 'Surely, I am coming quickly.' Amen. Even so, come, Lord Jesus" (Apoc., chaps. 21–22).

ΧΡΙΣΤΟΣ

Η ΧΩΡΑ ΤΩΝ ΖΩΝΤΩΝ

Part II

4

Christ on Earth—The Land of the Living

Jerusalem, Pentecost, 2000[1]

Here we are in Jerusalem, in the year of our Savior Two Thousand. Here we are in the City of God, on Holy Sion, the Mother of all Churches, the Metropolis of the Old and New Adam, the Old and New Israel.

What do we as the Church of God—the One, Holy, Catholic and Apostolic Orthodox Church—have to say at this place and time (εἰς τὸν χωροχρόνον)? What testimony do we give, and to what do we bear witness before the Third Millennium of Christianity in the history of mankind?

∴

One wise man said here in Jerusalem about three thousand years ago: "The thing that has been, it is that which shall be; and that which is done is that which shall be done: *and there is no new thing under the sun. Is there any thing whereof it may be said, See, this is new? It has been already of old time, which was before us*" (Eccl. 1:9–10). The one who said this was the wise and glorious King Solomon, builder of the first Temple to the God of Abraham, Isaac and Jacob here in Jerusalem, the most wise philosopher, storyteller and poet, the Holy Prophet and Ecclesiast, that is, the *preacher of the Church.*

Some fifteen centuries after him, again here in Jerusalem, another Jerusalemite, St. John Damascene, regarding these words of Solomon, gives another new testimony, which is also our testimony here today in Jerusalem, and that is: that there is Something *New under the sun*—this is the Event of *Christ on Earth.*

---

[1] Lecture given at the Pan-Orthodox Symposium at the Patriarchate of Jerusalem on the general theme "The Witness of the Church in the Third Millennium," Holy City of Jerusalem, June 11–19, 2000.

53

"For by the good pleasure of our God and Father," says St. Damascene, "the Only Begotten Son and Word of God and God, Who is in the bosom of the Father, of one essence with the Father and the Holy Spirit, Who was before the ages, Who is without beginning and Who in the beginning *Is* (ὁ Ὤν), and is with the Father and is God, He, being in the form of God, bowed down the heavens (over the sun and under the sun) and descended to earth, and condescended to His servants with a condescension ineffable and incomprehensible, and revealed God's great *pleroma* of love toward man. For He, being perfect God, becomes perfect man, and brings into being the newest of all new things, the *Only New Thing under the sun*,"—and, we would add, over the sun and over all suns. And thus here in Bethlehem, in that "House of Bread," adds St. Damascene, "the Logos was made flesh of the Holy Spirit and the Ever-virgin Mary, the Theotokos, and became the Messiah—the Mediator between God and men, as the only Lover of Man."[2]

He descended *here and now* upon the Holy Land two thousand years ago. He came, therefore, upon the earth and into the cosmos, our Lord and God and Savior Jesus Christ, incarnate God and God become man: the God-man. And in the Face of Jesus of Nazareth the apostles and the small number of Christians—who at first were comprised of Jews and then of Hellenes—saw and recognized the Son of God, the Messiah-Christ, the God-man, the Savior of the entire world, of all cosmic space-time (χωροχρόνος), and of everything in space and time, all God's creation, visible and invisible.

The apostles, the first Christians, the early Church, saw in the Face of Christ precisely that which the church preacher, presbyter and monk, John Damascene, proclaimed: the Newest of all things new—*the Only New Thing under the sun*. That is, they saw both the One Who is the primordial Creator of the entire world and all the ages, as well as the One Who, at the end of the age and of history, comes and is coming as the New Creator and Savior of the entire world and the human race. They saw in Jesus Christ the One promised and foretold by God, and awaited by all peoples (Matt. 12:21; Is. 42:4; Gen. 49:10), the Messenger of God, the Messiah-Christ; and in His Face they recognized, experi-

---

[2] *Exact Exposition of the Orthodox Faith* 3.1 (PG 94:984).

enced, tasted and communicated with the Divine and universal Alpha and Omega, the Beginning and First, and the End and Fulfillment of all space-time, all the heavens and all eternity. They saw and experienced in Christ the realization of that which was prophesied by the prophets and foreseen by the seers: the revelation and actualization of the *Great Counsel* of the Holy Trinity (Is. 9:6 LXX), the counsel and plan, the meditations and will of the Preeternal *Good Pleasure of God* regarding the world and man—of God's preeternal intentions regarding man, from before the beginning of the world until man's eschatological fulfillment in the eternal life of the Kingdom of God.[3] And this is the same as that which the Holy Apostle Paul wrote to the Ephesians: "Blessed be the God and Father of our Lord Jesus Christ, Who has blessed us with every spiritual blessing in the heavenly places in Christ, as He has chosen us in Him before the foundation of the world ... in love having predestined us to adoption as sons by Jesus Christ to Himself ... having made known to us the mystery of His will, according to His good pleasure, which He purposed in Christ, that in the dispensation of the fullness of time He might gather together in one all things in Christ, both which are in heaven and which are on earth" (Eph. 1:3–10).

This is the transcendent and wondrous *Mystery of Christ*, of which, after the Apostle Paul, the divinely inspired Holy Fathers speak, particularly St. Maximus the Confessor,[4] witnessing that in this theanthropic *Mystery of Christ* is revealed the sincerest and deepest abyss of the Father's Good Will (Εὐδοκίας—the All-gracious Will and Goodness of God), the first and final purpose for which everything has been created, and its significance. That purpose is: that Divinity and humanity be united in one Hypostasis—in the Person of Christ the God-man—without loss, change or diminution of the fullness of either the divine or human essences and natures. And all this is the act of God's love and philanthropy, as the Holy Fathers Athanasius and Maximus say: God, out of love, becomes human in order to make man divine. Or,

---

[3] See St. Maximus the Confessor: "The Great Counsel of God the Father is the quiet and hidden mystery of the Economy of salvation that the Only Begotten Son revealed, fulfilling it by the Incarnation; and so He Himself became the Angel (Messenger) of the Great and preeternal Counsel of God the Father" (PG 90:1136).

[4] St. Maximus, in the well-known *To Thalassius* 60 (PG 90:620–25).

in other words: "The Son of God becomes the Son of Man in order to render man a son of God."[5]

That mystery and event, which is called *Christ on Earth,* was foreseen and prophesied three thousand years ago by the same aforementioned Jerusalemite Solomon when, in his Proverbs, from the mouth of the Wisdom of God Himself, he said: "The Lord made Me (ἔκτισέ με—'created me,' according to the translation of the Septuagint; while Aquila, Symmachus and Theodotion translated the Hebrew verb *qanani* as ἔκτησέ με—'found me,' 'possessed me') the beginning of His ways for His works; He established Me before time was in the beginning ..., before all hills He begets Me" (Prov. 8:22–25).

And again, fifteen centuries later, another Jerusalemite, St. Cosmas the Melodist, Bishop of the city of Maiuma (near Gaza) and half-brother of St. Damascene, reinterpreted those words of Solomon in a thoroughly *Christological* way, in which Christ Himself as the Wisdom of God says: "The Father before time begets Me as Creative Wisdom; He creates Me in the beginning of His ways for His works, which are now mystically accomplished. For I, as the Word of God, by nature uncreated, adopt the names of that which I have taken upon Myself (having become man)."[6] It is well known to all people of the Church and to all theologians that here St. Cosmas, in interpreting the quoted words of Solomon's Proverbs, applied them to Christ at the Mystical Supper, to Christ in the Divine Liturgy-Eucharist; applied them, therefore, to the *Mystery-Event* which is called *Christ on Earth;* he concretized that personal-communal event of Christ the God-man to the highest degree, when Christ indeed becomes for us in the Church the *Bread of Life* and the *Land of the Living.*

This Mystery-Event of Christ consists both of the fact that He is truly God and truly Man, and of the fact that He is the one and unique God-man, assembled from His two natures, and eternally remains in His two perfect natures, wills and energies, as the One composite *Hy-*

---

[5] St. Athanasius the Great, *On the Incarnation of the Word* 54; St. Maximus, *Two Hundred Texts on Theology and the Incarnate Dispensation of the Son of God* 5.74.

[6] Canon of Great Thursday, ode 9, in praise of Christ's Mystical Supper with the Apostles on Sion. Even before St. Cosmas, St. Athanasius of Sinai wrote similarly: *Questions and Responses* 42 (PG 89:593).

postasis (μία σύνθετος ὑπόστασις) of the one and unique God-man, but not "one composite nature" (μία σύνθετος φύσις) as is mistakenly taught by the heretical Monophysites, for in that case our human nature is lost in Christ and thus also our actual and eternal salvation.[7]

This interpretation of St. Cosmas in his hymns on the Mystical Supper of Christ and our participation and communion in it—that is, in the Holy Eucharist of Christ Himself incarnate—is based on the well-known interpretation of St. Athanasius the Great, when the great Alexandrian archbishop and patriarch, one of the greatest witnesses of evangelical Orthodoxy in the heretofore two-thousand-year history of the Church, interprets[8] Solomon's expression in Proverbs 8:22: "The Lord created me the beginning of His ways for His works," and says that the expression "created me"[9] shows and proves that Christ, as the Preeternal Wisdom of God, as the Eternal Only Begotten Son of God, the Almighty Creator and Artist of the entire creation, the Same who by His voluntary and saving Incarnation and Becoming Man, became *creation—man*, for the salvation of man, His creation, and of all His creation. That is why St. Gregory the Theologian says (as repeated by St. Damascene in the divine hymns of our Church): "The One Who is (exists) from eternity, now comes into being (ὁ Ὢν γίνεται) by becoming man; the Unoriginate One now begins (ἄρχεται—receives beginning); the Fleshless One is incarnate, the Logos of God is embodied."[10]

In a word: the interpretation of St. Athanasius on Christ as the Wisdom of God, Whom God the Father *possesses* as Son of God, but Whom He also *creates* at the time of Christ's Incarnation as man, witnesses to the faith of the Church, that by His Incarnation the Son and Word of God, the Wisdom of God, "came to that which is His own" (John 1:11). Thus He came into the world—in the world and in the man whom He created and who belongs to Him, because God is Fa-

---

[7] See St. Sophronius of Jerusalem, *Synodal Encyclical* (PG 87c:3168–72).

[8] In book 2 of *Against the Arians*, particularly ch. 64–80.

[9] Even if this be considered an incorrect translation of "possessed me." Such "errors" serve to better demonstrate that Orthodox theology does not depend upon language or words, and philologizing or philosophizing about them, but upon the facts and events of divine revelation.

[10] Cf. St. Gregory the Theologian, *Oration* 38.2.

ther, creating the world and man *through the Son and for the Son* (Paul's δι' αὐτοῦ καὶ εἰς αὐτὸν—Col. 1:16), everywhere and in everything sealing and signing His *name*, so that when the Son comes into the world and becomes man, everywhere He will find His *words*—His *logoi* and "logos-ness," according to Fr. Justin Popovich.[11] These are those "οἱ λόγοι τῶν ὄντων" (rational, noetic, intellectual principles of being) which, according to the Holy Fathers, particularly St. Maximus the Confessor, are found mainly and ultimately in man as the *image* and *likeness* of God, in human beings as icons and likenesses of Christ, i.e., beings of Christological composition and Christocentric by determination. This is the true Gospel, the *Eternal Gospel* (Rev. 14:6)—the Eternal *Good News* of God about man, for man, and in man, in the heart of all creation. This is the Good News of the Holy and Man-loving Trinity, the Preeternal *Great Counsel* of the Good Will and Love of God, that is, of the Life-giving Trinity as Archetype of the *Council-Church-Eternal Community*. For, according to the God-inspired words of the Holy and Great Photius, "The unity of the Holy Trinity made the Church (ἐκκλησιάσασα) by the decision of Their singular will"[12] in Their Preeternal *Great Counsel* (cf. Is. 9:6 LXX); and thus the Trinity created the whole world and the human race, intending it to become in Christ the *Body-Church-Council* of all the children of God and of all things created by the Holy Trinity.

∴

This is that Gospel of God, the *new, all-joyful Good News* of the salvation and deification of all men and all creation in Christ the Godman, and this is that which we today, as the Orthodox Catholic Church of Christ, the Church of the Holy Trinity, witness and preach before the world and humanity at the end of the *Second* and beginning of the *Third* millennium of Christianity. This is that well-known Orthodox Christological cosmology and anthropology, soteriology and eschatology, of which we have testified these twenty full centuries through numberless constellations of saints: Apostles, Martyrs, Hierarchs, Confessors, Ascetics, Faithful disciples and followers of Christ, all those "clouds of Witnesses," as they are called by the Holy Apostles Paul and

---

[11] Fr. Justin presents the theme of *logos-ness* in all his works, especially in *Filosofskim urvinama* (Philosophical abysses) (Munich, 1956).
[12] St. Photius of Constantinople, *Homilies* 9.9.

John, all those who faithfully follow after Christ, all those who have as their Head, in their midst, and as their End the *"Author and Perfecter of the faith"* Jesus—the Preeternal *Lamb of God.*[13]

Therefore, for the Orthodox understanding and sensibility, for the true knowledge and experience of the Church, the entire structure and quintessence of the world is anthropological and Christocentric. True salvation for the world and history, for all χωροχρόνος (space-time), is found only in Christ incarnate and become man, in Christ the supra-cosmic and cosmic, in Christ Divine-human and Heavenly-earthly, in Christ ecclesial and liturgical, in Christ Crucified and Resurrected. From this St. Maximus the Confessor, that rare Christologue and myst-agogue among the Holy Fathers, rightfully testifies that "The mystery of the Incarnation of the Logos (Christ) contains the power and meaning of all the riddles and types (figures) in Holy Scripture, as well as the knowledge of created things sensible and intelligible. And he who comes to perceive the mystery of the Cross and Burial (of Christ) perceives the logoi (principles, meanings) of the abovementioned. But he who is ini-tiated into the ineffable power and meaning of the Resurrection per-ceives the purpose for which God first established everything."[14]

∴

We all know very well that today, as before, a wide variety of "salva-tions," "new world orders," and "self-realizations" for men and for the world are offered to men on the world market or fair. The great Serbian spiritual father and theologian Justin (Popovich) rightly said in our day that this world of ours is a "bazaar of gods," where every one of these pseudo-gods brings out its ready-made recipe for a "religion of salva-tion," and its pseudo-worship, or, better to say, idol-worship or man-worship. But it is man's great responsibility in this world and in this life—because he will not receive another life, nor will it be repeated in

---

13 Heb. 12:1–2; John 1:29; Rev. 5:6; 7:13–17. St. Symeon the New Theologian writes: "Christ is the First, the Middle and the Final Perfection, because He is ev-eryone: the first ones, the ones in the middle, and the ones at the end. For in Him there are no differences among them, as there is no Barbarian or Scythian, Greek or Jew, but Christ is all and in all (cf. Col. 3:11)" (*Theological and Practical Chapters* 2.1, *Sources Chrétiennes* 51 [Paris, 1980], p. 120). On Christ as *Lamb of God* see I Peter 1:19–20 and St. Maximus the Confessor, *To Thalassius* 60 (PG 90:620–25).

14 *Two Hundred Texts on Theology and the Incarnate Dispensation of the Son of God* 1.66 (PG 90:1108).

some other "cycle"—to choose the Real and True God, the One Who is "the One thing needful" (cf. Luke 10:42).

We Orthodox, knowing in Whom we have believed (cf. II Tim. 1:10–12; I John 1:1–3) and having as confirmation and guarantee of the truthfulness of our Faith the Spirit Comforter (cf. John 14:16–17, 26; 15:26; 16:13; I John 3:23–24), confess and testify of Christ, the Son of God and Son of Man, as the only "Way, Truth and Life" (cf. John 14:6), as the Only Savior and the only true and eternal salvation of the world and mankind. For we know through the One continually invoked in the Church, the Holy Spirit, given us from God the Father, Who prays within us in the Church "with sighs too deep for words" (cf. Rom. 8:15–16, 26), and invisibly but perceptibly announces and issues grace-filled epiphanies and testifies to us and the world—and particularly in these days of Pentecost which we are celebrating—that *there is no other name under heaven given among men by which we can be saved* (Acts 4:12), that is, other than the Name of Jesus Christ, and Him *Crucified and Resurrected*, in Whom we have life eternal, adoption by the Father, deification by the Holy Spirit, and "theanthropification" in the God-man.

Only Christ, manifested on earth by the Incarnation, Cross and Resurrection, witnessed to by the Spirit and glorified by the Father as the Only Begotten Son of God and Firstborn Son of the Virgin, has revealed to the world and the human race the Only Living and True God, Whom "no one has seen," nor would ever be able to see or know, had not the same "Only Begotten Son of God, Who is in the bosom of the Father," **revealed** Him (ἐξηγήσατο—shown, declared, made visible and revealed—John 1:18), and manifested Him in Himself, and led us to Him and united us in that eternal divine community of love and life. For, in the words of St. Gregory Palamas, without Christ's Divine Incarnation the most that we men could know about God would be some pale and impersonal traces of Him within us and in the world, *some mere energies observed in created things* (ἐνέργειά τις μόνον ἐνθεωρουμένη τοῖς κτίσμασι), as spoken about by some ancient unwise wise men, and as now spoken about by the misguided followers of Barlaam,"[15] or narrowly trained followers of Einstein, which are all the same.

---

[15] St. Gregory Palamas, *Homilies* 16.19.

This divine *manifestation* and *revelation* of God through His Only Begotten Son, this divine ἐξήγησις, as St. John the Evangelist would say, is nothing other than the self-hypostatic (self-personal) Christ the God-man Himself, Who, in becoming truly man, *with Himself and within Himself,* and not only by His teaching or by the Christian religion, revealed and declared and manifested God, eternally Alive and True. For He did not become a star, or an angel, or some other being or creature, but became man: "For verily He took not on Him the nature of angels; but He took on Him the seed of Abraham," that is, human nature, "wherefore in all things it behooved Him to be made like unto His brethren"—that is, like men (Heb. 2:16–17), for by becoming incarnate and becoming man He has made Himself our relative and kin.

This truth and this event have immeasurably great, foundational, the most pivotal and the highest possible significance and importance, and it is to this that we again bear witness today: that our Christian God, revealed in Christ, is *God* the *Lover of Man,* to Whom man is the dearest of all created things, of all beings heavenly and earthly; and that He shows and proves this precisely by Christ's manifestation on earth, His Incarnation, His becoming man.

The reason why this is so important and significant for us men is related by St. Diadochus, Bishop of Photiki in Epira, in the Balkans (beginning of the fifth century), in his vision and words: "In the person and glory of the Only Begotten Son is manifested the invisible, *formless* (ἀνείδεος) God the Father, for so it pleased God that His Word come by way of incarnation and become our human likeness and form, remaining in His almighty glory, so that we men—beholding His glorious human body, His visible and tangible likeness (for likeness looks and sees likeness)—may, when our likeness is cleansed, look upon the beauty of the Resurrection as upon God (ὥσπερ ἐπὶ Θεοῦ).... For, indeed, it is even appropriate that those whom God will rule in the future age, will be able eternally and with recognition to look upon their Lord, which would be impossible had not the Word of God, by becoming man, come in our human form and likeness."[16]

---

[16] St. Diadochus of Photiki, *The Vision* 21, *Sources Chrétiennes* 5 (Paris, 1966), pp. 175–76.

This philanthropic, original, preeternal will of God and this Christ-centered divine act of the salvation of the entire world in Christ as the God-man means that God determined that, in His Only Begotten Son, Who is eternally "in the bosom of the Father" (John 1:18), man and all human nature would be *adopted* by God in His Only Begotten Son (cf. Eph. 1:4–6), Who became, and eternally remains, Son of Man, so that "those whom God foreknew He also predestined to be conformed to the image of His Son, in order that He might be the Firstborn among many brethren" (Rom. 8:29). Thus, in hypostatic union with the Eternal Son of God, our *adoption* and *acceptance into the arms* of God the Father, is given by the Gospel of God[17] only to men among all God's creatures, but is not given to the angels, who therefore "long to look into" that God-given Gospel of Christ the Savior and into that which it contains and bears and gives with itself (cf. I Pet. 1:12).

And what is so great and beautiful in the Gospel, what even the angels long to *look into and see*, and be reflected, is pointed out to us by St. Athanasius of Sinai, another witness of Christ from this Holy Land, both God's and ours. "It appears to me," claims this saint, "that the angels long that, if it were possible, in their nature as well, just as the Word of God came to dwell in our body, He would dwell in theirs also, because He also created it. They desire also that their nature be worshipped and glorified by us men, and that their nature, sitting on the throne of Cherubim, in the bosom of the Father, as in the case of our nature in Christ, be honored by worship from men and from all visible and invisible creatures.... I say that they desire the Cherubim and Seraphim to have such boldness and freedom before Christ as the beloved disciple (John) had when—at the Mystical Supper—he leaned his head on His breast, and as had the sinful woman who anointed and perfumed His feet. And may I say something greater than all else: Christ says that when He comes on the day of judgment, the Powers of Heaven will turn away from Him in fear and trembling, but He will seat the righteous men at His table and will serve them Himself as their Cre-

---

[17] And according to the Holy Fathers Maximus and Gregory Palamas: "The Gospel of God is sent by God to men through the incarnate Son, Who gives to those who believe in Him eternal deification."

ator and Savior. These and such things are the good things given to us by Christ, into which the angels long to look, that is, to enter."[18]

❖

Man was created as a Godlike and Christ-yearning being, and that is why he yearns at the deepest levels of his being for his Archetype and Proto-likeness, for the Proto-icon and the First Image—Christ, the Only Begotten Son of God—and for the All-holy and Life-creating Trinity, Who is in Him and with Him. Man as a *person* greatly desires and yearns for *personal communion and togetherness,* for the achievement of fullness and of a personal *community of life and eternal love,* because it was for this that he was created, designated, endowed, given talent, and made capable. There is no man who does not have talents and gifts, and who is incapable of love and life in a personal and social community.[19] This is because God the Holy Trinity—as an eternal and immortal Community of Three Divine Persons, Who are Their own selves but also a Communion of Immortal and Ever-living Persons—is the source and the hearth, the heart and the nucleus of man, of personal and fully human beings. Thus, the source of salvation—which is the fullness, the true realization, and the perfecting of man—is found only in the Holy Trinity, in the Community of Eternal Love and Eternal Life of the Father and the Son and the Holy Sprit.

This, then, is what Christ the Savior, as the God-man, through the Church—or, more exactly, as the Church, a theanthropic Community of God and men—achieved and made possible; this is what He materialized and personally, collectively actualized for the human race and for all of God's spiritual and material creatures when He came to the Earth two thousand years ago, and became for us the true and eternal **Land of the Living,** as we have named the second half of our theme. This, too, is our faith, our confession, and our testimony as we face the world at the end of the second and at the beginning of the third millennium of Christianity.

[18] St. Athanasius of Sinai, *Questions and Responses* 77 (PG 89:705).
[19] That is why St. Basil the Great (*Longer Rules* 3; PG 31:917)—in contrast to Aristotle's definition that man is "πολιτικὸν ὄν," which is usually translated as "social being"—showed that man is "κοινωνικὸν ὄν," that is, a *communal, sociable being,* and therefore a *personal-communicative being.*

It is known to all of us that today in the world there are many "models" of "salvation" and "happiness" for man and humanity. Many gods and divinities are offered and forced upon us, along with many *images,* that is, idols and idolatrous cosmologies. One of the more well-known is the idolatrous cosmology of "eternal return" and "recycling"—of so-called metempsychosis or reincarnation, "the return of all things to the beginning" and "starting again and again." This "vicious circle" or circles, without beginning or end, without true *living* and a true entrance into *true and non-artificial life,* and without an actual (that is, an even more unrealizable) exit—namely, the achievement of transcending mortality, the achievement of a non-mortal, non-transitory and incorruptible goal and fullness of life—except in the certainty of death and of the grave without resurrection (regardless of what grave we are thinking of—a grave in the earth or the freezing or burning of everything in the universe): this *idolatrous cosmology* or *worldview* was known to the world before Christ, and is inevitable in a world without Christ, where "the last enemy that shall be destroyed is *death*" (I Cor. 15:26), and where the last destination of every path and journey is the grave and "food for worms" (cf. Job 21:26). The God-man and Savior, the Resurrected Christ, the Vanquisher of death and Destroyer of Hades, is the **Only New Thing under the sun** and is above all suns, galaxies and universes, because by becoming true man and remaining True God, He entered with His whole human nature, united with the Divinity, into death and hell. He vanquished death and destroyed eternal Hades from the inside, along with the devil—the creator of death—whom He bound and disarmed (cf. Heb. 2:14; I John 3:8), and by this act He opened *a new and a living way,* eternal and immortal (cf. Heb. 10:20; I Cor. 15:20–23; Rom. 6:4, 22–23). The Resurrection of Christ and our resurrection with Him, after Him, and in Him, is the only temporal and eternal meaning and fullness of humanity, life and immortality. That is why our Orthodox Christian Faith is faith in Resurrection, and not faith in *progress*—the "mill of death."

In essence, the situation is not made better by various mystics and mysticisms, which all, more or less, tend toward one end—which tell us that our end, the conclusion and termination of everyone and everything, is the death and finish of the living psychosomatic man, personal death and depersonalization. Even if this end be called "bliss," it is without those who are *blissful;* though it be called "life," it is without those who are truly *living;* though it be called "cosmic sympathy" or "love," it is without *those who love* and *those who are loved.* This is "Nirvana," in which we disappear into *Something* or *Someone,* into the absolute *All* or *Nothing* (which are one and the same in the end), which can perhaps even be called "God," but surely not the **Living and True,** Personal, Tri-hypostatic, Tri-Person-Communal God, Who has been revealed and has appeared to us in Christ. Such a "God" is rather some "Divine *Urgrund,*" *Abyss* and *Infinity,* a metaphysical "Black Hole," which devours everyone and everything, like the ancient Greek mythological Cronos, who devours his own children; or it is like the goddess Hera, the intelligent Zeus, or the wise Athena. These gods did not succeed, nor could they lead the world of antiquity out of the "all-devouring nethermost regions of Hades,"—nor can this be achieved by our modern, super-technical, electronic, silicon civilization, be it in California or elsewhere.

It is true that the Holy Fathers of the Orthodox Church say and testify that God is an endless and transcendent "sea of the essence of being" (πέλαγος οὐσίας, as St. Gregory the Theologian says).[20] At the same time, however, they show that this divine essence is not the cause of the Living and True God: God as Trinity, or God as Creator of all beings and creatures. Rather, the *cause* and the *source* is in God, in the All-loving, Eternal, and Supra-essential Hypostasis or Person of God the Father—Who preeternally begets and has His Only Begotten Son and sends forth and has His Most Holy Spirit. The Christian God—revealed and manifested to the world and man as the Consubstantial and Indivisible Trinity—is the *Cause* without a cause and the sovereign Source of all being and beings, of all life, love and immortality, of each living, personal and loving man, and of the human, personal community of mankind, the race of Adam. Christ, as "One of the Holy Trinity," came to earth from the Preeternal Father and became the true Man, *the New Adam* and the Founder of the renewed human race, and as such He remains the true God-man unto all eternity. With Him and

---

[20] *Orations* 38.7 and 45.3.

after Him the world and man are given "another Comforter," the Holy Spirit (John 14:16, 26), Whose thearchic, life-creating, renewing and transforming *Descent* we celebrate these days here in Sion, as the historical and eschatological Pentecost of the Church and the world.[21]

∴

But let us return to the second part of our theme: Christ the *Land of the Living*.

One of the great problems of the day, which is becoming greater and more tragic, is well known to all of us: the ecological problem—the question of mankind's environment. Our human surroundings are no longer just our home or the garden around the house, or the village or the city, but the whole sooty planet Earth and the whole universe around us. The pollution of the earth and of everything that is around us and within us is becoming greater, more layered, and more complex, so that today everything that we eat, breathe, and wear, and with which we feed the plants, animals and fields, has become so polluted and infected that we have to expect consequences which we have not even thought of or anticipated. (For instance, according to the testimony of one experienced agronomist from the Serbian region of Banat, several years of curing and "raining away" of contaminates from the soil would be necessary in order for the new crops to be safe for human consumption.)

Along with this, and more importantly, our human existence, life and surroundings are much more infected, contaminated, and surrounded by sin and evil—especially today, when there are all kinds of narcotics

---

[21] For more about the historical-eschatological importance of Pentecost see St. Maximus the Confessor, *To Thalassius* 65, schol. 44 (PG 90:780–81). Let us add here, in connection with *mysticism*, something that is paradoxical but true, and has been confirmed by the grace-filled experience of the Church. The Holy Fathers, including St. Dionysius the Areopagite and St. Maximus the Confessor, testify that Christ is, according to the apophatic expression, the "Most-divine (Supra-divine) God-man"— Ὑπέρθεος Θεάνθρωπος—as He is also called in the Church services (Exapostilarion of the 6th tone). With this expression, and with the spiritual-liturgical experience of the Church that forms the basis of such language, the true biblical, New Testament, truly Christian, grace-filled *mysticism* of the personal-communal Church of Christ has surpassed all cosmic, religious and pantheistic mysticisms of the "dark depths." According to the knowledge and experience of the Holy Fathers who worship the Living and True God, such mysticisms are demonic manifestations which are destructive to man, spiritually deadly, and depersonalizing.

and drugs; spiritual anti-ecological infections, psychophysical diseases, and corruption; and all types of demonic putrefactions and stenches, by which man and his world are stained, rotting, and deformed. The world certainly did not come from the hands of the Most-pure and All-holy Creator in such a state; for, in the words of Holy Scripture, "God created man (and the world) to be immortal.... Nevertheless, through envy of the devil (and the willing cooperation of man), (sin and) death came into the world" (Wisd. of Sol. 2:23–24; cf. Rom. 5:12).

Due to these·*ecological*—or, more accurately, *soteriological*—reasons, Christ came from heaven to earth as a God-given Savior: not only that He would bring and grant health and salvation to man and the world, but that He Himself would become and remain our *life* for all eternity (cf. I John 1:2, 3:9), our eternal salvation (cf. Heb. 5:9), our true spiritual and bodily *health*, immortality, and Life Eternal. (The original meaning of the word salvation—σωτηρία—is to be healthy, σῶος: healthy, whole, chaste.)

This is why, in Orthodoxy, *Ecology* (οἰκολογία) is closely connected with *Economy* (οἰκονομία)—that is, of course, with the *Divine Economy* of the salvation of the world and man. In the languages of Orthodox Slavs, the latter word is correctly translated in a literal manner: *Economy* is the "domestic organization" of salvation (*Domostroi spaseniya*). Therefore, *Ecology* should be translated as "domestic-word" (*Domoslovie*), and the ecological question should be translated as the "domestic-rational" question (*domoslovesny vopros*), because man is a rational (*slovesny*, of the word) being. Hence, the organization of man's home, environment, and surroundings should be *rational* (Christ-rational, Christ-logical), that is, divinely wise and humanly sensible—in the true tradition of Slavic domestic stewardship, as our Orthodox people say. Orthodox theologians who follow after the Holy Fathers, like Fr. Alexander Schmemann or Metropolitan John Zizioulas, call this a *liturgical* approach to the world and life—a *eucharistic* service and management of the material world and environment.[22]

---

[22] Cf. Fr. Alexander Schmemann, *For the Life of the* World (Crestwood, N.Y.: St. Vladimir's Seminary Press, 1963), and Met. John Zizioulas' article "The Eucharistic Vision of the World," published in *Vidoslov*, Nativity, 1993.

Unfortunately, in contemporary Western civilization and in our pro-Western civilization (most of the world is Westernized, and in our times it is even worse—it is Americanized), this world—which has been bestowed upon us by God for living and for the development of the *Economy*, i.e., for cultivation, service and use, but also for the stewardship of the material world around us, of that which is good and useful for man[23]—has discontinued every connection and relationship with the *Divine Economy* of the salvation of the world and man. It has become only horizontal, only consumeristic and exploitative (regardless of whether it is communist or capitalist); it has become a naked *Economy*, and therefore has inevitably caused rising ecological problems.

(Some contemporary "ecological movements"—the so called "greens" or similar political parties—are only latecomers, and are usually doomed to failed attempts at stopping the rushing train of the so-called "progress" of mankind, which, with increasing speed, is plunging toward catastrophe. The measures that these "movements" propose or implement do not place at the center of attention the spiritual and psychosomatic health and salvation of **Godlike man**, both as person and as community. [It is very indicative that in Western civilization the **human person** is replaced with the "individual," and the **"human community"** with "society," whereas the fate of the planet and of the created order depends on Godlike man.] Their center of interest is the "nature" around man, and not the *nature of man;* and thus through their understanding of ecology they manifest the old pagan physiolatry, that is, the glorification of impersonal nature, or Nature, and in such a way they move the center of interest from the Godlike and Christ-yearning man elsewhere.)

Particularly true and moving for us here is the Gospel testimony of a real *ecological* tragedy and of its *salvific* conclusion. This is contained in Christ's parable about the Prodigal Son, who left his father and "took his journey into a far country, and there wasted his substance with riotous living." (In the Greek this is even more poignantly stated: "He

---

[23] Because "every creature of God is good, and nothing to be refused, if it be received (εἰς μετάληψιν) with thanksgiving (μετὰ εὐχαριστίας): for it is sanctified by the word of God and prayer" (I Tim. 4:3–5, cf. Gen. 1:31)—hence this God-given *Economy* of the material world, for which it was created and given to free and Godlike man for use even in Paradise (cf. Gen. 1:28, 2:7–15).

wasted his whole essence living in an unhealthy and un-salvific [ἀ-σώτως] way.) He was seized by hunger and "poverty"—literally, "hysteria"—so that he wanted to satisfy his hunger, if only with swine's food; until finally, in great existential difficulty, he "came to himself," and through a renewing and health-restoring *repentance* (μετάνοια—transformation of mind and heart), he returned to his Father's House, as the Church of Christ is called.[24] Meanwhile, the man-loving Father had already started rejoicing when his son was "still a great way off"—because "this my son was dead, and is alive again; he was lost, and is found" (Luke 15:11–32). This is the reason and the purpose of Christ's coming to earth: that man should truly find himself, and be saved. Having been deadened by his separation and estrangement from God, he should return to God and himself, and find himself eternally alive in the Father's House, in the *Land of the Living*.

∴

God's love towards man is so great, and His love for humanity so immense, that "He gave His Only Begotten Son, that whoever believes in Him should not perish, but have everlasting life" (John 3:16). That is why God, through the Prophet Jeremiah, told mankind, including the people of the present age at the end of the *Second Millennium* of Christianity: "The Lord has appeared of old unto me, saying, Yea, I have loved thee with an everlasting love: therefore with loving-kindness have I drawn thee" (Jer. 38:3 LXX; 31:3 KJV). And this is supported by the Prophet Habakkuk, in his testimony about the All-good and Man-loving God of revelation: "His virtue covered the heavens, and the earth was full of His praise" (Hab. 3:3), followed by that which can be translated either as "He established His power as great love," or as "He established great love as His power," (Hab. 3:4), which means that God's Love is His real *power*, and that when God's great power is manifested, even then it is *love*, because the Christian God has an essential name: "God is Love" (I John 4:8, 16).

Out of love for man and the world, God the Father sent God the Word, His beloved Son, into the world, into the wholeness of man's

---

[24] Cf. the extraordinary ecclesiological essay by Fr. Georges Florovsky, "The Father's House," which was published by Fr. Justin Popovich in Serbian translation in his periodical *Christian Life*, 1926, nos. 1–2.

psychosomatic nature, so that Christ—as the God-man; as the Only Begotten and the "Firstborn among many brethren" (Rom. 8:29); as *personal-communal;* as the Communion and Union of God and man; and therefore as the **Church**, which St. Gregory the Theologian, together with David the Psalmist, calls *"God ... in the congregation of the gods"*[25]—should be for us and for all creatures God's true and eternal *Land of the Living,* more sublime and more perfect than the first Paradise planted in the East.

Christ—God incarnate and become man—is the Living Space of all men and for all men, of all creatures and all creation in all of God's realms. God did not create death, and He did not create the world and the human race for death, but for life—that is, Eternal Life, "Life in abundance," as Christ Himself said (cf. John 10:10). This is why David the Psalmist says: "For Thou hast delivered my soul (= my life) from death ... that I should be well-pleasing before God in the *light of the living"* (Ps. 55:13); and in another place, "I will be well-pleasing before the Lord in the **land of the living**" (Ps. 114:9). (Light and life are synonymous in Holy Scripture, which is why Christ said, "I am the Light of the world," and, "I am the Life of the World.") Interpreting this Psalm, St. Basil the Great says: "This fallen world of ours is mortal and is the land of the dying ... whereas the *land of the living* is the abode of those who do not die because of sin, but live a true life in Jesus Christ."[26]

Christ as the *Land of the Living* does not include only heaven and only eschatology. For us who are in Christ, entry into the *Land of the Living* and life therein begins here on earth, in the world and in history. In this, our God-given space-time *(chorochronos),* which is in Christ, in the Church, the grace of the Holy Spirit sanctifies and transforms the saints, and through them their surroundings. They shall be fully transformed in the Second Parousia of the Lord, when Christ will become our eternal and incorruptible space-time, our eternal and immortal

---

[25] Psalm 81:1 and St. Gregory the Theologian, *Oration* 30.4.
[26] *Homily on Psalm 114.* Cf. St. Athanasius the Great, *Commentary on the Psalms:* "The land of the living is the name of the heavenly Jerusalem (Heb. 12:22–24), in which those who have lived in God and who struggled, and who as winners have pleased God, will hear the words: "Well done, thou good and faithful servant: thou hast been faithful over a few things, I will make thee ruler over many things: enter thou into the joy of thy lord" (Matt. 25:21).

Land of the Living in the Living God and Truth, in the Council and bosom of the Holy and Life-creating Trinity.

In the Orthodox liturgical, *ecclesial* (= *church-catholic*) understanding and in experiential, grace-filled knowledge, Christ the God-man is at the same time both One and Unique, the Head and the Foundation and the First-place-holder of the Church of the people of God—the *Only Begotten* Son of God and the *Firstborn* among His many brethren. He is the same *within* the Church and *as* the Church, simultaneously catholic, collective and communal, as the *Living Abode*, as the *Space for Life*, as the **Land of the Living**—of everyone and everything. This is why St. Gregory Palamas, the great theologian and ascetic struggler of Orthodox *hesychasm*—by whom we Orthodox lived during our Middle Ages and thanks to whom we survived our difficult five-century-long Muslim enslavement—testifies in his works that Christ in the saints becomes myriad-hypostasized (composed of millions of persons), because He gives Himself wholly to all and is wholly in all, and all are in Him as the God-man—within His theanthropic Body, the Church, which is "the fullness of Him Who fills all in all" (Eph. 1:22–23), because it was the preeternal Will and Goodness of God that "He might gather together in one (unite, bring under one head, recapitulate—ἀνακεφαλαιώσασθαι) all things in Christ, both which are in heaven, and which are on earth" (Eph. 1:10).

In conclusion, we quote this testimony of St. Gregory Palamas of Thessalonica: "The Son of God not only united His divine Hypostasis (Person) with our nature—oh, His unimaginable love for man!—and took upon Himself a body animated by a rational soul, and appeared on earth and lived with us men (cf. I Tim. 3:15–16, Baruch 3:37), but He also—oh, miracle that exceeds all majesty!—united Himself with human persons themselves, joining Himself to each believer through the communion of His Holy Body (*in the Eucharist*), becoming to us a 'co-body' (and we to Him—cf. Eph. 3:6), and making us temples of the Whole Divinity, because in Him, that is, in Christ's Body, 'dwells all the fullness of the Godhead bodily' (Col. 2:9)."[27]

There! That is our testimony today—the testimony of the Catholic Orthodox Church in the ensuing *Third Millennium*.

---

[27] *In the Defense of the Holy Hesychasts* 1.3.38. *Works* of St. Gregory Palamas (Thessalonica, 1962), vol. 1, p. 449 (in Greek).

St. Gregory Palamas (1296–1359),
fresco from Vatopedi Monastery, 1371.

5

The Anthropology of Hesychasm

Athens, 1988[1]

Hesychasm as a term emerged in the fourteenth century, during the time of the ascetic and dogmatic struggles of St. Gregory Palamas and his fellow strugglers. They defended ancient Orthodox spiritual knowledge and theology against Latinized and Latinizing theologians and philosophers who came from the West to Thessalonica and Constantinople, spreading anti-Orthodox ideas and acquiring a number of followers. The fourteenth century was an extremely significant time for the Orthodox Church because the Holy Fathers, with exceptional strength and vigor, brought forth a new testimony of the experience of evangelical spiritu.l life and of true biblical, divine-human theology, in contrast to the challenges of anthropocentric theology coming to Byzantium from Italy and the West, from Scholasticism and the mere humanism of the so-called Renaissance.

The Renaissance, which began at that time, placed the *question of man* at the center of its interest. Orthodox hesychasm also placed *man* at the center of its interest and struggle, as well as of its life and thought, but it provided different answers than those of the Renaissance. This Orthodox teaching emerged from the depths of the authentically Christian Church life and theology of God's Holy Fathers. This was the authentic Orthodox testimony about man experienced in Christ the God-man. Here we will discuss this Christ-centered *hesychastic* anthropology, which we could also justifiably call the patristic Orthodox anthropology because the two are one and the same.

[1] A lecture held in Athens in 1988 in the hall of the Archaeological Society, and organized by the "Friends of Mount Athos."

Throughout the Orthodox Balkans, *hesychasm* has always made, up to today, a very important contribution for each individual as well as for Orthodox peoples. Hesychasm was the expression of the living, evangelical faith and grace-filled experience of the Orthodox Churches, and it kept and preserved, in faith and practice, the evangelical, apostolic, and patristic Tradition. By contrast, the Christian West took a different path—disregarding the Tradition of the Church. A contemporary scholar of hesychasm is correct in saying that the line of demarcation between the Orthodox Christian East and Western (Latin and German) Christianity was traced by grace-filled hesychast presence and influence.

For us Orthodox Serbs, the hesychastic ascetics, spiritual fathers and theologians were particularly significant because, just before the political annihilation of the medieval Serbian state, they were decisively important in preparing the people nationally, ecclesiastically, and spiritually to endure the long Turkish yoke, as well as the upsurge of Western Uniate propaganda—a twofold pressure on their identity. Hesychasm brought a true spiritual and cultural rebirth to the Orthodox Church, thus strengthening national well-being and the souls of Orthodox Christians in their struggle against the conquerors and oppressors—the subjugators of the national and Christian spirit and body. This resistance came from strength of spirit, from the Christian way of life, and from the struggle for the Heavenly Kingdom during difficult periods. Hesychasm was the principal upholder of endurance and national renewal through its evangelical philosophy of life and the world, surviving all the historical changes during the transition from the Middle Ages to modern times.

Hesychasm was a way of thinking about the world and human life that bridged the transcendental abyss between this world and the other world. That is why the hesychastic experience of human destiny was so optimistic. It did not negate the drama of human historic life but transfigured it by connecting it with lasting, holy values: true asceticism and martyrdom for the sake of the Kingdom of God. Hesychasm also connected individuals and peoples with the Church as a living organism, as the Body of the Crucified and Resurrected Christ the God-man, Who remained at the center of hesychasm and hesychastic theology.

It must be said that the spiritual and theological experience of St. Gregory Palamas and other hesychasts was not different from the centuries-old, living Orthodox tradition in the East. After all, in the Palamite texts, especially in the well-known Synodical Tomos of 1351, it is written that hesychast theology is only ἀνάπτυξις—a *development* and *furtherance*—of the faith and theology of the Sixth Ecumenical Council and the early Church Fathers. This means that, in the fourteenth century, hesychast theology—and therefore hesychast anthropology—grew out of evangelical and patristic Christological experience, and from the context of biblical-ecclesiastical faith and experience, whose witness and inspired interpreter at that time was St. Gregory Palamas.

According to St. Gregory Palamas, who only repeated what was said by St. Maximus the Confessor, everything God said about man is contained in the Gospel of Christ. And what is the Gospel? "This is God's Gospel," says St. Gregory after St. Maximus: "God's mission to people through the incarnate Son, Who grants to all those Who believe in Him eternal deification."[2] These words of St. Gregory Palamas show the importance that Orthodox hesychasts attach to their anthropology, because they identify the final aim of the human being with the Gospel of God—and therefore with Christ's becoming man and our becoming deified in Him. In other words, the final fulfillment of the human being lies in man's *"christification,"* his *deification.*

∵

But a question can be posed: does not this lofty definition of man also mean the alienation and loss of man? Orthodox hesychasts respond that this development and sublimation of man, and his achievement of deification in Christ the incarnate God-man, is the only guarantee of the authentic survival and affirmation of man, whereas every other definition leads toward the alienation and final loss of man. Only deification (christification) brings man salvation from degradation and alienation. In order to make this clear we will simplify the problem without leaving our topic.

In the history of the human race there are two main approaches to man and two solutions to the problem of man. One is theocentric, and

---

2 See *To Thalassius* 61 (PG 90:637A).

the other anthropocentric. The first is known since Classical times and is summed up in Plato's saying: The measure of man is God. The second is also known from antiquity and is expressed in the saying of the Sophist, Protagoras: The measure of man is man. In the anthropological understanding of Orthodox hesychasts, neither of these "measures" is the real *measure* of man—in history, and especially in eschatology. Because if the measure of man is God, this means that ultimately man has to disappear into God or Divinity (depending on the meaning of "god" in a particular religion or religious philosophy).

Even with Plato and other great philosophers and religious mystics, the final aim of everything is that all should become one with God and in union with God. In other words, everything should become one *pantheistic unity* of all and everything—a unity in which man does not and should not exist as an individual being. This has been proclaimed by almost every mystic in the history of humankind, including Plotinus, Gautama Buddha, Spinoza, Jakob Böhme, and Meister Eckhart. In this view, if anything remains, it will be "blessedness" rather than *blessed ones;* there will be bliss but not blissful ones; there will be eternal life but not eternally living ones; there will only be some *Being* or some *Nirvana* (it is not important if this is a kind of existence or pure non-being). In the experience of Christian Orthodox hesychasts, it is inhuman and ungodly that man should disappear, regardless or whether he disappears into some divine Nothingness or into some absolute Non-being—into an Abyss of depersonalization and dehumanization. For man is created to exist and to live, and not to disappear; he is personal and divinely personalized, to live eternally and personally.

The other approach to man, according to which "the measure of man is man," is also inhuman in the view of Orthodox hesychasts, because in that case the real and full man is lost. The real human purpose is not achieved because man cannot give himself immortality and eternal life, and all his efforts are similar to those of Baron Munchausen, who tried to pull himself out of a hole by pulling his own hair. Through the mere sophistry of anthropocentrism and modern humanism (or "hominism," as Fr. Justin Popovich called it), man is condemned to destruction and self-annihilation (as testified by the great prophet Dostoyevsky). All self-defined aims and man's self-realization reveal nothing but man's voluntary entrance into a cage of his own limitation and self-imposed futility, where everything is only "vanity of vanities," as the wise Solomon said. In this way man remains an eternal prisoner of his own and cosmic *Nature*, which continues to pressure and smother us in this life, as it did to much-suffering Job in the Bible. However, the aspiration of man and humanity to overcome what he is, as well as the world as it is, testifies that man is not a "measure" of his own—that he always gravitates, in one way or the other, toward self-overcoming, and not toward self-nullification or self-extinction. Man gravitates toward *deification* as the attainment of fullness.

That is why the holy hesychast strugglers and thinkers set God's *Gospel* about man as the measure worthy of man and the human race. This Gospel, as we have seen, is Christ the God-man Himself, the incarnate and eternal Son of God, who became true Man and the Son of Man. For this reason, Christ became the true Savior and Deifier of man. In His divine-human person He united, in the most perfect and most salvific way, God and man, divine and human nature, without the diminishing, loss, or alienation of either God or man. That is why, for hesychastic anthropology, Christ as God and man—i.e., as the God-man—is the only real and perfect *chrono-type* of man, the real measure and measurement, the real *fullness* in this world, in this life, and in the eternal Kingdom of immortality. In other words, according to hesychast anthropology the secret of man is connected to the salvific *Mystery of Christ*, spoken of by the Holy Apostles (especially St. Paul) and the Holy Fathers (especially the hesychasts).

With Christ and in Christ the God-man, man overcomes the tragic failure of self-fulfillment, for which he yearns. This same yearning was experienced by the Greeks. The ancient Greeks constantly relived the tragic failure of man, and spoke of it and described it with bitterness: through myths, in philosophy, in art, and particularly in tragedies. The Holy Church Fathers, who for the most part were Greek, continually lived and relived the tragedies of the ancient Greeks and subsequently embraced Christ, not just as a Teacher, or as a Sage, or even as a God who reveals holy or eternal things, but as the actual, real God Who became Man, as the true *God-man*, true "in Himself" (cf. Eph. 1:4–10; John 1:18), Who revealed God as a living, historical person.

On the basis of this Christology, St. Gregory Palamas develops an authentic and real hesychast anthropology. Only Christ is the key which enables us to come to God without losing ourselves—our otherness. He enables human self-realization without destroying the God in us and without abolishing the human. The *Mystery of Christ* is not just a dogma of our Faith but also a great gift of God—the Way in which God, as the *Land of the Living* (Psalm 26:15), gives Himself to man and accepts man in Himself, without abolishing either.

The great theology of St. Palamas regarding divine "uncreated energies," which I will speak about, is nothing more than the theological exegesis of following events and facts. It follows from the fact that God and man are united in Christ, and that not only is Christ united with human nature but that, in Himself, He unites God with us. This is how we have the *living Church*, one *Body*, one *organism*, one *"deified community,"* as St. Gregory Palamas said, a "community of gods" ("God in the midst of gods," according to St. Gregory the Theologian—cf. Psalm 81:1), in whose center we find God the Trinity as the everlasting Communion of Three Persons.

In other words, the theology of St. Palamas stems from Christology, from the great truth that God became actual man. For this reason the struggles and efforts of the Holy Fathers were equally for defense of the doctrine of the Divinity of Christ and for the doctrine of His humanity. They upheld the teaching that the Person of the Son of God became the Son of Man in order to show, proclaim and fulfill the Great Counsel (i.e., decision) of the Triune God concerning the creation of man, which has as its aim that man become the adopted son of God and that humanity become a family of "the Firstborn among many brethren" (Rom. 8:29). I will dare to say, along with the words of St. Photius, that God's aim is that everything become one integral Church in the image of the Divine Trinity, the primordial, preeternal Church. St. Photius calls the Church the Great Counsel of the Holy Trinity. He says, "In making in Itself the Church (ἐκκλησιάσασα) before the ages, the Holy Trinity created the world and man."

This joining of anthropology with Christology, together with this leading of Christology into the only true framework of Triadology, opens up the dimensions of Orthodox anthropology. The latter is not only theocentric and anthropocentric, but Christ-centered, God-man-centered. Proper Christology has both God and man in the center, embraced in eternal Love and Community, in universal life, will, love, light and glory, abolishing neither God as the Triad of persons, nor man as a person, all together as a "community of persons in the Holy Spirit." In other words, that which is expressed in the anthropology of St. Palamas and other hesychasts is the essence of our Faith, not just a chapter of its theology. The truth is expressed that the entire creation of the world serves only to reveal God's preeternal Great Counsel. God's good pleasure and His will (εὐδοκία—Eph. 1:5) is that we discover, in the incarnate God-man Christ, God's great and unending Love, the goal of creation and the entire history, economy, and salvation of creation. The end is that of which the Lord spoke in His great High-Priestly prayer after the Last Supper and before Gethsemane: "That all may be one, as Thou, Father, art in Me, and I in Thee; that they also may be one in Us" (John 17:21). It is this love that embodies the essence of Divine Life. For St. Palamas, "God is Love" means that God is a Community of the Father, the Son, and the Holy Spirit. And God leads us into this Trinitarian Community so that we, too, might be participants and communicants in this Divine Life, which can also be called Grace, Love, Light, Energy, Glory, Deification, and the like. In this way, man will be saved: the *created* man, who was created out of nothing by the energy of God but was predestined for the fullness of adoption, embraced in the bosom of God the Father, where His Son, His Logos, lives eternally (cf. John 1:12–18, 17:3, 17:23–24).

Numerous passages in the works of St. Palamas, as well as hesychastic life and practice, bear witness to this: that God sent His Son "that we dwell in Him, and He in us" (cf. I John 4:8–13). This life is the Love, Grace, and Energy of the Holy Spirit. These are not just God's "promises," "laws," "commandments," or ideas, but reality. For "the Word was made flesh, and dwelt among us (and we beheld His glory)" (John 1:14). We become partakers of this glory. Even now the Kingdom of God is upon us. It was not only revealed on Tabor: Tabor was only a preview of the glory revealed to those baptized holy ones who experience, ascetically and liturgically, grace-given knowledge.

The holy hesychast Fathers of the monastic epoch desired to show that man is "a great thing," not just a small historical thing in terms of the universe and the cosmos. God, in His primordial Counsel in the creation of the world, knew of the fullness that Christ would bring to us through Himself and His Incarnation, Crucifixion and Resurrection; and that the descent of the Holy Spirit (Pentecost) would make us witnesses of the Holy Trinity in His Church. The experiential knowledge of true and real salvation is not only the forgiveness of sins or the "improvement" of our morals, but the community of the Father, His Son, and the Holy Spirit ("translating us into the Kingdom of His dear Son"—Col. 1:13): the entry into the eternal, non-material, uncreated, relationship of the Father and the Son. In this way, man becomes a communicant of eternal life, becomes a god by grace, not ceasing to be man. This is how the Gospel is realized: the "coming and the Incarnation of Christ, Who gives uncreated deification (θέωσις) as a reward and fulfillment to those who believe in Him."

In this context, St. Gregory Palamas repeats the familiar words of St. Maximus that in this unification of man with Christ, in this celebration of man by the grace of the Holy Spirit, man becomes "without beginning and without end" (ἄναρχος καὶ ἀτελεύτητος). He enters into the beginningless, uncreated, and endless love of God—love which is not an idea, psychological feeling, or instinct, but rather an envelopment and permeating of divine life. It is an *ecstasy* of God, Who, in creating man and the world, *stepped* out of Himself in order to give Himself to us, without losing Himself and without achieving an identity of essences (κατ' οὐσίαν ταυτότητα), as St. Palamas would say, but rather achieving an identity of His communion, love, and energy with ours. This is the personality of the living God of the Bible, Who reveals Himself and gives Himself to us in a manner in which man can accept Him—without man annihilating his own essence, but remaining always dissimilar, of a different nature, alongside the uncreated nature of the Triune God.

However, man, like God, is not only his nature; he is not only man by nature. He is an icon of the personal God and enters into communion with the personal God. The content of his existence is not exhausted in his nature. He is a godlike community of life—which means a community of persons. Man is, therefore, not only a *natural* but also a *personal* being.

St. Palamas would say: Even God is not primarily a being or essence. He is primarily and above everything "I AM" (the Existing One, Сушти, ὁ Ὤν, Exodus 3:14). Should we want to identify the "origin" of God, we would say: I AM does not come from His being (essence), but His being (essence) comes from I AM. The primordial existence of God is personal and, more precisely, it is communal. It is the tri-hypostatic reality of God's I AM (ὁ Ὤν): Father and Son and Holy Spirit. Personal man was created in keeping with this formula and prototype; thus he too participates in a community of persons, and elevates his nature to a supernatural state which is divine, without annihilating himself. He ascends to and glorifies God, and thus he is fulfilled as a person in a community of love with the personal God. For man, this is the only possibility of self-realization, without annihilating himself or God.

In the mystical experience of Plotinus, Gautama Buddha, and many other mystics old and new, man can perhaps taste something otherworldly, can become one with "god," whatever that might be; but after that neither man nor god can exist. Man can exist, if at all, when life without living is achieved, or eternal happiness without those who are happy! So, we have depersonalization and de-signification (the creation of meaninglessness) in this pantheistic and naturalistic ideology.

Hesychasm, and above all personal hesychasm, can be called an ascetic-liturgical testimony. This theological expression testifies that man's purpose is not to disappear into some divine *Totality*, into some impersonal and depersonalized abyss, but to be united with the personal God in a community of love, which affirms those who participate in it and which reveals people as real gods by grace and as eternally alive—not just as "eternally existing" but as "eternally alive." "I am come that they might have life, and that they might have it more abundantly," says Christ (John 10:10). This refers to living people deified in Christ, alive in the abundance and glory of God, eternally alive through the energies of God and through all that St. Palamas ascribes to God— God Who is not only One and Tri-personal, but is Almighty (παντοδύναμος) (the Confession of Faith by St. Gregory Palamas). .

"Almighty God," according to St. Palamas, does not mean primarily that God can do everything, but that He has all might and means, all force and energy, the divine *abundance* from which He creates the

world, deifies it and saves it, bringing everything in relationship to Himself in order to glorify it. The human body and the nature around us—the entire creation of God—are intended for the Community of Divine Life. Already here on earth this life, from Baptism to the Eucharist, shows itself as a betrothal and a beginning, a foretaste of the Kingdom which comes *"in power"* (Mark 9:1). Historically, this may seem like not much, and the contemporary man might remark, "Fine, these hesychasts experienced contact with God, a communion, but is that all?" "That is not all," said St. Palamas, "for man is not only that which he is, but he is more so that which he *will* be"; and the guarantee and beginning of this is already given in Christ. This is the *deposit* of the Holy Spirit that is given to us in Christ (cf. II Cor. 1:22, 5:5) and with Christ in the Church. In Christ, we already have everything—a beginning and an end. Eschatology exists as reality in Christ. But, taking into consideration that man is a living and free person, the Church has been made as a place for the fulfillment of this dynamic relationship and progression, with man's free participation. It is a place for *struggle*, a place for the manifestation of faith and for becoming Christ-like in love. For man is a being of growth and progress.

Love is not simply a deed or an experience, but rather a lasting state of living life, a new way of being, a new existence of man, a new life, and a life in Christ, the dynamics of which will continue into eternity. In other words, the perfection of the holy ones will continue even there, and God will forever be new to us, as we are to Him and to our own selves. Eternal life will be a joy, and "no law under the sun" will be valid except for Christ's, Who is "the only new thing under the sun," Who "makes all things new," and Who is eternal Life and Joy, Love and the source of Love and Joy (cf. Eccl. 1:9; Rev. 21:5). This is not a closed circle or *anadiplosis* (doubling back) with respect to ourselves, or a turning back of God toward Himself, but real life and growth, a source of joy, growth "from glory to glory" (II Cor. 3:18), and "grace for grace" (John 1:14–16). St. Palamas says that God was not satisfied to be true only unto Himself. Rather, this is a God Who out of love comes to us and makes us children of God. St. Gregory, speaking to Barlaam, who argued for a kind of essentialist God (that is, a God of essence or nature only), said that we need to seek the Living God, Who "stepped out" of

Himself without losing His identity, in order to meet man, out of love and freedom, not out of any kind of need, inner or otherwise.

St. Palamas writes to Barlaam: "We need to look for a different God [unlike the god of Barlaam], Who is not only self-fulfilled, self-sufficient, and observes Himself through Himself (ἑαυτὸν δι' ἑαυτοῦ θεωρούμενον), but Who is also of goodness and love. Being such, He is not satisfied with a motivation that comes only from contemplation of Himself. Being not only self-sufficient, He is over-filled and over-abundant [with love]. He is Almighty through His will, not unable to do good; and He is not just motionless, but sets everything in motion (οὔτε μόνον ἀκίνητον ἀλλὰ καὶ κινούμενον). In this way, He is present in creative and providential 'goings out' and energies (προόδοις καὶ ἐνεργείαις). Simply said, we need to seek a God in Whom we can participate (Θεὸν ὄντα μεθεκτὸν—God in whom we can commune), and in Whom each of us can enter into communion in his own way. According to the analogy of communion, we will exist (be—ὄντες), and live, and become deified (ἔνθεοι ἐσώμεθα)."[3]

This quotation, which is so linguistically complex (even though we would expect the language from the fourteenth century to be somewhat simpler—but what a great treasure it is!), shows us that the God of the holy hesychasts—and that of all Orthodox Christians—is the Living and True God of the Bible, Who is rich in His freedom, and Who moves not out of necessity but out of love, not out of a mighty outpouring of His nature, but out of the abundance of His free and good will, out of His goodness. He created everything from unselfish motives, and He wants to embrace, within His bosom where His eternal and beloved Son is, us who are free and loving, to take us in Him and with Him into the eternal Triune Community of life and love.

All this God does "for the glory of God," as the Holy Scripture says (John 1:14; Eph. 1:6–12, 18; Col. 1:27). This glory is in fact "our glory" (cf. John 17:22, 24; Rom. 8:18, 9:23), because the glory of God is the celebration of man; the glory of God is the salvation of man, and man's glorification. These are not just promises and portents, but a reality given and incarnated in Christ, and that is why the holy hesychasts

---

[3] *In Defense of the Holy Hesychasts* 2.24.

claim that God can be seen here on earth, and that the Heavenly Kingdom can be foretasted and experienced, just as our human nature experienced in Christ the God-man. For this reason He, as the Eternally and Only Begotten Son of God, became the Firstborn among many brethren (Romans 8:29)—the First *New Man*, the New Adam, the ancestor of New Humanity.

When St. Gregory Palamas says *Christ*, he means Christ's whole body, which is united with people and becomes that which St. Gregory says of the Holy Eucharist: "The Son of God not only united His divine Hypostasis (Person) with our nature—oh, His unimaginable love for man!—and took upon Himself a body animated by a rational soul, and appeared on earth and lived with us men, but He also—oh, miracle that exceeds all majesty!—united Himself with human hypsostases (persons) themselves, joining Himself to each believer (ἑκάστῳ τῶν πιστευόντων συνανακιρνῶν ἑαυτὸν) through the communion of His Holy Body, becoming to us a 'co-body' (σύσσωμος ἡμῖν), and making us temples of His All-encompassing Divinity, because in Him, that is, in Christ's Body, 'dwells all the fullness of the Godhead bodily' (Col. 2:9)."[4]

The Divine Eucharist, according to the holy hesychast ascetics, is not only one Sacrament but is in fact the greatest Sacrament of the Church and of the Kingdom: the coming personal participation (communion, fellowship) in the Heavenly Kingdom in power, the communion (κοινωνία) of the Living Personal God with us, and of each of us with Christ, and among ourselves in Christ.

It is amazing how St. Gregory Palamas and other hesychasts experienced the salvation and deification of man eucharistically, and not only ascetically, not only through struggles. From the Holy Eucharist they interpret the Holy Tradition: an ascetic experience which is not only monastic but is also apostolic-martyric, consisting of absolute love for and devotion to Christ. It is the committing of one's whole being to Christ the Lamb of God, following Him wherever He may go (cf. Rev. 7:14, 14:4). Just as God presented and gave His whole self to man, so too man, according to the holy hesychasts, should present and give his whole self to God, and thus the salvation of man is completed. (Fr. Justin

---

[4] *In Defense of the Holy Hesychasts* 1.3.38.

Popovich used to say: "For man's salvation, the whole God and the whole man are needed, nothing less.")

The ascetic experience which is spoken about and testified to by Orthodox hesychasts is nothing other than the fulfillment of the grace of Holy Baptism. For Baptism is the first and main struggle (*podvig*) of man, the struggle of freedom and faith by which one embraces Christ our God and Savior and unites with Him; and a further adoption and multiplication of baptismal grace, "the deposit of the Holy Spirit," is given to one immediately after Baptism through Holy Chrismation. Holy Baptism is fulfilled and known in its fullness in the Holy Liturgy. Only through these three basic and inseparable Holy Sacraments is "life in Christ" known in its fullness. This is what the holy hesychasts say and testify, particularly the contemporary of St. Gregory Palamas—St. Nicholas Cabasilas (in his two famous works, *A Commentary on the Divine Liturgy* and *The Life in Christ*). (It is interesting to note how Sts. Gregory Palamas and Nicholas Cabasilas mutually support one another in the exposition and exegesis of the Orthodox ascetic-liturgical experience.)

What is asceticism for St. Palamas? It is the preparation of man, not for mystical flights, and not for an escape from the world, but for union with Christ—a union that has ecclesiological or Churchly dimensions even if the ascetic is a desert dweller or is a martyr who is exiled far away, for this is for the honor and glory of the Church. And not only that, but asceticism is in fact a *new life* in the Church, a new grace and new realization of the eschatological event of union with Christ. In this manner, the martyrs and strugglers are the riches and enrichment of the Church, not so much by their personal accomplishment and crowning (i.e., with the crown of martyrdom and struggle), but by being a success and joy for the Church. In this way an ascetic or desert dweller becomes an incarnation of a dogma—of a Churchly event. However, in the liturgical experience this condition is not simply an ascetic state but is above all the struggler's state of *prayer*, the state of *epiclesis*. Our entire historical life, including that of the Church, is an *invocation* of the Holy Spirit. We have accepted the deposit and the beginning, but at the same time we plead to the Holy Spirit "to come and abide in us, to cleanse us and fill us"; and this *epiclectic* (prayerful) state of the Church is identical to the *epiclectic* state of the hesychasts who engage in the Jesus prayer. Therefore, we should not create polarizations, as we often do, by falling into extremes and one-sidedness; we should not think: what is more important, to be alone or part of a community (in eremitic or coenobitic monasticism)? In the experience of the hesychast ascetics there is no difference between these two positions. That is why Orthodox monasteries, since the beginning, have focused on the Liturgy, and found that it is the Liturgy that gives meaning to and fulfills the experience of the Orthodox ascetics.

However, we should not think, as is often the case, that the Liturgy is only a "sacrament," something holy and sacerdotal, which we automatically accept and make our own. It is rather the revealing of the entire *mystery of union* with God in Christ, which presupposes both freedom and struggle. This entails the dynamic and living stance of man here on earth as the son of God, as the one whom God created uniquely in His own image and incorporates into the community of His Son—into the Church Body. Man is called to the eschatological fullness of his union with God, a union in the community of persons, not in some sort of impersonal blessedness. In short, the summit of the ascetic struggle is in the catholic Church, in which Christ recapitulates God's whole creation.

The hesychasts gave the Orthodox people such an ethos. A few years after St. Gregory Palamas, conquerors entered the Balkans. However, it is of primary significance that we in the Balkans have not only survived the Turkish enslavement, but have until this day preserved the apostolic, martyric, ascetic-liturgical ethos, so that even now we can say that the Orthodox hesychasts are witnesses and teachers for contemporary Orthodox people. What is more, we should transmit this fullness of man to Western Christianity as well.

I could add one personal testimony of something that I believe is significant to our people, who went through the experience of Marxist rule which was and still is a type of inhuman totalitarianism. Communism is not anthropocentric, as we customarily believe. It is a naturalistic ideology, a materialistic, pantheistic ideology, pessimistic and inhuman because it totally depersonalizes man. Our Serbian people defied it only due to the experience which I have called hesychastic. We have therefore tasted another type, another "flavor" of man, and, may I be allowed to say, a different person of God from the one that is customarily depicted in religions, philosophies, faiths, mysticisms, and so on. If we do not preserve within ourselves this knowledge which we have termed hesychastic—and which is nurtured not only on Mount Athos, not only here or there, but wherever Orthodoxy is really practiced, wherever the Gospel is fulfilled—we will end up without both God and man. The Gospel is, according to St. Palamas, the complete work of God and man, the complete *economy of divine operation and dispensation* of Christ; the Gospel is the totality of Christ, Who is God and man.

The God of India, although he is All-God (πάνθεος), has nothing essential to offer man, who remains poor, unhappy, unredeemed, and unfulfilled. I don't care to speak on this too long but I must mention it, since for us Serbs and Greeks Islam has remained a sensitive and relevant subject. The Allah of Khomeini, and also of Mohammed, has nothing to offer us because he has never revealed himself to anyone nor does he intend to reveal himself in eternity. He neither speaks nor has anything to say or offer us. Not only is this kind of God not interested in us, but even all our devotion to Him—Islam means *submission*—ultimately leaves us wounded and defeated, as it is stated in a verse of the Koran. A great Yugoslavian writer, a Muslim of Serb origin, but a very subtle man, Mesha Selimovich, said, "Man is always at a loss with Allah." What a tragedy is contained in these words! How unhappy is Allah's man! His Allah, if he exists at all, is not the God of the Bible, History and Revelation. I seriously doubt any kind of connections between Mohammed and biblical tradition, with regard not only to the Islamic tie with Isaac, but also to the tie with Esau or Ishmael. In any case, this Islamic God has nothing to tell us or offer us, and this has great and direct anthropological consequences. (It has also sociological consequences, but mainly anthropological ones.)

Impersonal gods have nothing to tell us. The absence of God—as I would call atheism—does injustice to man and damages him greatly. It strips man and leaves him despairing and sorrowful in this life, which is just a small foretaste of personhood: personhood that is not simply the subject of psychology or sociology, but has the existential meaning of *person*. When someone tastes love, then he understands the high purpose for which God has created us. "I am wounded with love" (Τετρωμένη

87

ἐγὼ τῆς ἀγάπης), says the human soul and every human being (Song of Songs 5:8).

Only the God Who became man, Who became Christ, Who accepted human nature, human existence, and a human body, and Who in this body, in this existence and in this human love, bestows true fullness—this is the God worthy of man. This is not what ancient *eros*—erotic love—meant. As was nicely shown in the introduction to Plato's *Symposium* by John Sykoutris of Athens, the ancient Greek *eros* is a type of envelopment and returning to oneself, whether it be to the "One" god of Plotinus or Plato, or just to man. Only love as "ecstatic eros" (to use the phrase that St. Palamas borrowed from St. Dionysius the Areopagite); the love of a loving God (ὁ ἀγαπῶν Θεὸς), a God Who "goes out" from Himself in order to meet another, in order to lead man, not to crush man with Himself; the love of a God Who would rather fulfill man and glorify man in a communion of love—only such a love can personalize man in full. Only love affirms and fulfills and celebrates man. Only in Christ does love offer us a guarantee, an assurance, a true confirmation of man, and also that which is for everyone—a unity of all people with God, which is first of all a Community, as is very nicely emphasized by the Metropolitan of Pergamon, Professor John Zizioulas. Both God and man represent the realization of a community: a communion which has the Holy Trinity as the measure of perfect, all-encompassing Love. This Love reveals the wealth of a person, and calls man, in a debt of gratitude to Christ, to taste this abundance, here in this world in His Body, His Church, in the attainment of the *community* of the Holy Spirit, and not only somewhere in the distant, eschatological future. It is eschatology that will show the *fullness* and will reveal what man will really be. This was affirmed by what St. Palamas said, following the Apostle: "When the Son of God appears, then we will be like Him, we will be similar to Him, and we will see Him as He is, but we will also see ourselves in Him, as we truly will be" (cf. I John 3:2).

Thus, Orthodox hesychastic anthropology appears as a doxology, and in fact it is a doxology—there is no greater glorification of God than that of man in Christ.

However, this path is the *path of the Cross*, the path of Death and Life. Holy strugglers and hesychasts knew very well the fullness of the

Orthodox tradition. There exists no other path than the *path of the Cross of Christ*, the path of witness and martyrdom, the path of St. Ignatius—of his "crucified love" for Christ, the path of "the everlasting existence of man, open to the grace of the Holy Spirit." The purpose of man is not simply the development of a dynamic human nature, as the Early Church Fathers said of ancient philosophies. Man lost his God-likeness in Paradise, and he could not fulfill himself and the dynamism of his nature. Even if this were possible, it would again be a sentence of poverty, lack of redemption, self-limitation, and unredeemed grace, for man remains unredeemed without a Communion of Love with the Living God.

To express the view of St. Palamas: man does not seek the Kingdom of God, but seeks the King Who comes to His Kingdom.

Eternal life is nothing other than Christ and man in Christ—that is, the Church. But, in history, the path to this passes through the Cross. There is no other path, and that is why ascetic life means the Cross. The entire progress of the Church in the world and in history is the Cross: let us never forget that. This was the ethos of the Apostles, the ethos of the martyrs, and the ethos of the hesychasts.

Perhaps God gave to us Orthodox people this testimony out of a Love which we do not deserve. Perhaps because we have shown just a slight openness, a certain *inclination*, as the Holy Fathers said: inclination in the sense of man being fully open with faith, love, and struggle to accept the communion of God's love toward His Son and His Holy Spirit. Thus, there is no reason for self-praise, but neither is there reason for disappointment or the depreciation of our exalted nature as human beings—and even more so as Orthodox Christians and as Orthodox nations in the ecclesiological sense. This nation, truly being blood and body, is after all Christ's limb, and it is not of man's will but of God's. This meaning was important for the hesychasts in the fourteenth century and for Orthodox people in the Balkans.

It has not always been like that in recent times, and I say this with my Serbian people in mind, for it has often been thought that "body and blood" will inherit the Kingdom of God. But we know the Kingdom of God will be inherited by the new body and new blood—by our new birth, our rebirth in Christ, Who unites us in the same cradle, from the same Mother and Birthgiver, and from the same Mystery of the Incarnation of God, of the creation of the Church, and of our gathering in Christ.

From all that has been said, it is clear that the anthropology of the holy hesychasts is the message of the entire Gospel and, repeating the words of St. Palamas, nothing less than the Gospel, with its entire divine-human program.

6

The Creation of the World and Man[1]

The biblical account of the creation of the world and man contains a pan-human truth—a tradition recorded by all the major religions of the world—that man is of divine origin. Of course, the biblical testimony concerning the creation of the world and man contains more elements than those of other religions. First of all, we are told that man was created after the rest of the world was created, and that this was a personal, creative act of God supplying man with divine characteristics, thus making him an image of God. The Bible, therefore, says the following about the creation of man: "And God said, 'Let us make man in Our image, in Our likeness'... So God created man in His own image ... male and female He created them" (Gen. 1:26-27). The Bible then goes on to give a more elaborate description of the psychophysical being of man: "And the Lord God formed man from the dust of the ground, and breathed into his nostrils the breath of life; and man became a living soul" (Gen. 2:7). This biblical account contains several elements that need to be emphasized: first of all, man was created by a personal act of a personal God, and he is, therefore, a Godlike and a God-personal being; furthermore, man was created after the rest of the world was created, which means that the rest of the world is conditional with regard to man: the mineral, vegetative and animal worlds all precede man and are all his prerequisites.

Thus, man is part of the world, but he is also the peak, the crown of all creation; he is part of nature, but he is also the king of nature. He is a member of God's household that we call the world, but he is also the host of this household. He is, therefore, a microcosm within the macrocosm, or a world of his own within the grand world of God. However, man is

---

[1] A catechetical lecture given on TV Novi Sad, 1990.

greater than the world itself, since he is a child of God in this world which is God's household, and, at the same time, he is a son of God.

The biblical narrative on the creation of the first man—Adam—does not contain any pessimistic or dark elements. As observed by an excellent scholar of world religions, Mircea Eliade, it gives an optimistic view of man and the world. Man's creation was not meant as some sort of a punishment to him; neither has this world, or man's body, been created as some sort of a dungeon for him. On the contrary, man is a Godlike being, a child of God, but, at the same time, he is closely connected to the rest of the nature by being the very crown of that nature. This shows that God gave man the great role of being a sort of summary, a synthesis of all nature, of all the elements of the world. When it is said that man was made of the "dust of the ground," this would mean that the entire material world (mineral, vegetative and animal) has been incorporated into his physical, bodily being. And, when it is said further on that man became a "living soul," this speaks of his soul and psyche, i.e., the spiritual side of man; it means that the whole of the divinely created spiritual and angelic world has also been incorporated in him. This psychophysical unity in the human being does not represent any kind of dualism; man is soul and body, but first and foremost he is a unique, Godlike person. It is exactly this quality that makes man singular and distinct from the rest of God's creation. It means that man has been designated to communicate with God in a communion of love, and this is why man's place in creation is above all nature. Man is the synthesis of all nature. He is nature's purpose and designation. He has a beginning since he has been created, but he has been created for immortality. This is how human history begins—it has its beginning, but is destined for eternity

This understanding of man—this Christian, biblical anthropology—we the Orthodox call an open anthropology, since man is a dynamic being, having a combination of the material and spiritual worlds within his person. There is no polarization, no dualism, but there is dynamism. Man is dynamically directed to unify the material and spiritual worlds and to bring them both to God. This is his great purpose, his freedom, his history, and, we might say, his destiny. But, since man is Godlike, meaning that he is free, the world's entire destiny is related to him. Therefore, the biblical account of the creation connects the world with man. This is an aspect of modern thought, since the question of ecology—man's living environment—is closely connected with man, his personal relationship with nature, and their common relationship with the Living God. The biblical history of the creation of man is in fact the beginning of human history. It is dynamic, open, positive, creative. Inherent in it are full responsibility and freedom, which are the inseparable companions, factors, and constitutive parts of man.

If this biblical narrative of the creation of man is elaborated by including other biblical narratives that speak of man, we will be able to see that, according to the Bible, man was not created for death, but for immortality. Man was not created to die and decay, but to live eternally. This is why it is said in the Bible that "God did not create death" (Wisdom 1:13), but that everything, being good and for preservation, was created to have its being (cf. Gen. 1:31, Wisdom 1:14). In the book of Wisdom, King Solomon says that God created man for immortality, and that He created him after His own eternal being; death came into the world through the devil's envy (cf. Wisdom 2:23–24). This biblical testimony indicates that the original designation of man is not death or decay. It was in the history of man's creation and life that he, being influenced by the devil, introduced death into this world; that is, in his freedom man chose a way that did not lead to God and immortality, and death came as a consequence. This is why death is a historical phenomenon that is neither natural nor necessary; it is tied to man's nature through sin, but it is not part of his true nature. However, the Bible adds that God also made the salvation of man possible. This salvation is a historical phenomenon and an event in history, too, since God came to save man, to deliver him from death, and to enable him to enjoy immortality and everlasting life.

It is in man's freedom and in his responsibility for his own destiny that one must search for the historical reasons for the existence of death and decay. If we now make a summary of the biblical narrative on the creation of the world, on man's nature and his purpose, then we can briefly say that man's nature and his final designation are connected to the fact that he was, as the Bible says, created in the image and likeness of God. However, these are both in the domain of man's freedom, since he is a free, rational, but also responsible person—responsible for his personal behavior and historical actions. This is why Christ, the Son of God, became man—so that He would save man as a living image of God and reestablish him as a child of God designated for immortal life.

∴

When the Holy Bible says that man was created in the image and likeness of God, this means that man is a personal, rational, conscious, self-determining and responsible being. The image of God in man and his likeness to God indicate that man has his own mind, his own will, his feelings, his freedom, his love, and that he is both an individual and a communal being. According to the Holy Bible, the Christian Faith holds that man, being a person, has as an undisputed value, and that he has solemn dignity. As such he can not and must not be sacrificed or subordinated to anything or anyone. This high dignity elevates man above the rest of nature, above all living beings, as a person, conscious and free, and personally capable of communion. As a Godlike person man needs to become even greater, even more perfect in order to achieve Godlikeness. This is done not only through individuality, through man being a unique individual, but also through the development of a relationship of freedom and love with other individuals. First and foremost, this is to be done in relation to the very prototype or "original" of individuality—that is, in relation to the Living God—and then in relation to other Godlike men. Resembling a cross, man was created to be both an individual and a communal being. His individuality is being formed through communion, and true communion is being formed only through an interaction of individuals. Here lies the Godlikeness of man, after the image of the eternal communion of the Holy Trinity.

The Bible says that man was not only created in the image of God, but was also designated to achieve Godlikeness—to achieve a greater similarity to God, to become like God through freedom and love. This is the eternal purpose of man.

The Godlikeness of man gives meaning to the rest of nature, since man was created as the peak and the crown of all nature, being both a member and the head of the entire creation. Greek wisdom says that man is a microcosm within a macrocosm, but the Holy Bible and Christianity say that man is a macrocosm within a microcosm, meaning that, owing to his Godlikeness, man as a world is much greater than the rest of the world at large. For, within himself, man unifies, heads, and recapitulates the whole of nature. As a free being in a communion of love with God and other men, he brings the whole of nature into communion with God. Man's Godlikeness is his personhood and his capacity for communion, and this provides the meaning and purpose of the whole of nature. This is what makes man the very link between the created spiritual, angelic world on the one side and the created material, mineral, vegetative and biological worlds on the other; he is also the link between the created world and God, Who is the source of all nature and of man's personhood.

We have said that man—as an intelligent, free and responsible person—is Godlike also because he is a being originally created to be communal. In this sense man was created in the image of the biblical Living and True God—in the image of the Holy Trinity. This is the Christian God, Who is both One and communal at the same time, Who is Three Persons: Father, Son, and Holy Spirit in a communion of divine love and freedom, everlasting life and immortality. Thus, man was created to develop as an individual, to develop his God-given and Godlike potentials, virtues, talents, capacities and creativity. But he was also created to develop his communion with other men and God. Both in the capacity of an individual and of mankind as a whole—as a communion of sons of Adam who were designated to be sons of God—man is invited to grow, to perfect himself, so that the whole of mankind will become an eternal communion in Christ, that is, the Eternal Church.

When we say that God created man, we do not mean that everything was concluded and finished as far as the creation of man was concerned. For God created man to be a free and a self-creating person—so that man could participate in his own creation, thus growing into those potentials, talents, gifts, powers and capabilities of his mind and will, of his body and soul. This is all summed up in his psychophysical constitution, not only in the psychological sense, but also in the ontological, existential, personal and social sense. Man builds his own self (his otherness), having God as his model, and this is why the image of God lying in us as a potentiality seeks to achieve the likeness of God, i.e., to achieve similarity, almost sameness with God, through our perfection and growth in God. The basic characteristics of that image of God are love and freedom, but they are all left to man himself to build upon.

Only in the capacity of a mutually connected and conditioned love and freedom does man achieve growth and perfection; only in such a capacity does he develop as an individual and a communicant with other human beings. God sent His Son, our Lord Jesus Christ, Who is man's "original," to help man and bestow on him the capabilities of developing Godlikeness within himself, so that he also might become a son of God and achieve, with other men as his brothers, perfect communion in the image of the Holy Trinity. This communion is the Communion of the Church, within which each individual is being preserved by the preservation of perfect communion. The Christian God is the Holy Trinity: Father, Son, and Holy Spirit, the unity of Three Persons in the communion of the Divine. That is why man was created in the image of the Holy Trinity: for Communion, for the Church. As such he reaches his full meaning within the Church, and in this context Christian anthropology is perfect, since it is an open anthropology—an anthropology of the progress, creativity, eternal life and perfection of man through the God-man Christ.

Part III

7
The Holy Sacrament of Baptism: Entrance into and Living in the Church[1]

Introduction:
The Prerequisites and Theological-Ecclesiastical Context
of the Holy Sacrament of Baptism

Baptism, like everything else in our Christian Faith and our Orthodox Church, can never be seen as independent of the remaining truths, sacraments and realities of our Faith and Church.

The fundamental prerequisite and context of the Sacrament of Baptism is the *catholic, general* Divine Economy of salvation, which includes the creation of the world and man, man's sin and fall, and especially the saving act of Christ's Incarnation, Death and Resurrection, as also Pentecost—the outpouring of the Holy Spirit.

To correctly (in an Orthodox manner) understand Holy Baptism, one must have in mind the creation of man according to the image and likeness of God, i.e., an *open Christian anthropology* by which man is a dynamic being made in God's image, open to life, immortality, deification (θέωσις), communion (κοινωνία) with the God-man, and community—that is, the Church, which is the mystery of the Holy Trinity.

Through sin the dynamic movement of man toward God was ended, and man reached a "paraphysical" (unnatural) state in corruption and death. However, his image was not completely depraved and corrupted. From this derives the possibility of salvation and of returning man to his original designation. And that is done through the saving act of Christ: His Incarnation, Baptism, Crucifixion, Death, and glorious Resurrection, and the gift of the Holy Spirit. In one word, it is

---

[1] A lecture given to the Orthodox Youth, Melbourne, Australia.

through the founding of the *Church* as the new reality, the new means of being and life for man.

1. The Context of the Church: Entering through Baptism

By means of Baptism, one enters into the Church as a *Community* of people in Christ, with God the Father, through the grace of the Holy Spirit. Through Baptism, one enters into the "Economy of Grace" of the Holy Trinity. It is a new creation of the world and man—a *re-creation* (ἀνάπλασις), a *rebirth* (ἀναγέννησις). The new and last (eschatological) "creation" is therefore in the Name of the Holy Trinity: "... is baptized in the Name of the Father, and of the Son, and of the Holy Spirit" (cf. Matt. 28:20, St. Basil and St. Nicholas Cabasilas).

The prerequisite of Baptism, of entering into the Church, *is faith* in Christ the Savior-God-man, and, through Him, faith in the Holy Trinity. This is the Triadological context of the Christian faith in Christ (for that reason the entire Creed is read before the Baptism, and the Baptism itself is not only, as with the Protestants, "a baptism in the Name of Christ," since the reception of the Holy Spirit is also necessary, i.e., a full adoption by God the Father, through the Son in the Spirit): the Holy Trinitarian character of the Orthodox Christian Faith and Baptism, as of everything else in the Church.

True faith assumes *repentance:* a rejection of Satan and evil works and sins, and a turning to the Living and True God. Thence come the *exorcisms* before Baptism, since there neither is nor can be a community between God and Satan, light and darkness, good and evil, life and death, Paradise and hell, the Kingdom of God and the kingdom of death (cf. II Cor. 6:14–16). Repentance is the path of return from the fall of Adam: the reinstatement of obedience and love toward God, of humility in the place of pride. The old man, as a son of the old fallen Adam, by *repentance and faith* turns back to the New Adam, Christ. Through Christ, the old man, like the Prodigal Son, returns to his Father, and the Father returns to him his dignity and inheritance as a son. Repentance, faith and Baptism: this is the returning to life of the dead, the finding of the lost, the resurrecting of those who have passed on. Baptism is a *new birth* or a *new creation* of the new and last communion. It is not only a sacred (sacramental) action for the sake of receiving forgiveness and for personal salvation, but also a partaking of membership in Christ, an "in-churching" (ἐνσωμάτωσις and ἐνχρίστωσις, ἐκκλησιοποίησις). It is a dying with and *being crucified* with Christ, an immersion (βάπτισις—immersing) in the death of Christ and, by this, a dying to sin and death. Baptism is, then, a *resurrection* with Christ into a new, spirit-bearing life. It is an incorporation into the Corpus (Body) of Christ, an incarnational "in-churching" (cf. Rom. 6:3-11).

This becoming a member in Christ takes place by the power and action and grace of the Holy Spirit. "For by one Spirit are we all baptized into one Body," the Body of Christ (I Cor. 12:13). This *pneumatological* character of the Holy Sacrament of Baptism is very important in Orthodoxy. As Christ was *anointed* by the Holy Spirit at His Incarnation and Baptism, so is the newly baptized also anointed and sealed by the Holy Spirit, Who is the Spirit of Christ, so that he—a Christian—also becomes a *"christ"* (an anointed one) of the Lord. The Holy Spirit forms Christ in him (cf. the *Prayer of Baptism:* the last one in the rite of the blessing of the water, before the Baptism itself).

An analysis of the rite and order of the Sacrament of Baptism (according to the Book of Needs), demonstrates, in short, that in the Sacrament of Baptism a *cosmological* dimension is also included: Baptism as an immersion in water, the basic element of matter and the world. Through Baptism, all of creation is consecrated also; and this takes place through man, who is again united with God. Thus all of creation "waits for the revealing of the sons of God" (Rom. 8:19, see also 8:20-26).

Immediately after Baptism follows *the Holy Sacrament of Chrismation*—a sealing and filling with the Holy Spirit. Without this, Baptism is not complete, since it is not a Sacrament "for itself" and "by itself," but rather an entering into membership in the community of the Church, entering into a living relationship with God and with brethren, i.e., with all other people who desire to believe in Christ for eternal life.

This Communion and community is the *"Koinonia* of the Holy Spirit" (II Cor. 13:14), and, through this, "the Communion of the Holy Trinity." Through Baptism we become "partakers of the divine nature" (II Peter 1:4). This means that we begin to live according to the mode of the life of the Holy Trinity: a community of Holy Persons in the Unity of Nature, Life, Love, Being, Energy. Thus is Baptism our *new being* ("genesis"): Τὸ κατὰ Χριστὸν ὑποστῆναι ("existing by Christ"), as says St. Nicholas Cabasilas. In Heb. 3:14 we read: "For we have become partakers of Christ, if we hold the beginning of our confidence [i.e., our *new existence,* our *new mode of life* in Christ and by Christ] steadfast unto the end."

Besides being closely tied with Holy Chrismation, Baptism is also closely bound to the *Holy Eucharist,* i.e., the Divine Liturgy. In fact, Baptism is performed together with the Liturgy. (So it always was and so it should be even today. This is shown by the ecclesiastical calendar, in which periods of fasting occur before the Feasts of the Nativity of Christ and Pascha, and at the Liturgies on the Eve of Nativity and Great Saturday Baptisms are performed, and the newly baptized are introduced to the Liturgy and receive Holy Communion). The practice should be renewed of baptizing children before the Liturgy, up until the Small Entrance, and afterwards giving them Communion at the Liturgy. It is only at the Divine Liturgy that the newly baptized fully becomes a member in the Church as the Body of Christ, becomes a member of a concrete community, of the Eucharistic Church, of the Catholic, Orthodox, Apostolic Church of Christ, of God.

2. Baptism as the Beginning of a New, True Life in the Church

The Holy Sacrament of Baptism is not a magical action that will automatically effect a change in a Christian without his living faith and active participation in the new Christian existence and life. Baptism is found within the general, wider context of the relationship between God and man, of the freedom of God and the free will of man. That relationship is based on a free *cooperation* (συνεργία), on a co-action and co-living (συμβίωσις), where the love of God freely invites man, and man accepts freedom in love, cooperation and co-living.

By means of Baptism, one enters into the army of Christ (St. Gregory of Nyssa), but a soldier still needs to prove that he is really a fighter, i.e., an accomplisher of deeds, a zealous worker, an active participant in the new reality. (For example, if a player who joins a large team does not train and is not active, he will not have anything except membership; constant *training* is necessary for him to remain in good *condition* and to continue to show results.)

In the section of the Epistle to Romans that is read at Baptism, the Apostle Paul says that our rising with Christ is shown as a dying to sin and a continued *living for God, the carrying out of a new life.* That is the dynamic task of our Christian existence. That is the area of our Orthodox *achievement* (in Greek, ἄσκησις; in Slavonic, *podvig*), i.e., the working, training, and functioning of our renewed powers and the energies of our new being in Christ, restrengthened by the grace of the Holy Spirit. It is a new life of *bearing the cross and following Christ,* a life of a sacrificial *feat of love,* the practice of fidelity to the Lamb of God, a witnessing (μαρτυρία) to the everyday newness of Christ's gift of eternal life. It is "worshipping God in Spirit and in Truth" (cf. John 4:23), "walking in Truth" (II John, v. 4), and "doing the Truth" (cf. John 3:21). The life of the baptized is a Liturgy of all life (the first meaning of the word *Leitourgia* (λειτουργία) was the using and functioning of God-given powers and abilities for the good of all, i.e., the Church).

Orthodox asceticism emerges from the grace of rebirth in Baptism. It is the developing, growing and multiplying of God-given talents, for the sake of the *pledge* of the Holy Spirit. It is the experiencing and growing of the seeds of grace through works of virtue. It is the manifestation of the Energies of the Holy Spirit, by Whom we are sealed, confirmed. It is being sure that the light of the Spirit constantly burns and does not go out; it is the offering (priestly service) of one's entire being to God, the bearing of fruit through good deeds for Christ and for the Church.

If we are baptized as children, then Baptism needs to be renewed by *Repentance* (the Holy Sacrament of Repentance and Confession), by salvation-bringing tears of the water of Holy Baptism, which needs to be activated, to be made dynamic and active through faith and will. This does not mean that Baptism is performed more than once, but rather that the grace has hidden itself, pushed back by our negligence, inactiveness and our return to old sins and old dead works. Repentance is not "re-baptism," but rather a renewal of the water of the grace of Holy Baptism through the warm tears of repentance (*St. Diadochus of Photiki* and *St. Mark of the Desert*).

Baptism was, for us, becoming a member of the community of the Church; now repentance needs to renew that ecclesiastical (communal) character of our being and life. One must live actively, dynamically, ascetically, "with all the aints" (Eph. 3:18). For salvation in the Church and life in Christ are not given only once, but are a constant task to be fulfilled. It is not only forgiveness and justification, but also a *new life,* walking in the renewal of the Spirit by means of what is new and newly creating. "Behold, I make (create) all things new," says Christ (Rev. 21:5). For that reason all the Orthodox saints are miraculously new, and the Gospel is always newly created in them.

Baptism is the beginning of evangelical existence. It is the constant, active, ascetic living of the *life in Christ*, through the grace of the Holy Spirit, which is received in the Sacraments, beginning with Baptism and continuing on, and developed and multiplied in virtues, in good deeds. All this together reveals the Orthodox universal-catholic character of Baptism, and shows that it is not something isolated from everything else in Christianity, from the rest of ecclesiastical being and life. The Holy Eucharist requires, as a prerequisite for participation in it, not only the act of Baptism, but also the constant manifestation of a baptized *existence* and the *life* of grace in Christ.

Conclusion

The Holy Sacrament of Baptism is a mystery (a mystical-charismatic reality) of our Faith and our Church, which is linked with the whole Christian vision of God, the world and man. Baptism is also thus linked with the Orthodox Christian *open anthropology*, according to which man is an open, dynamic being, created for eternal communion of life and love with God in Christ.

Human sin had broken and made impossible that communion, but Christ's economy of salvation once again opened up and realized that divine-human communion. Baptism is, in fact, our incorporation into Christ through living faith, our practical participation in the community of the Church, through the grace of the Holy Spirit.

Baptism is the beginning of a *new existence*, an act of charismatic-virtuous growth in cooperation and symbiosis with God. Baptism is the basis—and our further life in the Church is the development and strengthening—of our *theosis* (θέωσις, deification), through our willing co-crucifixion and co-resurrection with Christ. In Baptism is given the entire program of our life in Christ, here on earth as well as in eternity. For only life in Christ the God-man leads man out of the dungeon of sin, death and existential destruction, and leads him into the eternal life of the God-man, for which the human race was created.

8
Liturgy and Spirituality
Athens, 1976[1]

1.

The Liturgy[2] is found at the very center of the life, experience, and understanding of the Orthodox Catholic (*Sobornaya*) Church of God and therefore at the center of Orthodox theology. The Liturgy establishes, but also expresses, the being and life of the Orthodox Church, because the very being of the Church of Christ is *liturgical*, and her life is *eucharistic*.

The whole creation of God, the whole world, is conceived (ἐννοήθη, in the words of St. Gregory the Theologian) and fashioned by God in such a way as to become one great *Economy* (οἰκονομία—

---

[1] A lecture held at the Second Congress of Orthodox Theological Schools, Athens, 1976.

[2] The word *Liturgy* is used here primarily in the meaning of an Orthodox church *gathering* of the faithful ἐπὶ τὸ αὐτό, usually held in the temple for the purpose of celebrating the Holy Eucharist. Liturgy denotes the Holy Eucharist of the Church. Furthermore, the expression *liturgy* is used in a wider sense as Orthodox worship in general, celebration of liturgical actions of the Church, which is recapitulated by the Holy Liturgy of the Church. Finally, we use the word *liturgy* in a wider context, allowed by the eucharistic, church-cosmic dimensions of the Divine Liturgy, in the sense of the true and normal *functions* of every created being: the real function (service) of every living organism, every created thing, the whole of God's creation (since the original meaning of the Greek word "lit-urgy" [λειτ-ουργία] is a public act, performing, work, function, general and public labor for the people, doing works for the good of all). On the other hand, the word *spirituality* (even though we might expect to find the idiom *spiritual life* in the title of this work in order to contrast it with the Western understanding of "spirituality") is used in accordance with the Orthodox Church's ascetic experience: in the sense of a condition or state (quality, virtue) of created beings, primarily man, achieved by the act of the grace-giving Holy Spirit (cf. Gal. 5:22–23). This state is always the result of the energy or influence of the spiritual grace of the Holy Spirit in human existence and life, with man's cooperation in freedom and love, in synergy with the Holy Spirit.

from οἶκος and νέμω) of God in Christ, "the *Economy* of the grace of God" (Eph. 3:2), in the words of the Apostle Paul. This means that the created world is to become one *communion* (κοινωνία) comprising God and creation; to become the *Church*—the *Body* of Christ and the *House* of the Father in the Spirit (cf. Eph. 1:22–23, 2:21–22); to become one "blessed kingdom" of the Father and the Son and the Holy Spirit, the kingdom of "the grace of our Lord Jesus Christ, and the love of God the Father, and the communion of the Holy Spirit" (II Cor. 13:14, and the Holy Liturgy).

The whole world, including man, was fashioned as God's "Economy" (household) and destined to become the Kingdom of God. The whole world had its *liturgy*, its *function* or service, which consisted of a free and loving communion of creation with God the Creator in the Holy Spirit. It was said concerning the Creation of the world that "the Spirit of God moved upon the face of the waters" (Gen. 1:2), because the Spirit of God hovered above the whole material creation—over the world and at the creation of man. "The Lord God ... breathed into his [man's] nostrils the breath of life; and man became a living soul" in the Holy Spirit (Gen. 2:7, cf. I Cor. 15:45, cf. St. Irenaeus of Lyons, St. Basil the Great, etc.). From this it follows that life and the true functioning, action and operation of this God-created world, and especially of man as its crown, should be one continuous *liturgy*—a continuous communication, a living *fellowship* with God in the Holy Spirit. In other words, it should be one continuous liturgical, *eucharistic* way of living, existing, acting and behaving, and, together with this, a eucharistic way of participation (*communion*) in God through the Holy Spirit. In this eucharistic way of living everything is received from God as a *gift* of His goodness and love, and everything is returned to God with *gratitude* (εὐχαριστία means *gratitude*) and offered as *liturgy*, so that again everything might be returned to us by Him as divine grace (χάρις, meaning gift) for life and immortality. "Thine own of Thine own we offer unto Thee, in behalf of all and for all"—this is what our Church confesses and how it acts in the central moment of its Liturgy.

However, through the fall, by which man became "naked"—i.e., without the grace of Holy Spirit—the communion of man and of all created matter with God was cut off. The liturgical and eucharistic way of existing and functioning, and the offering up of man and everything in the world to God became disfigured, corrupt, and finally severed. It stopped functioning correctly and salvifically; it was deformed into a quasi-function (παρὰ-λειτουργία), and so the salvific and life-giving fellowship with the Living God was interrupted. For this reason man, and with him all creation, entered into a nonfunctional state; in other words, man and all creation fell under the destructive and deathly "law" of captivity, alienation and corruption, the "the law of sin" and "the law of death" (cf. Rom. 8:2, 19–22), since there is and can be no life free of corruption, decay and death without the *eucharistic* life in God and with God, without eucharistic liturgizing in Spirit, and without the eucharistic (God-centered, *Spirit*-ual) way of living and existing—in other words, without the eucharistic functioning of man's being and life. Through his fall and his falling-away from God, man descended and sank into an unnatural and anti-natural, sick state of "living in death" and living "for death." Instead of having a true and normal ("natural" for the Godlike and God-centered human being) life in God and a real psychosomatic life in the Holy Spirit, with the attainment of human fullness and authenticity, man fell away from God. This came about because he began living, as has been very well said, "a non-eucharistic life in a eucharistic world."[3]

Since then, instead of freely and lovingly serving and liturgizing before the All-blessed and Man-loving God in Spirit and in Truth with thanksgiving (*eucharistically*), and instead of celebrating (*liturgizing*) the spiritual service (πνευματικὴ λατρεία in the words of the Holy Liturgy) and finding the one true spiritual life (πνευματικὴ ζωή), man was made captive by the chains of "bodily desires and pleasures." For this reason man could no longer *liturgize* (λειτουργεῖν), could no longer offer (προσφέρειν) and function as a *liturgist*—a cosmic priest who sacrifices and offers up to God his whole being and life and the whole world around him, the whole of creation, and through this way of life and sacrifice participates in God's life and holiness (the *spirituality* of God) (cf. I Peter 1:14–16; II Peter 1:3–4; Heb. 12:10). In the words of the Lit-

---

[3] Alexander Schmemann, *For the Life of the World* (Crestwood, N. Y.: St. Vladimir's Seminary Press, 1963), p. 19.

urgy of St. Basil the Great: "No one who is bound by the desires and pleasures of the flesh is worthy to approach or draw near or to serve Thee, O King of Glory"—for He is the only *Holy One,* and the Holy things are given only to the holy.

However, although man forsook God and severed his communion with Him, and although he thereby departed from his true liturgizing, from his salvific functions, activities and duties, God did not leave man, but rather established and realized through His Only Begotten Son a "second communion" (δευτέραν κοινωνίαν)[4] between God and man. This *new communion,* which was realized through Christ's *Economy* of salvation, was firmly established through Christ's Incarnation and voluntary Passion, through His voluntary sacrifice on the Cross, through His glorious Resurrection and Ascension, and finally, through His sending down of the Holy Spirit upon all flesh and all creation on the day of Pentecost (cf. Acts 2:17). Furthermore, the new community not only abundantly overcame the sin and fall of man, but also superseded the first liturgy, the liturgical function and ministry of man and of the world. Since, in Christ the God-man, victory is achieved over the fall of man and its consequences, this new community is created and brought into the world. This Church of the God-man Christ is this new assembly and gathering (σύναξις, σύνοδος) of God and His people, as the community (κοινωνία) of the "Firstborn" and His "many brethren" (Rom. 8:29), as the communion of the Body and Blood of Christ (cf. I Cor. 10:16–17), and as the communion of the Holy Spirit with us all (cf. II Cor. 13:14).

The fulfillment and realization of this salvific event, and the reality of the Economy of God in Christ—the community of the Only Begotten Son of God and those adopted as sons of God—is in fact the Holy Liturgy of the Church, the Divine Eucharist as a spiritual liturgy, i.e., a divinely called meeting of the heavenly *synaxis* and *assembly* of the people of God, in the Holy Spirit and by the Holy Spirit—the people gathered and united in one Body, *the Body of Christ,* through the participation and communion of all the faithful in one Bread and one Spirit (cf.

---

[4] An expression of St. Gregory the Theologian from his Paschal Homily 45.9 (PG 36:639). St. Maximus the Confessor also lauded this "second communion" in *To Thalassius* 54 (PG 90:520).

I Cor. 10:17, 12:12–13; Eph. 4:3–6). Thus the statement of St. John Damascene is theologically quite justified and correct, that the service of the Holy Mystery of the Eucharist, that is, the Holy Liturgy, "fulfills the complete spiritual and supernatural Economy of Christ's Incarnation (πᾶσαν πληροῖ τὴν πνευματικὴν καὶ ὑπερφυῆ οἰκονομίαν τῆς τοῦ Θεοῦ Λόγου σαρκώσεως)."[5]

We consider that everything which has been said thus far is sufficiently clear and that it is not necessary to continue further on this subject. Every Orthodox theologian, we believe, will agree with the truth that the Liturgy of the Orthodox Church of Christ encompasses and is identified with the fullness of the Economy (οἰκονομία) of Christ's Incarnation for our salvation and deification.

2.

But why does St. John Damascene, in the above-cited text, characterize the Divine Economy of salvation (οἰκονομία) with the word *"spiritual"* when speaking of the *Incarnation* of God the Logos? Why is it said that Christ's Economy is "spiritual" when the Liturgy (*Eucharist*) of the Church, as the fulfillment and achievement of that Economy, is undoubtedly and truly the actual bread and wine and then the no-less-real *Body* and *Blood* of the incarnate Christ, our true food and drink?

The fact that the Incarnation of the Son of God is real and bodily and that His Body and Blood in the Eucharist are also a reality and actual physicality does not interfere with the fact that these are at the same time *spiritual*. The Divine Economy (οἰκονομία) and Divine Eucharist (Liturgy) are truly human or, more correctly, divine-human realities, because both are *spiritual* and "of the Holy Spirit and the Virgin Mary," as we confess in the Creed. Just as the Incarnation and becoming man of the Son and Logos of God were accomplished through the Holy Virgin Theotokos and were accompanied by the descent of the Holy Spirit (cf. Luke 1:35), so the gifts of the Church, the bread and wine of the Holy Eucharist, which the Church offers to God at the Eucharistic gathering, truly become the Body and Blood of Christ only through the *"invocation and*

---

[5] *On the Body and Blood of Christ* 2 (PG 95:408C).

descent of the Holy Spirit," as St. John Damascene has said.[6] This has been confirmed by many other Orthodox theologians throughout the centuries of Orthodox tradition, especially by the liturgical Holy Fathers: St. Cyril of Jerusalem, St. Basil the Great, St. John Chrysostom, and others.[7] It is precisely because of this priestly and sanctifying activity of the Holy Spirit in and over the Church that the Liturgy is called, in the Orthodox theological-liturgical tradition, the "spiritual mysteries" (πνευματικὰ μυστήρια), "spiritual service," "spiritual sacrifice," "spiritual feast," even "spiritual body," "spiritual food and drink," "spiritual chalice," "the source of the Spirit (πηγὴ Πνεύματος)," and similar names.

Accordingly, the Liturgy of the Orthodox Church is entirely *spiritual* just as the complete Economy in the body (ἡ κατὰ σάρκα οἰκονομία) of Christ the God-man is spiritual. However, this is not in the sense of an "idealization" or "spiritualization," or of any *dematerialization* of the liturgical holy gifts and liturgical service and serving (function and practice), because the bread and the wine with water in the Holy Liturgy are material realities of this world which are not merely changed in appearance (κατὰ δόκησιν—Docetically, seemingly), but truly changed into the true reality of the Body and Blood of Christ. The divine liturgical service of the Church is *spiritual* and her eucharistic gifts are *spiritual* because they are accomplished, blessed, sanctified and *spiritualized* by the power and action of the Holy Spirit of God—in other words, they are infused by the divine grace of God, Who is a *Spirit* (cf. John 4:24). This is also why the Church Fathers say that in the Divine Liturgy, the Eucharistic gifts which the Church offers and celebrates, and of which all the faithful partake, are not only bread and wine which become the Body and Blood, but are at the same time infused with the Divinity of Christ. "If Christ is God and man," says St. Symeon the New Theologian, "then His Holy Body is not just a *body* (σάρξ) but a body and God indivisible and commingled, for He is body—the bread which is visible to our eyes—and He is the invisible Divinity, Who is seen by the eyes of

---

[6] *The Exact Exposition of the Orthodox Faith* 4.13.
[7] The key liturgical-theological question here is about the *epiclesis* during the Holy Liturgy, where the Roman Catholic Church and its liturgical praxis and theology have diverted from the ancient Christian tradition.

the soul."[8] St. John Damascene says that, in Holy Communion, we the faithful "are united with the Body of the Lord and with His Spirit.... For the Body of the Lord is a life-creating spirit, since It is conceived by the Life-giving Spirit. For 'that which is born of the Spirit is spirit' (John 3:6). I say this not to detract from the nature of the Body, but to show Its life-giving character and Its Divinity."[9]

We do not think it is necessary to dwell much longer on this theological truth, that is, to prove that the complete Liturgy of the Orthodox Church is *spiritual,* that it is of the Holy Spirit and in the Holy Spirit—in short, that the Holy Eucharist of the Church is the revelation and uncovering in the Holy Spirit of the all-embracing and ultimate reality of our Faith. This is confirmed by the Liturgy as the main act and central event of the Church and Church life, and it is undoubtedly confirmed by the texts of liturgical prayers (it is well known that the prayers of the Church are the best confessions and elucidations of the Faith of the Church). In these prayers throughout the Liturgy, the Holy Spirit is called upon to descend "upon us (the celebrating priests) and upon these offered gifts and upon all the people of God" with His divine power, to consecrate "the *spiritual* offering" on "the *spiritual* table" and to unite us all through "the one bread and cup," i.e., the Body and Blood of the one Christ, to unite into "the communion of the Holy Spirit" (Liturgy of St. Basil the Great).

This "communion of the Holy Spirit" (II Cor. 13:14) is the proof and guarantee of the *spirituality* of the Liturgy, because the spirituality of the Liturgy comes and arises from the *invocation* (ἐπίκλησις) and the descent and action of the Holy Spirit. This prayerful invocation (*epiclesis*) of the Holy Spirit, and of all Orthodox *epiclectic* spirituality in general, is characteristic not only of the Holy Eucharist and Liturgy, but also of other prayers, mysteries and ministrations, and of all the divine services of the Church—in short, of each sacred rite, activity, function and service, of all *spiritual* life on earth in the true and salvific Church of

---

[8] *Ethical Sermons* 10, ed. *Sources Chrétiennes,* no. 129 (Paris, 1967), p. 313. Cf. p. 272: "It is not only the bread and wine of Holy Communion through which forgiveness and communion of life are bestowed, but it is also through the Divinity which is mysteriously united with them and commingled."
[9] *The Exact Exposition of the Orthodox Faith* 4.13.

Christ. In his very important book *On the Holy Spirit,* St. Basil the Great confirms this when he says: "Is not the ordering (διακόσμησις) of the Church clearly and indisputably due to the action of the Holy Spirit?" Then, quoting the well-known ecclesiological verse of I Corinthians 12:28, he adds: "This order (τάξις) in the Church is *given and ordered* (διατέτακται) by the distribution of the gifts of the Holy Spirit."[10] In the liturgical service of Pentecost, this same idea is expressed even more clearly: "The Holy Spirit grants all things (χορηγεῖ—rewards greatly) ...; the Holy Spirit makes prophets, perfects priests ...; He constitutes and upholds (συγκροτεῖ) the whole institution of the Church."[11]

3.

If we accept what has been said so far—that the Holy Spirit, as the soul of the Church, truly permeates, animates, and accomplishes all things in the Church, and especially in the liturgical life of the Church, in its ministrations (hierurgical functioning), with the Holy Eucharist at the center and pinnacle—then it is natural to ask the following question: Is it then possible that the *life* of the members of the Church outside of the Liturgy and common worship are not from the Holy Spirit or are without the Holy Spirit? Is it possible that the "non-liturgical" life of the faithful in the Church (if one can speak of such a thing), the "moral" or even "spiritual" life of everyday existence and work, are not from the Holy Spirit or are without the Holy Spirit?

The total experience of the Orthodox Church throughout the centuries demonstrates the contrary. It confirms that all the rest of the Church's life in all her members—as limbs of the eternal God-man Christ—is also *spiritual* (πνευματική) life, since it is nothing less than the fruit and effect of the *Holy Spirit,* and since it comes about and exists by the activity and grace of the Holy Spirit with our free cooperation (synergy), with Him as our Life-Giver and Life-Creator. This other life is also called *spiritual life* in the Orthodox tradition, because it, too, is of the Holy Spirit and in the Holy Spirit.

But we should add that the common term *spiritual life,* used throughout the centuries of Orthodox experience and tradition, does

[10] St. Basil the Great, *On the Holy Spirit* 39.
[11] *Pentecostarion,* Great Vespers of Pentecost, sticheron on "Lord, I have cried," tone 1.

not mean merely what is usually called "moral" or "ethical" life, or "spirituality," or some "higher intellectual ideal," or something similar. From the perspective of Orthodox spiritual experience, all of these categories would come under the heading of bodily (σαρκική) life, or, in the best case, in accordance with the Apostle Paul and the Holy Fathers, they would just be psychological (ψυχική) life (cf. James 3:15; I Cor. 2:14). Calling this kind of life "spiritual life," as is usually done, is justifiable only in the sense that in the world there are many different "spirits" (cf. I John 4:1–3). Strictly speaking, "moral" or "intellectual" life or "spirituality," which is reduced to man's spirit and to immanent material things, regardless of whether they are only material or spiritual or both (this is where all natural religious experiences and various kinds of mysticism meet), is not *spiritual* life in Orthodox tradition, because it is life "without Spirit," life outside the Holy Spirit, life without the Spirit of God and Christ. And no matter how rich and elevated it is according to the measures of the world, in the end it is still very impoverished and deprived (cf. Rev. 3:17–18). It is a "naked" life, without the grace of God, just as our forefather Adam was naked after his fall and separation from the Living and True God.

The Orthodox understanding of spiritual life, and consequently of *spirituality*, has always meant life which springs from the Holy and Life-giving Spirit, a life with the Holy Spirit and in the Holy Spirit, or a life in Christ through the Holy Spirit—in short, the life of the faithful in Christ through the Holy Spirit; and this is life in its divine and divine-human fullness.

This Orthodox *spiritual life* of the faithful, the life of the faithful in Christ through the grace of the Holy Spirit, even though we have called it "non-liturgical," is entirely liturgical in its origin and character.

We have seen that the Liturgy of the Orthodox Church represents the realization and actualization of the entire Economy of salvation of Christ, which is the only way of overcoming and triumphing over man's fall, sin and death, and presents the true resurrection, revival and permanent salvation of man and the world through Christ's Resurrection and the bestowal of the Holy Spirit on man. This is why the entire Liturgy of the Church consists in "the proclamation of the death and Resurrection of Christ till He come" (cf. I Cor. 11:26 and the Liturgy of Basil the Great).

The entire spiritual life of the faithful in Christ consists of being co-crucified and dying with Christ, and of co-resurrecting with Him (cf. Rom. 6:4–14), which proves and confirms that the Christological truth of the Divine Liturgy (eucharistic Christology and soteriology) extends and is transmitted to the lives of all the faithful. In each Liturgy the whole Economy of the God-man, Christ the Savior, and His whole life are repeated and imparted, and are actualized liturgically *hic et nunc* (here and now). The consequence and continuation of this fact is the personal knowledge of Orthodox experience: that in the spiritual life of the Orthodox Christian the whole Economy (soteriology) of the life of Christ is repeated and relived, and only by living Christ's life does man triumph over the inherited fall and the personal fall of human nature, sin and death. The Holy Apostles, especially Paul and John, speak much of this, as do many Holy Fathers of the Eastern Church. St. Gregory the Sinaite, for example, writes: "Everyone baptized into Christ should pass progressively through *all the stages of life that are in Christ* (τὰς μεθηλικιώσεις πάσας τὰς ἐν Χριστῷ). For in baptism a person receives the power so as to progress, and he can grow and learn by keeping the commandments."[12]

Furthermore, the following should be emphasized: Just as Christ is actively and truly present in the Holy Liturgy as Savior and God-man—Who by the power and mercy of the Holy Spirit transforms the eucharistic bread and wine into His Body and Blood and gives Himself to the faithful—so too He is the same in the spiritual life of every one of the faithful who seeks salvation. He is there as the Savior and salvation, because by the same grace of the Holy Spirit he *forms Himself* (μορφώνει—is formed) in each believer by entering him and living in him (cf. Gal. 4:19; I John 4:9–13), so that everyone can repeat after the Apostle Paul those well-known words about the Christ-centeredness of true Christian life: "Not I, but Christ lives in me" (Gal. 2:20).

In this way, Christ, Who is one and the same in the Church's Liturgy and in the spiritual life of the faithful, reveals Himself not only as the Foundation and the Head of the Church (His catholic Body) and as the Bread of Life for all the faithful of the Church collectively as

---

[12] St. Gregory of Sinai, in *The Philokalia*, vol. 4 (London: Faber and Faber, 1998), p. 253.

members of His own Body, but also as their enduring *Life* (cf. John 6:51-56; Col. 3:3-4, 2:6, etc.) and "the beginning and foundation and hypostasis of every virtue in them."[13]

The Liturgy, and hence the liturgical life of the Church in general, is the basis and source of the whole spiritual life and effort of the faithful, of which their entire *spirituality* is the consequence and result. This spiritual life is the fruit and continuation of the one, same and unique life of Christ in the faithful. It is attained in the Liturgy in a spiritual-corporeal way (σαρκικῶς καὶ πνευματικῶς, in the words of St. Ignatius),[14] and after the Liturgy it overflows into the lifelong effort of the Orthodox Christian. This type of liturgical-ascetical experience and vision of life, this liturgical-ascetic *ethos* (ἦθος and ἔθος), reveals the fundamental truth of Christianity in general, the truth of the Gospels and of Holy Tradition: "In this the love of God was manifested toward us, that God has sent his Only Begotten Son into the world, that we might *live through Him*" (I John 4:9).[15]

In this way the liturgical-spiritual life of Orthodoxy is revealed as the *experiencing of the Mystery of Christ*, which is one and the same in the Liturgy and the liturgical life of the Church, and in the other life struggles of the faithful in the Holy Spirit. This unified liturgical-spiritual experience of Orthodoxy reveals, even during this lifetime, the ultimate eschatological truth and reality of the Mystery of Christ: On the one hand, the ecclesiological and personal reality of the experience of life in Christ, by which all the faithful are united and identified with Christ in the eucharistic assembly (σύναξις) and the Church Liturgy—as the Church, the *Body of Christ*—and all become "one in Jesus Christ" (εἷς ἐν Χριστῷ—Paul in Gal. 3:28), or, as St. John Chrysostom says: all become "one Christ" (πάντες Χριστὸς εἷς ἐγένεσθε, σῶμα αὐτοῦ ὄντες—"all of you became one Christ because you are His body").[16] On the

---

[13] St. Maximus the Confessor, *To Thalassius* 64 (PG 90:732B). Cf. St. Gregory of Sinai, in *The Philokalia* (Greek), vol. 4, pp. 43-44.

[14] Cf. St. Ignatius, Epistles to: Ephesians (8), Magnesians (1), Smyrnians (12).

[15] In the words of St. Nikolai (Velimirovich) of Zhicha: "Christ did not come into the world only to teach us life, or only to repair our life, but to become and be our life" (*Prayers by the Lake* [Belgrade, 1922], p. 75).

[16] St. John Chrysostom, *On the Epistle to the Colossians*, Homily 8.2 (PG 62:353).

other hand, thanks to the incorporation (ἐνσωμάτωσις)[17] into Christ through Baptism, Chrismation (anointing by the Holy Spirit) and the Eucharist (Liturgy), the faithful, in their life in Christ, become "anointed ones" (κεχρισμένοι), that is, they become *christs—χριστοί*, as St. Methodius of Olympus and many other Holy Fathers say: "Become christs through the fellowship of the Spirit (οἱονεὶ Χριστῶν γεγονότων τῶν πιστῶν κατὰ μετουσίαν τοῦ Πνεύματος)."[18]

In other words, in the liturgical and spiritual life and experience of the Orthodox Church, Christ is *all and in all* to all the faithful who are the living limbs of the eternally living Christ—τὰ πάντα καὶ ἐν πᾶσι (Col. 3:11).

4.

Even though Orthodox liturgical life and spiritual life are of a Christological character and are Christ-centered, we must emphasize immediately that they are also entirely of the Holy Spirit and through the Holy Spirit. The *Holy Spirit* is the One Who accomplishes and performs all things, not only in Baptism and the Liturgy, but also in the ascetical effort of the spiritual life of the faithful. He anoints and sanctifies the faithful by His grace and makes them Christ-like and Christ-bearers; He makes them holy, Spirit-bearers and *spiritual* (πνευματικοί). Without the grace of the Holy Spirit, Whose name is Holiness,[19] there is neither *sanctification* nor *holiness,* and consequently no *union* and *communion* (κοινωνία—fellowship) with God, Who is Spirit and Truth, Who is Holy and Holiness, Who is Life and the fellowship of Life in catholic fullness and catholic Trinitarian *perichoresis.* According to the Apostle Paul, therefore, people without the Holy Spirit are "alienated from the life of God" and are "without God in the world" (Eph. 4:18, 2:12). Many Orthodox Fathers of the Church speak of this *spiritual,* Paracletic character of Christian life. "Without the Holy Spirit," says St. Athanasius the Great, "we are foreign to and far from God, and only through partaking (τῇ

---

[17] Fr. Justin Popovich calls this *uhristovljenje* or *ucrkvljenje* (ἐν-χρίστωσις or ἐκκλησιοποίησις). See *Orthodoxy and Ecumenism* (Thessalonica, 1974), pp. 13, 15.
[18] St. Methodius, *Symposium (Banquet)* VIII.8, ed. *Sources Chrétiennes,* no. 95 (Paris, 1963), p. 220.
[19] Cf. St. Basil the Great, *On the Holy Spirit* 22, 46–48, etc.

μετοχῇ) of the Spirit are we united with the Divinity."[20] St. Basil the Great similarly says: "There is no sanctification (or holiness) without the Holy Spirit."[21] St. John Damascene testifies: "Union of God with men takes place through the Holy Spirit."[22] And, finally, St. Symeon the New Theologian says: "No one can be perfectly called a believer if he does not receive the Holy Spirit ... for only the gift of grace (cf. I Peter 1:13) of the Holy Spirit makes us communicants and partakers of the Divine Nature" (cf. II Peter 1:4).[23]

All these quotations and testimonies of the Holy Fathers confirm and reveal this other foundation of Christianity: namely, that the Holy Spirit is sent from God and given by Christ in the Church as the Life-creating and Life-giving Source, the Sanctifier and Savior of the faithful, the Animator and Inspirer and Comforter and Deifier. As St. Cyril of Jerusalem calls Him: "This good Creator of the holy things (ἁγιοποιός) of the Church and Helper, Ally, Protector and great Teacher of the Church, Ruler of souls, Guide of those in trials, Enlightener of the lost, Setter of the contest of the strugglers, and Rewarder of the victors, the Holy Spirit Comforter."[24] In the words of St. Cyril, St. Cyprian and many other Holy Fathers, only the One, Holy, Catholic and Apostolic Church of Christ has its Paraclete, and the reason that it is called Catholic (καθολική) is that it contains all the grace-bestowing gifts of the Holy Spirit. "It is called Catholic (καθολική)" says St. Cyril of Jerusalem, "also because it *catholically* (καθολικῶς—in totality) contains every type of virtue, in words and in deeds, and in every kind of spiritual gift (πνευματικοῖς παντοίοις χαρίσμασιν—all types of gifts of grace)."[25]

In view of what has been said, spirituality in the Orthodox Church—which originates and is fed in its entirety by the liturgical life of the Church, and which is given a liturgical character and function by this life—is at the same time entirely of Christ and of the Holy Spirit. It

---

[20] *Against the Arians* 3.24.
[21] *On the Holy Spirit*, 38.
[22] *Homily on the Nativity of the Theotokos* 3.
[23] St. Symeon the New Theologian, *Ethical Sermons* 4 (*op. cit.*, p. 36) and 10 (p. 294). See also St. Athanasius the Great, *Dialogue on the Holy Trinity* 1.7.
[24] *Catechesis* 16.14 and 19; 17.13.
[25] *Catechesis* 18.23; cf. also 17.29, etc.

is at the same time Christological and Pneumatological, meaning also *Triadological* because everything that is of Christ and of the Holy Spirit is also of God the Father. The life of the Holy Trinity is one and the same essence, energy and activity—one grace. Therefore, in Orthodoxy it is all the same: having and leading a true spiritual life and being a Christ-bearer, a true Christian and a spiritual man. It follows that a spiritual man is not some "bodiless" or "ideal" man, but a true and real spiritual-bodily man filled with the grace of the Holy Spirit. As St. Irenaeus of Lyons says: "According to the Apostle (I Cor. 2:15, 3:1), those who are spiritual are so by the participation of the Holy Spirit (οἱ κατὰ μετάληψιν τοῦ Πνεύματος ὄντες πνευματικοί), and not because they deprive their bodies or practice abstinence."[26] The "spiritual man" in Orthodoxy does not imply simply a moral-virtuous man (because such a man is only earth that is passible (γῆ πάσχουσα), as the early Christians used to say),[27] but a man who has the Holy Spirit, the Spirit of God, and the fruits of the grace of the Spirit (cf. Gal. 5:22; Eph. 5:9).

These fruits of the Holy Spirit can be called—as they are in the ascetic literature of the Orthodox East—deeds, ascetic struggles, and virtues. But these virtues and deeds are always to be understood as spiritual gifts of the free and loving cooperation between the grace-bestowing Holy Spirit and the entire psychosomatic man. It is characteristic of the Fathers of the Church to give the following names to these deed and fruits: "spiritual deeds," "spiritual *podvigs* (struggles)," and "spiritual virtues." These names embrace all the fruits of spiritual and bodily grace-bestowing ascetic struggles. In the grace-filled experience of the Orthodox East, everything that is done and experienced by the spiritual and hallowed man is also *spiritual*, hallowed, spiritualized, and consecrated by the grace of the Holy Spirit, because these "deeds" and "fruits" of the spiritual man are the results and fruits bestowed upon him by God the Holy Spirit, by Whom he is led (cf. Rom. 8:14; Gal.

[26] *Against the Heresies* 5.6.1. St. Irenaeus continues: "But if the Spirit be wanting to the soul, he who is such is indeed of an animal nature, and being left carnal, shall be an imperfect being, possessing indeed the image [of God] in his formation, but not receiving the likeness through the Spirit; and thus is this being imperfect." Ed. *Sources Chrétiennes*, no. 153 (Paris, 1969), pp. 75–77.
[27] The Epistle of Barnabas 6:9.

5:18). The spiritual man has the Holy Spirit as the *gift* of God, but in a certain way he has earned this gift on his own. This is what St. Seraphim of Sarov meant when he said that the aim of our Christian life is to "acquire the Holy Spirit."[28] Even though the Holy Spirit is given in the liturgical and sacramental existence and life of the Church, the faithful continually acquire Him through their God-pleasing struggles and virtues. This twofold truth of spiritual life is affirmed equally in the liturgical and ascetical writings of the Holy Fathers of the Church, which are the fruits of their liturgical-ascetic spiritual experience.

5.

A very specific and important theological and historical event took place during the fourteenth century. At that time the battle of hesychasm took place in Orthodox lands. It happened on two fronts, against two heretics who had opposing understandings of spirituality and spiritual life. On one side, it was a battle against the anti-Church and anti-liturgical "spirituality" of the heretical Messalians, and on the other side, it was a battle against Western Scholasticism, devoid of the Holy Spirit—that is, graceless "spirituality" (or, more exactly, a "spirituality" of *created grace*, i.e., non-divine but only ethical, moralistic, and humanistic)—which negated divine energy, the uncreated grace of the Holy Spirit, and was based only on the "created gifts" of God, which reduced Scholasticism to plain moralistic and humanistic "spirituality."

The old Messalian heresy of the so called Euchites, which resurfaced again after the seventh century in heretical branches of Neo-Manichaeism (Paulicianism and Bogomilism), and in pure Messalianism, negated and rejected the Church and its liturgical-sacramental life: the Mysteries of Baptism and the Eucharist, the ministry, the liturgical assemblies of the faithful in temples, and all common church prayers and services. Just like the ancient Gnostics, Manichaeans and others, the Messalians (the ancient ones and those of the fourteenth century) rejected the Church liturgical life in the name of a spirituality which was without church or liturgy and which consisted solely of individual prayer (hence their name, *Euchites*—those who pray) and of

---

[28] *Conversation with Motovilov.*

extreme ascesis, which included the avoidance of all relationships and ties with the material world (they fasted to extremes, rejected marriage and children, etc.). Such a "spiritual" life was preached by the Messalians, for they thought that these measures would expel the evil spirit which abides in man's heart, and so make room for the Holy Spirit. The Orthodox Church responded immediately in the fourteenth century, as it had earlier, and as a result of its true liturgical-hesychastic spirituality, anathematized the preacher of this heresy. Such spirituality of the Messalian type (and many such Christian and non-Christian "spiritualities" exist today: various forms of mysticism, non-grace-bestowing asceticism, spiritism, yoga, Zen Buddhism, and so on) is also rejected by true Orthodox spiritual understanding and experience, and by Orthodox theology. (The mistrust that some Western, mainly Roman Catholic, theologians have of certain saints—such as St. Symeon the New Theologian and St. Gregory Palamas—whom they suspect of "Messalianism" or "sick mysticism," is misguided. This view is unfortunately also shared by some Orthodox "professors of theology" who are under Western influence. In expressing such a view, these theologians only exhibit their pseudo-spirituality, primarily of the Western type.)

The condemnation of this Messalian "spirituality" by Orthodox hesychasts was a result of their profound experience and knowledge of Orthodox liturgical spirituality. For the hesychasts, all the Holy Mysteries of the Church (which were rejected by the Messalians as unnecessary)—Baptism, Chrismation, and the Eucharist—have always remained *divine sources* from which true spirituality springs and is nourished, as the true and salvific spiritual life of man. This was the message of St. Gregory Palamas to the Messalians of the fourteenth century. He was one of the main defenders of hesychastic spiritual life. He writes about the Holy Mysteries of Baptism and the Eucharist: "These two Mysteries contain our salvation, because these two mysteries combine and recapitulate the full *Theandric* Economy"—the entire divine-human Economy and dispensation of salvation of Christ.[29] Similar to him was St. Nicholas Cabasilas, who, in his important work *The Life in Christ,* shows in an unsurpassed way that the Orthodox spiritual life is

---

[29] *Homily* 60.3, ed. S. Oikonomou (Athens, 1861), p. 250.

entirely liturgical, sacramental and mysteriological. In the name of this true Orthodox and liturgical spirituality, the Orthodox Church and its theology have always condemned and rejected any Messalian or similar "spirituality," because it is impossible and nonsensical to represent or defend even the possibility of the existence of real spiritual life and the true experience of salvation outside the Church—the Body of Christ—and outside of the Church's liturgical, grace-bestowing life and her experience in the Holy Spirit.

The Orthodox hesychasts of the fourteenth century condemned and rejected with equal determination and just as unambiguously the Western moralistic and humanistic perception of spirituality. The spirituality and spiritual life of which Barlaam of Calabria was a representative reduced itself to a plain moral "imitation" (*imitatio*) of Christ, or some "habit of virtue" (*habitus*) gained through ascesis with the possible help of the grace of God—but of grace which was *created,* and not the eternal, uncreated divine and *divinely creative energy* of the Holy Spirit, as grace is experienced and understood in Orthodoxy. The understanding of this spirituality, whose representative in the fourteenth century was Barlaam of Calabria—a man who came from the West to Byzantium and found a following there—is an understanding which negates the reality of the experience of the Holy Fathers, who in their earthly lives experienced and acknowledged the anticipated eschatological reality of salvation and deification through the experience and adoption of the eternal and uncreated grace of God (which appears and is experienced as the energy of uncreated light, power, goodness, love of God, etc.). This spirituality had to be condemned and rejected by the spiritual experience of the Orthodox East and its grace-bestowing empirical theology. Barlaam's interpretation of spiritual life was actually a blasphemy against the Holy Spirit,[30] because it reduces our salvation in Christ and our grace-filled spiritual life in the Holy Spirit to the simple moral "improvement" of fallen human life, human virtue and morals, and it rejects the *deifica-*

---

[30] By defending the true faith in the Holy Spirit and in His uncreated grace, the Orthodox hesychasts also defended the Orthodox teaching about the Holy Spirit against the Latin heresy of the Filioque, since that Western non-Orthodox teaching, which demeans the Holy Spirit, inevitably had effects on the life, organization and spirituality of Western Christianity.

tion (θέωσις) of man and his *spiritualization* in body and soul as his crowning, his true meaning and designation, his glorification, and as his grace-filled *theanthropification* in the *Theanthropos* Christ.

This Western understanding of man's spiritual life was held by many moralists and pietists, both before and after Barlaam of Calabria, and it is held even today. Even though this understanding desires to be identified with the Church—in other words, with Church spirituality—it inadvertently and inevitably returns to the position of a para-church, Messalian, graceless spirituality, as St. Gregory Palamas himself concluded. He writes in *Tomos Aghioritikos:* "He who says that perfect union with God can come (τελεῖσθε) without the deifying (θεοποιοῦ) grace of the Holy Spirit, and that it comes only through imitation and relation (τῇ μιμήσει τε καὶ σχέσει), like those who share the same ethics (τοὺς ὁμοήθεις) and share common love for one another; and likewise he who feels that the deifying grace of God is only a habit (*habitus*—ἕξις) of intelligent beings acquired through imitation (*imitatio*—μίμησις), but does not consider grace to be the supernatural and inexpressible illumination and the Divine Energy, which is invisibly seen and incomprehensibly understood by those who are made worthy—such a man should know that he unknowingly has fallen into the error of Messalianism."[31]

From this hesychast text it should not be concluded that Orthodox spiritual life does not embrace true, natural human morality, man's ethical perfection and development, the moral-spiritual advancement of man, and, in general, man's struggle and aspiration to imitate God through virtue. (St. Basil the Great and other Fathers say: "Christianity is the imitation of the Divine Nature."[32]) This text wishes to emphasize the entire truth of authentic Orthodox spirituality, that is to say, that the Orthodox spiritual life is not confined only to morals, virtues, virtuous habits (*habitus*), moral "imitation" of Christ, or mimicking God. "Every virtue of ours and our imitation of God," says St. Gregory Palamas, "makes man more suitable (ἐπιτήδειον) for union with God, but that inexpressible union is accomplished (τελεσιουργεῖ) only by the grace of the Holy

---

[31] *Aghioritikos Tomos* 2, *Syngrammata* of St. Gregory Palamas, ed. P. Chrestou (Thessalonica, 1966), p. 570.

[32] *Homily on the Creation of Man* 1.17 (PG 44:273; this homily is attributed also to St. Gregory of Nyssa).

Spirit."[33] Orthodox spirituality is not simply human and humanistic, but a divine-human spirituality (*theo-human, theanthropic*, as Fr. Justin Popovich would say). This spirituality is made possible and given as a gift through the hypostatic union of God the Logos with our human nature. This is the spirituality generated in the Church by the Holy Spirit, through the Orthodox Liturgy and Orthodox spiritual life, and it is realized as grace-filled union and as the life of each true believer, in love and freedom, in communion with Christ, in the Living and True God.

From all that has been stated above it follows that Orthodox spirituality shows itself in all of its aspects as an ascetical-liturgical spirituality, because it is entirely Christological and Christ-centered (within the bounds and according to the measure of Orthodox Chalcedonian Christology), and because it is entirely of the Holy Spirit, Pneumatological (in accordance with the Orthodox confession of the Holy Spirit and His uncreated grace and deifying energy).

Along with all of this, it is necessary at least in the shortest of sketches to add the following truth of Orthodox spiritual knowledge and experiential theology. Orthodox spirituality is liturgical, and this liturgical spirituality has been shown to be anthropologically true and salvific for man, because it bestows rebirth and reestablishes the entire human psychosomatic being, the human spirit and human body, and the entire human life into that God-given *liturgy* and hierurgy of which we spoke at the beginning of this lecture. True spiritual life, known through grace-filled Orthodox ascetic experience and knowledge, creates and enables the liturgizing and functioning of the real Godlike and God-centered human being, healthy and functional as God created him, and as He designated him. The entire Orthodox spiritual-ascetic life is one continuous eucharistic, God-centered liturgy, and therefore the manifestations of the Church Liturgy are felt in each God-pleasing struggle: in the struggle of faith, in repentance and peaceful self-knowledge, in the struggle for the purification of soul and body, the struggle of prayer and fasting, the struggle of keeping to every divine commandment, and in every bodily and spiritual virtue—in short, in the entire struggle of the life and functioning of man. That is, it is the eucharistic

---

[33] *Aghioritikos Tomos* 2, p. 571.

practice and function of *giving* and offering up (προσφορὰ καὶ ἀναφορά) yourself and your entire being and life to your Living and True God— always through Christ and in the Holy Spirit. The frequent liturgical repetition and prayer, "Let us commend ourselves and one another and all our life unto Christ our God," is the liturgical program continually realized in Orthodox asceticism and in spiritual life, as continuous service and ministering, as a never-ending liturgy and liturgizing to the Living God "in spirit and in truth" (John 4:24). This, according to Holy Apostles and Holy Fathers, is a continuous sacrifice to God: "Present your bodies a *living sacrifice*, holy, acceptable unto God" (Rom. 12:1), an offering up of *"spiritual sacrifices,* acceptable to God by Jesus Christ" (I Peter 2:5).[34]

6.

Finally, let us say a few words about the connection between Orthodox spirituality and authentic theology.

True spiritual life in Orthodoxy has always been closely connected to theology. Over the many centuries of Orthodox tradition true spirituality has not existed without theology, nor true theology without spirituality. A well-known saying of an ancient ascetic and theologian shows its full value and application here: "If you are a theologian you will pray sincerely, and if you pray sincerely, you are a theologian." (Εἰ θεολόγος εἶ, προσεύχῃ ἀληθῶς, καὶ εἰ ἀληθῶς προσεύχῃ, θεολόγος εἶ).[35] Even though it is thought that this wise thought, truly born of spiritual life, belongs to Evagrius of Pontus, this does not mean that such spiritual knowledge concerning the mutual dependence of theology and spirituality was unknown to Church Fathers and ascetics before and after Evagrius, and independently of him. On the contrary, we find this knowledge recorded by St. Gregory the Theologian in his *Theological Orations,* where this extraordinary theologian and ascetic expounds

---

[34] The service books of our Church often speak of this "offering up" of oneself as a *sacrifice* to God, and this is found even in the texts of the Holy Liturgy. Many Holy Fathers speak of this (theologians, bishops, ascetics, and monks). St. John Chrysostom especially speaks of this in his numerous works.

[35] *Chapters on Prayer* 61 (PG 79:1179). This work is attributed to St. Nilus the Ascetic, but it is thought to be by Evagrius of Pontus.

from his spiritual experience on who can theologize, and on when and how he can do so. "It is necessary that mystical matters should be spoken of mystically, and holy things in a holy way."[36] Hence, "not everyone can philosophize (theologize)[37] about God, but only those who have been tried, who have attained to contemplation (ἐν θεωρίᾳ), and who have previously purified their soul and body, or are at least in the process of purifying it.... I am not saying this in the sense that one should not always remember God in his mind (i.e., pray to Him). On the contrary, one should always bear God in his mind (i.e., pray to Him) more than one breathes (μνημονευτέον γὰρ Θεοῦ μᾶλλον ἤ ἀναπνευστέον), and so to speak, one should do nothing but that" (i.e., continually, prayerfully think of God, and pray to Him).[38] From the quoted words of this holy theologian-ascetic and ascetical theologian, we can see the unbreakable connection and interdependence between spiritual life and true theology.

According to the formula of the greatest and most essential theology of the Church—and this is the Holy Liturgy and the prayerful (ministerial) theology of the Church—theology in the practice of Orthodox spirituality is always a prayerful and doxological hierurgy, a doxological ministry, which lays the basis and nourishes real spirituality, but at the same time is also nourished and energized by that spirituality. The words of St. Irenaeus of Lyons, "Our belief is in accordance with the Eucharist, and the Eucharist confirms our belief" (Ἡμῶν δὲ σύμφωνος ἡ γνώμη τῇ Εὐχαριστίᾳ, καὶ ἡ Εὐχαριστία πάλιν βεβαιοῖ τὴν γνώμην ἡμῶν),[39] confirm that the Church's Liturgy and the Church's faith are identical, and consequently identical with theology. Hence our Orthodox spirituality, which comes from Baptism and Chrisma-

---

[36] *First Theological Oration (Oration* 27) 5 (PG 36:17).

[37] The expression *philosophy*, used by St. Gregory the Theologian and by some other Holy Fathers, designates, as far as "our philosophy" (i.e., Christian) is concerned, above all the true Christian (ascetic) life in faith. "First it is necessary to cleanse yourself with practical philosophy, and then to open the mouth of your mind to receive the Spirit" (*Oration* 6.1). "Our philosophy is by nature humble, but it is exalted in a hidden manner and it lifts one up to God" (*Oration* 25.4). Therefore, "to philosophize about God" refers here to true and befitting theologizing about God.

[38] *First Theological Oration (Oration* 27) 3–4 (PG 36:13–16).

[39] *Against Heresies* 4.18.5.

tion and is eucharistic in origin, is entirely in accordance with the faith and theology of the Church, and this shows and confirms the authenticity of the theology of the person who bears that spirituality and theologizes in accordance with it.

The aim and the content of Orthodox spirituality is *fellowship* (κοινωνία) *with God,* which is also the aim and the culmination of authentic Orthodox theology. In Orthodoxy, therefore, theology is not only "τὸ περὶ Θεοῦ λέγειν" (speaking about God) but first of all "τὸ συγγίνεσθαι Θεῷ" (to be together with and to be united with God), as St. Gregory Palamas says.[40] Only on the basis of the experience of this *fellowship,* the experience of community with God, can theological declarations about things seen and witnessed (cf. I John 1:1–3; II Peter 1:16) be expressed in "God-pleasing words" (ἐν θεοπρεπέσι λόγοις), in concepts and "categories" worthy of God, and in God-pleasing and salvific confessions and doxologies.

7.

Truly, we all know—and the Holy Fathers before us knew—the "theology" learned from books, and from human ideas and categories. However, according to the Holy Fathers, this "learned" ("scientific") theology can never be a self-sufficient, certain and true theology. Especially if the theologian is puffed-up, pretentious and condescending, lacking humility and humble-mindedness, his theology is most often only plain "technology"—i.e., skill or a play of words. Furthermore, this theology is also dangerous, because it can become enticing words (πιθανολογία), which beguile (παρὰ-λογίζεται) (cf. Col. 2:4). In other words, it can become a purposeless and merely tempting phraseology that produces fantasies and leads one into delusion. St. Symeon the New Theologian says: "For if it is only through learning and study that we are given true wisdom and knowledge of God [i.e., theology], to what end, then, do we need faith, Divine Baptism, and Communion of the Holy Mysteries?"[41] Here the saint and true theologian of the Church wants to says that, without living fellowship in faith (communion) and in the

---

[40] *Triads* 1.3.42, *Syngrammata,* vol. 1 (Thessalonica, 1962), p. 453.
[41] *Ethical Sermons* 9, *op. cit.,* p. 226.

Holy Mysteries of the Church, i.e., without the divine grace which comes from the living faith and liturgical life of the Church, theological scholarship and education is far from true theology. The same holy theologian-ascetic continues: "May no one be deceived by empty and sophisticated words, and think that it is possible to understand the Divine Mysteries of our faith without the Holy Spirit, Who instructs and illuminates (ἄνευ τοῦ μυσταγωγοῦντος καὶ φωτίζοντος Πνεύματος—without the Spirit mystically initiating and illumining); neither can anyone become a vessel of the gifts of the grace of the Holy Spirit without the virtues of meekness and humble-mindedness."[42]

St. Gregory Palamas is even more precise in this distinction between "learned" theology (as a science derived from books and the human mind) and authentic grace-filled theology. In his well-known *Triads,* written as a defense of hesychastic, grace-filled experience and theology, he writes: "There is a contemplation (θεωρία) which consists of a kind of knowledge of God and His dogmas, which is also called theology." According to the saint, however, this is not certain and sure theology; hence, he adds: "The natural use and natural movement (activity) of our psychic powers and bodily organs creates and brings some kind of transformation of the rational image (τῆς λογικῆς εἰκόνος) within us, but this is not the perfect beauty of our exalted nobility, nor does it grant us supernatural unification with the Divine Illumination. This kind of union (with God) allows and enables us to *theologize with certitude,* because our psychic and bodily powers are in their natural state and functioning normally."[43]

As is clear from these passages of St. Symeon the New Theologian and St. Gregory Palamas, there is no true theology without liturgical life in the Church, and there is no true, reliable faith or authentic theology except that which proceeds from the spiritual life and living experience of

---

[42] *Ibid.* In the continuation of this text St. Symeon adds the following words: "It is undoubtedly necessary for all of us that we should above all place the foundation of our faith deep into our soul, and then build in ourselves through various types of virtues true piety as a strong wall; and when the soul is secure from all sides and is based inside as on a secure foundation of virtue, the roof should be placed—and this is the Divine knowledge of God (theology)—and that is how the whole edifice of the Spirit is built."

[43] *Triads* 1.3.15, *op. cit.,* p. 425.

the union of man with God, and from the grace-bestowing fellowship and living contact with the Holy Spirit. In other words, there is no theology apart from the fruit of the spirituality of the Holy Spirit. These and similar ascetical-theological testimonies can be encountered innumerable times throughout the many centuries of Orthodox spiritual tradition.

We will cite some of these texts. For example, Diadochus of Photiki writes: "God does not give the gift of grace of theology (τὸ τῆς θεολογίας χάρισμα) to one who has not prepared himself."[44] St. Kallistos Kataphygiotes is even more precise: "When the life-creating and unoriginate power and energy of the Holy Spirit enters and abides in the heart of one who lives in virtue and in peace of mind ... this greatly and abundantly illumines his spiritual powers, so that the mind of this man and the grace [of God] become 'one spirit' (I Cor. 6:17); then the mind ... through the energy and light of the Life-creating and Holy Spirit, reaches the revelations of Divine Mysteries ... and by humbling himself and praying, [man] is made active (ἐνεργούμενος) by God Himself in the Holy Spirit. In this state he does not depart from theologizing (οὐδὲ τοῦ θεολογεῖν ἐστιν ἐκτός), but becomes a real and true theologian (ἐστὶν αὐτόχρημα θεολόγος) and cannot but continuously theologize."[45]

Finally, let us cite yet another very characteristic passage of St. Symeon the New Theologian, an exceptional theologian-ascetic and ascetic-theologian of the Orthodox Church. Speaking about a man who was found truly worthy to have Christ abide in him, he writes: "If you honor Christ and accept Him and give Him a peaceful place (ἡσυχίαν) in yourself, then know very well that you will not lay your head on the breast of God, as God's beloved disciple John did, but you will rather carry in your breast the entire Logos of God, and you will theologize new and old theologies (θεολογίας θεολογήσεις καινάς τε καὶ παλαιάς), you will understand very well all the already-written theologies, and you will become a sweet-sounding organ which will speak and sound far better than any music."[46] These words of St. Symeon the New Theologian, the experienced spiritual ascetic and theologian of Orthodox spirituality, clearly show the true relationship between spiritual life and proper

---

[44] *Gnostic Chapters* 66, ed. *Sources Chrétiennes*, no. 5 (Paris, 1966), p. 127.
[45] *The Philokalia* (Greek), vol. 5 (Athens, 1963), pp. 51–52.
[46] *Ethical Sermons* 11, *op. cit.*, p. 348.

theology. Besides this, the cited words show that in the genuine liturgi-cal-ascetic spirituality of Orthodoxy and Orthodox theology, the prob-lem and the dilemma between "conservatism" and "progressiveness" in theology—which surfaces especially in our times—is actually overcome. The life-creating Holy Spirit, as the Comforter and Instructor of the Church, Who instructs her in everything and guides her to every truth (John 14:16, 16:13), is the eternal Inspirer, as He was of the ancient Ap-ostolic preaching and ancient patristic theology, and He teaches those who are initiates in the mysteries of the Kingdom of God, so that as good householders they also bring forth out of their treasure (the Church) "things new and old" (Matt. 13:52).

The cited words of St. Symeon the New Theologian about true the-ology are simply a rewording of the liturgical hymns by which the Or-thodox Church praises and glorifies her Holy Fathers, the *Theologians.* She calls them "harps of the Holy Spirit" and "pure golden mouths of the Word," that is, mouths through which God the Logos spoke (theo-logized). These Holy Fathers "clearly gave to the Church the *mystery of theology*"[47] in one catholic, polyphonic symphony and harmony.

From all that we have said, the close relationship between genuine Orthodox theology and true spirituality becomes obvious. Both are *li-turgical* and *grace-giving;* both are the spiritual fruit of the Holy Spirit and man's free and loving cooperation with Him. Without the grace-be-stowing experience of this type of spiritual life, it is difficult for an Ortho-dox theologian to escape the danger of becoming like "the many who corrupt (καπηλεύοντες) the word of God" (II Cor. 2:17), for in that case he is not theologizing in accordance with the words of the Holy Apostle: "as of sincerity, ... as of God, in the sight of God speak we in Christ" (II Cor. 2:17). He cannot theologize because the spiritual face of his soul and mind does not reveal and reflect the transforming and deifying glory of God "by the Spirit of the Lord" (II Cor. 3:18); he does not have God's *spirituality,* and has not become the vessel and home of the grace-bestow-ing spiritual life of the Holy Spirit and of His fruits. Orthodox spiritual-ity, as asceticism and life in the Spirit, as service to the Spirit, represents a

---

[47] *Pentecostarion,* The Sunday of the Holy Fathers, "Glory" verse from the "Praises," tone 8.

tried and tested theological-ascetical school, a school of continual experience through ascetic struggles and blessings, a school of new life and of consecration into the mystery of the Living and True God, a school of initiation into the mystery of liturgical sanctification (mystagogy), in which the Holy Spirit makes us worthy and capable of "offering up the *Orthodox abundance of theology* (ὀρθόδοξον πλουτισμὸν θεολογίας) to the God and Savior of our souls."[48]

The Divine Liturgy,
Aer (*vozdukh*) in Hilandar Monastery, 15th century.

[48] Service to the Nativity of Our Lord, "Glory" verse from the "Praises," tone 6.

9
Eschatological Dimensions of the Church[1]

Within the general theme of "The Icon and the Kingdom," our theological faculty has been entrusted with the particular theme of "The Church and the Kingdom." In the framework of that theme this paper will deal with the eschatological character of the Church as a whole and the eschatological perspective of everything in the Church. This means that what is necessary for an authentic and full Orthodox eschatology is the eschatological dimension of the Church, which organically links the Church with the Kingdom of God.

For the beginning of the evaluation of our theme and as a proper context we shall take a biblical event described in three places in the Holy Scriptures. That event is the appearance of God to Moses on Sinai when He ordered him to erect the Tabernacle (the Tent of Witness). References to this manifestation are made in the Book of Exodus 25:40, by Protomartyr Stephen in Acts 7:44, and finally by the Apostle Paul in the Epistle to the Hebrews 8:5. If we combine these three references we shall get the following text: "See," said God to Moses, "that you erect the Tabernacle, and everything in it, according to the type (κατὰ τὸ τύπον) which was shown you on Mount Sinai."

There is abundant literature concerning this event and its interpretation. What does this event mean, and which interpretation is possible? In addition, what is it that is shown by God to Moses on Sinai, and what did he see? What was the basis for his making the Tabernacle? Why did Deacon Stephen refer to this matter just at the moment of his martyrdom for Christ, when he himself "being full of the Holy Spirit, gazed into heaven and saw the glory of God, and Jesus standing at the right hand of God" (Acts 7:55)? Why, then, did the author of the Epistle to the Hebrews come to consider the same event that happened to Mo-

[1] Report at the Congress of Orthodox Schools at Holy Cross, Brookline, Mass., 1992.

ses and Stephen, that is, the event that they both had seen, each in his time and in his own way?

It would take too long to retell the whole Epistle to the Hebrews, but we are bound to turn our attention to the leading thread which, in reference to the aforesaid event, is woven throughout the whole epistle. At the outset, I would like to remind you that the same theme was treated by the Church Fathers, particularity St. Gregory the Theologian and St. Maximus the Confessor.

St. Gregory the Theologian writes: "From time immemorial (i.e., throughout history) there have been (γεγόνασι—it happened, it took place) two great and public transpositions (μετάθεσις—transfer) of human life (= historical living), which are also called two covenants (δύο διαθῆκαι) and earthquakes, due to the great significance and majesty of the matters themselves. One transfer was from the idols to the Law, and the other one from the Law to the Gospel. We preach (εὐαγγελιζόμεθα) a *third earthquake* as well—the removal (μετάστασις) from here (from the earth) up to there (to heaven) of what is shaken 'in order that what cannot be shaken may remain'" (Heb. 12:26–27).[2] Then, as is known, he speaks of how the Old Testament preached the Father clearly, and the Son in opaque fashion, like a shadow. The New Testament manifested the Son, and only pointed to the divinity of the Holy Spirit. And now we live together with the Spirit (ἐμπολιτεύεται νῦν τὸ Πνεῦμα) and He gives us a more ready manifestation of Himself.[3]

Let us briefly quote the commentary of St. Maximus the Confessor. Here, although he does not directly address the Epistle to the Hebrews, he does so indirectly through his well-known *Scholia* on the text of Dionysius the Areopagite, *On the Hierarchy,* in which he comments on the Divine Liturgy: "Everything of the Old Testament—that is the shadow (σκιά), and everything of the New Testament—that is the icon (εἰκών), and the state of the *Aion* to come (τῶν μελλόντων), of the good things to come, of the Kingdom is the truth (ἀλήθεια)."[4]

From these two references it is apparent that the Fathers speak about a gradual, stage-by-stage, divine revelation and development of

---

[2] St. Gregory the Theologian, *Fifth Theological Oration* (*Oration* 31) 25–26 (PG 36:160–61).

[3] Ibid.

[4] St. Maximus the Confessor, *Scholia on Church Hierarchy* 3.3.2 (PG 4:137D).

sacred history, about the epiphany of God to those of us who are in the world, which leads us to knowledge of God and communion with God. This is what the whole Epistle to the Hebrews speaks about, and we are going to consider this now, as well as the event of Moses' vision on Sinai, on which is based the *typos* of the Old Testament Tabernacle.

The Epistle to the Hebrews begins with the prominent statement: "In many and various ways God spoke in times past [in the Old Testament] to our fathers by the Prophets; but in these last days [in the New Testament], He has spoken to us by the Son [the incarnate Christ], Whom He appointed Heir of all things, through Whom also He created the world" (Heb. 1:1–2). It is obvious that Paul speaks here about the gradual revelation of God: before Christ, during the earthly life of Christ, and later on in the future *Aion*. What is said about the past, the Old Testament, is indisputable; this is likewise true about what is said about Christ's time, the New Testament, but one has to underscore especially that the author of the Epistle to the Hebrews clearly points out the eschatological future as well. For, later on, he says that God made it that Christ, His Son from eternity and the Creator of the world and the ages, Whom He as the "First-born brought into the world," and after He had suffered for the "purification of [our] sins," now "was seated at the right hand of the Majesty on high" (Heb. 1:3–6 and the whole context of chapters 7 to 10).

This three-member scheme, that is, this vision (understanding) of the revelation in three stages, is observed by the Apostle throughout the Epistle to the Hebrews, especially in chapters 5–10, where he elaborates on the theme of the Old Testament high priest, and on Christ as "the High Priest of the good things to come" (τῶν μελλόντων ἀγαθῶν, or τῶν γενομένων ἀγαθῶν, i.e., of the realized goods, as it appears in other manuscripts—Heb. 9:11).

However, can we really speak about three stages of world history and about God's relation toward the world? And what do these three stages mean, and what is the relationship among them? Or, to resume our first question: What did Moses really see on Sinai?

Although it is said that "the Lord spoke to Moses face to face" (ἐνώπιος ἐνωπίῳ, Ex. 33:11), Moses nevertheless did not see God's face, but only God's "back" (τὰ ὀπίσω, Ex. 33:23) while he (Moses) was covered and preserved by God's hand during his passing by and when Moses was in a cleft of the rock. St. Gregory the Theologian sees in Moses' vision the coming Incarnation, the manifestation of the Christ incarnate, by which men were enabled to have a vision of God.[5] This interpretation by St. Gregory gives us at the same time a proper key to the comprehension of Moses' vision of the *typos* on Mount Sinai, upon which he erected the Tabernacle. Without doubt, that was the vision of the future reality of Christ's Church, according to which, although it is still to come, Moses erects the Old Testament tabernacle as a shadow of the future reality (Heb. 10:1; 8:2, 6–7).

However, here we have to put a question: of which future reality? That of the historical Church in the New Testament or that of the Church in the eschatological Kingdom? That is, did Moses see on Sinai the coming historical Church, the one which came into existence in the world with the Incarnation and Pentecost, or the heavenly Church such as will be after Christ's Second Coming, in His Kingdom? Moreover, another question is raised: are these really two realities—are these two different Churches? From all these questions one point is clear: we find ourselves embroiled in our theme concerning the relation between the Church and the Kingdom.

This biblical and especially apostolic and patristic understanding of Moses' vision and its interpretation obviously are characteristically eschatological, of course in the sense of true Christian eschatology, in which the perspective is not primarily chronological but Christological as well as eschatological, where the past, present, and future are interwoven, linked together and sometimes interactive.[6] Therefore, Moses' vision of *typos* on Mount Sinai does not refer to the past, or to the "world of eternal ideas," but to the eschatological "future goods," the "future reality," which is to become, although it appears as already existing, as "preexistent." For this reason some of the Church Fathers talk about the

---

[5] St. Gregory the Theologian, *Second Theological Oration* (*Oration* 28) 3 (PG 36:29).

[6] St. Maximus the Confessor, *To Thalassius* (PG 90:284A): "Ἔθος ἐστὶ τῇ Γραφῇ τοὺς χρόνους μεταλλάσσειν, καὶ εἰς ἀλλήλους μεταλαμβάνειν· καὶ τὸν μέλλοντα ὡς παρῳχηκότα, καὶ τὸν παρῳχηκότα ὡς μέλλοντα· καὶ τὸν ἐνεστῶτα, εἰς τὸν πρὸ αὐτοῦ καὶ μετ᾽ αὐτὸν χρόνον ἐκφωνεῖν, ὡς ἔστι δῆλον τοῖς αὐτῆς πεπειραμένοις."

"preexistence of the Church," so that the Church existed even in Paradise, in spite of the fact that St. John's Apocalypse shows that Paradise is an eschatological reality, an idea especially developed by St. Ephraim the Syrian in his inspired *Hymns on Paradise,* in which Paradise is seen as the basic point or the axis of all of history, and is apparently for St. Ephraim a primarily eschatological and protological reality.

It becomes clear from what we have revealed that the biblical vision of world history, and of God's revelation in it, is eschatological vision and understanding. Although a biblical and especially Christian understanding of history is an extraordinary novelty in relation to the world of antiquity, nevertheless this biblical, Judeo-Christian understanding of history, for the Orthodox, should be conceived from this eschatological perspective. History so conceived is understood not merely in the linear sense, in the sense of historic continuity, historical processes, and successive chronological movements and developments, but rather in a unique eschatological event, where time and history are contained and at the same time are transcended, overcome, and brought into the new eschatological *Aion* of the Kingdom.

This Event is Christ, or Christ's Mysterium, according to the wording of St. Paul and St. Maximus. We shall discuss this event-mystery because it is actually the key question for our theme of the Church and the Kingdom.

The event of Christ or Christ's mystery (τὸ μυστήριον τοῦ Χριστοῦ— Eph. 3:4, 9; Col. 1:26-27, 2:2) is dealt with not only in the Epistle to the Hebrews, but also in some of the other of Paul's epistles, and the whole New Testament as well. It is the very reality which contains in itself the whole truth, the whole reality of the Church, and also the whole truth and reality of God's Kingdom. Christ as the incarnate God-man (Θεάνθρωπος) is both the *Alpha* and *Omega* of God's entire revelation, God's *oikonomia* of the salvation of the world and humanity, the *Alpha* and *Omega* of history, and of the whole of eschatology. Christ became so because He made Himself incarnate, became man in history; and that historical event became the center and focus of history, where the beginning and the end join, the ἀρχή and τέλος of all created beings. Due to the fact that all creation, all beings created by God's will and

135

love, are directed to the future, to their goal and destination, to their *pleroma* and perfection (which is not in the past, but in the future, in eschatology), the incarnate Christ has been placed from the beginning as the mover (moving force) of all beings and of history, as their "anticipated and predestinated goal"—πέρας and τέλος, according to St. Maximus the Confessor.[7] One must also compare Maximus' other texts, where he says that "the mystery of the Incarnation of the Logos" contains the key to everything that is said in the Holy Scriptures. For both a proper and full knowledge of all creation, the event of Christ's Resurrection contains the full mystery (reality) of eschatological content of *pleroma* and *telos*, of everything that God created and for what He designated them.[8]

It is not necessary to belabor the basic theological truth that Christ, the incarnate and resurrected, is the center and *telos* of history and the *pleroma* of eschatology; consequently, He as God-man (Θεάνθρωπος) is the center both of the Church and of the Kingdom. The whole Church and its history, which is at the same time the history of all creation, of the whole world, is determined by the Incarnation of Christ, Who is the aim, fullness, and perfection of every created being. However, at the same time we must emphasize that the eschatological end (*telos*) has by Christ's Incarnation entered into history and become its part and its inner mover (moving force) toward ultimate finality. So, in Christ is fully embraced also the whole Old Testament, the past, the aim and designation of which is to inspire movement toward Christ. In Him is also embraced the whole of world history, the history of salvation, because He is the core and heart of the history of humanity, so that Christ's mystery, the Church (for the Church is the Body of the incarnate Christ, and is identified with Christ) is the central focus of history. The Church is the evangelical leaven and the firstfruits (ἀπαρχὴ) of the true future world history, of eschatology, and so it is at the same time liberation from its (history's) limitedness, corruptibility, perdition, and mortality.

---

[7] St. Maximus the Confessor, *To Thalassius* 60 (PG 90:620–25). "Ὁ προεπινοού-μενος Θεῖος σκοπὸς καὶ τέλος ... τὸ τῆς προνοίας καὶ τῶν προεπινοουμένων πέρας" (PG 90:621A).

[8] St. Maximus the Confessor, *Two Hundred Texts on Theology and the Incarnate Dispensation of the Son of God* 1.66 (PG 90:1108AB).

So Christ in the Church and with the Church (by Himself as the Church) introduces the *eschaton* already here into history. He brings the *new Aion* of the Kingdom here and now *(hic et nunc)*.

How does this *New Aion* happen? Such is the meaning of the eschatological character of the Church, which is our theme. However, we need to make it more explicit.

By indicating the Christological and Christocentric character of the Church, in its history and also in eschatology, in the Kingdom, it is necessary to point out an important truth of Orthodox theology concerning full and authentic Christology, which is linked with Triadology, and especially with Pneumatology. In other words, we should bring to the fore the Orthodox, apostolic, patristic vision of catholic, integral Christology in all its theanthropic dimensions, and not treat Christology separately and individually (as "Christomonism"), as often happens in traditions foreign to Orthodoxy.

In this way we come to the truth that Christ and Christ's mystery are one and the same, that the Church and Christ are the same, that Christ and the Kingdom are the same, that the Church and the Kingdom are the same. But this identification is not just philosophical; it has its theological, Orthodox character, where an identification does not mean an abolishment of the unalterable difference between the uncreated and the created, between God and man, between the ontological reality of two natures, as we are taught by the dogma of Chalcedon. This identification primarily indicates that the uncreated and the created, divine and created being, are brought into communion in Christ, into the unity of personal communion, into the unity of the true life, which cannot be interrupted any longer either by nature or by any limitedness, corruptibility, perdition, or mortality.

In Orthodox Christology, viewed in this way, the focal point of the relationship between the Church and the Kingdom is the Holy Spirit. Christology in Orthodox theology is most closely connected with Pneumatology, and they presuppose each other.

We should bear in mind that, according to Orthodox theology, the role of the Holy Spirit is great and very significant in the whole *oikonomia* of salvation, realized in Christ and in the Church. It is precisely the Holy Spirit Who in the *oikonomia* opens the entire history of salvation for "*ta eschata,*" for the eschatological reality of the Kingdom, and it is He who liberates history from every limitation, from perdition and death, by bringing, through the Church, God's grace and life of the *New Aion* into the world and history; consequently, the Holy Spirit presents eschatological reality. Only by the grace of the Holy Spirit can the Church be—and is—that which Christ said: "not of the world" (John 17:16). Christ's Kingdom has started with the Church in the world, in history, but that Kingdom is not of this world. So the Church, thanks to the Pentecost of the Holy Spirit (and not only to the Incarnation), is not a mere historical reality, a human historical society—a "religious community," which historically continues throughout the centuries and has a certain mission in the world—but is much more. It is a reality with an eschatological character.

The eschatological character of the Church is manifested primarily and most fully in the Eucharist, in the Liturgy of the Church, as an eschatological *synaxis* of the faithful and of all creation in Christ by the power and grace and energy of the Spirit, the Comforter. It is in the Liturgy that the historical reality of the Church is connected by the Holy Spirit with the eschatological reality of the Kingdom. It is the Holy Spirit Who connects all the members of the Body of Christ with Christ Himself, and all the members amongst themselves (a theme which is elaborated at length by St. Paul in his epistles, especially in the more eschatological ones). The Holy Spirit connects in the Eucharist of the Church both present and future, history and eschatology. For this reason, by the Holy Spirit the Eucharist of the Church, in its character, is always eschatological. But this does not mean that history is denied in the Eucharist, in the Liturgy; rather, the historical events and the lives of the faithful are connected with the eschatological event of the encounter of and union with the Kingdom and participation in the Kingdom, which is the realization of the living community of God the King. Let us now in more detail deliberate upon this matter of the Holy Eucharist in the context of our theme concerning the Church and the Kingdom.

We have quoted the words of St. Gregory the Theologian and St. Maximus about the stage-like development of the history of salvation, about the Old and the New Testaments and about the future *aion*. We are especially reminded of Maximus' words that the Old Testament is the shadow, the New Testament the icon, and the future state, the truth.[9] Obviously, Maximus here follows the Apostle Paul, especially in the Epistle to the Hebrews, but he also follows St. Dionysius the Areopagite and the whole patristic tradition of the Orthodox East.

However, the problem is this: could it be said that the reality of the New Testament Church is only icon, and not yet truth?

In symbolic interpretations of the Divine Liturgy, most prominently by St. Dionysius the Areopagite,[10] the Eucharistic gifts are often referred to as symbols. St. Maximus applies this thinking to some extent in his *Mystagogy*. However, some time later, when iconoclasm appeared, the Orthodox theologians in Byzantium sharply reacted against the thesis of the iconoclasts that, while it would be impossible to paint Christ in an icon, the only true and real icon of Christ would be, according to their teaching, the Body and Blood in the Eucharist.[11] The holy Patriarch Nicephorus I and St. Theodore the Studite emphatically repudiated the statement that the Gifts in the Eucharist are only the "icon." They state that they are the "mysteries of the truth itself" (τὰ τῆς ἀληθείας μυστήρια) and that the holy Eucharist is "the contents and recapitulation of the entire *oikonomia* of salvation" (συγκεφαλαίωσις τῆς ὅλης οἰκονομίας), according to St. Theodore the Studite.[12] According to St. Nicephorus of Constantinople: The Eucharist is not the "*typos* of that Body" (of Christ), but "although symbolically performed, it is the deified (θεόθεν) Body of Christ," because "by the *epiclesis* of the priest and by the descent of the Holy Spirit, they (the Gifts) change into the Body and Blood of Christ," because the incarnate Christ himself is "our High Priest, and Lamb, and Sacrifice."[13]

From all this we can conclude that the meaning of the icon in the quoted passage of St. Maximus obviously has another meaning, not the classical Hellenistic one, used also by the iconoclasts. Such a patristic

---

[9] St. Maximus the Confessor, PG 90:137. See also St. Maximus the Confessor, PG 91:1253.

[10] *On the Church Hierarchy.*

[11] See Mansi, *Collectio Conciliorum* 13.261–64.

[12] PG 99:340.

[13] PG 100:336.

meaning of the icon, as suggested by Metropolitan John Zizioulas,[14] is the biblical understanding, apocalyptic and liturgical, which under the word "icon" shows the vision of eschatological truth primarily in the person, in personality, so that one might say that the Son of God is the "icon of the Father," which absolutely does not mean that He is not the truth, but that He is in a living and personal relationship with the Father, and that one reflects in the other as in a "mirror." This is precisely the same as what St. Paul says in the First Epistle to the Corinthians, that we now see in a mirror dimly and we know only in part, but when *"to teleion"* (fullness) comes, then we shall see face to face and the "in part" will be fulfilled.

Strictly speaking, I think that for the Orthodox, it is clear that the Old Testament cannot be seen as a pre-stage of the New Testament, neither can the New Testament be seen in the same measure, as a pre-stage of the eschatological Kingdom. Of course, a gradualness has to be taken into account, but it is not the same measure and distance between, on the one hand, the Old and the New Testaments, and the New Testament (in which the Resurrection of Christ took place) and the Kingdom on the other. Why? Because it is in the New Testament that the "great mystery of pious adoration" occurred: "God was manifested in the flesh," and since then the Church became "the pillar and bulwark of the Truth" (I Tim. 3:15–16), because "grace and truth came (ἐγένετο) through Jesus Christ" (John 1:14–17). Therefore St. Maximus, who wrote the previously quoted passage about the shadow, icon, and truth, could also say that "Christ's mystery—τὸ κατὰ Χριστὸν μυστήριον—is more mysterious (μυστηριωδέστερον) than all divine mysteries, and is the determinative (ὁριστικόν) mystery for every existing and future perfection (τελειότητος), and stands above every limit and end (ὅρου καὶ πέρατος). This mystery teaches us that with the incarnate and perfect God-man, the Logos is and does exist with the human body which He took from us, and which is of the same essence (ὁμοούσιον) as ours, and which is united with Him by the hypostasis (καθ᾿ ὑπόστασιν), by which

---

[14] John Zizioulas, *Being as Communion* (Crestwood, N. Y.: St. Vladimir's Seminary Press, 1985), pp. 67–122.

He ascended to heaven, 'above all rule and authority and power and do-
minion, and above every name that is named, not only in this age but
also in that which is to come' (Eph. 1:21), and where He is sitting now
and for the endless ages together with God the Father, having sublimat-
ed all the heavens and placed Himself above them; and He will come
again for the sake of renewal and transformation of everything (ἐπὶ
μεταποιήσει τε καὶ μεταστοιχειώσει τοῦ παντός) and for the salvation of
our souls and bodies."[15]

Next to this highly significant thought of St. Maximus, we must
not forget some other noteworthy apostolic-patristic testimonies to
Christ's mystery of presence and identification with the Church in the
Holy Eucharist here and now *(hic et nunc),* with which the mystery of
eucharistic communion and unity of the whole Church with Christ in
the future Kingdom is identified.[16] So, the eschatological heavenly
Kingdom will not be anything other than the eucharistic meal of the
Kingdom, the eternal Liturgy and the Trinitarian *koinonia* with all of
us (cf. Rev. 19:9, 17; II Cor. 13:13). Consequently, the Holy Eucharist,
ever since the Last Supper, has been the eschatological meal of God's
people in history. Hence, it is in the Holy Eucharist, both as *anamnesis*
and as *epiclesis,* that the Church experiences a sublimation of division
of time, an overcoming of the past and the present and the future; it
experiences their organic unity, so that the past has a new reality in the
present, and in that same liturgical present the future already becomes
the present reality. As has already been observed by Orthodox theologians, the Church experiences in the Eucharist not only the "actualization of Christ's sacrifice on the Cross," but also the eschatological Kingdom of the resurrected Christ as an already present reality.[17] All that is
possible, of course, thanks to the eschatological dimension of Pentecost, permanently present in the Church, which is the descent and effect of the Holy Spirit. This explains why eschatology is emphasized in
Orthodox ecclesiology and in Orthodox theology in general.

[15] St. Maximus the Confessor, *Ambigua* 2.42 (PG 91:1332).
[16] John 6; Luke 22:29–30; St. Nicholas Cabasilas, *Commentary on the Divine
Liturgy* 38 and 47 (PG 150:452–53 and 461–65).
[17] John Zizioulas, "The Eucharist: Some Biblical Aspects." In Marne, ed., *The Eucharist* (Paris, 1970).

Nevertheless, Orthodox theology emphasizes an organic, but also a dynamic, so to speak, dialectical relationship between history and eschatology. It is one and the same: the community of Christ's Body, the Church of God's people in history and the "Church of the firstborn" in the heavenly Kingdom (Heb. 12:22–23). However, there is still an arena of spiritual effort and movement. One and the same reality is effected, but it is the living organism in its growth, in the living dynamic movement of those not yet quite grown up as children of God, going from one spiritual effort to the other, "from grace to grace." Such is the living charismatic, sacramental growth of the Church as the Body of Christ: "for the equipping of the saints, for the work of ministry, for the building up of the Body of Christ, until we all attain to the unity of the faith, and the knowledge of the Son of God, to the measure of the stature of the fullness of Christ," the resurrected One (Eph. 4:12–13).

This dynamic vision of Christ's growth is important for the right comprehension of the relationship between the Church and the Kingdom in historical life and in the movement of the Church toward eschatological *telos* and fullness. There cannot be any of this fullness as long as death is present in the world, in creation and humanity (cf. Rom. 8:19–23)—that is, until the *parousia* and the universal resurrection come.

This belief is actually what allows for the iconic understanding of the New Testament in its relation to the future *Aion,* not only by St. Gregory the Theologian and St. Maximus the Confessor, but also by such eucharistic-oriented theologians as Saints Ignatius of Antioch and John Chrysostom. For example, St. John Chrysostom rightly observes, in reference to the question of what God's Kingdom is, that it is "Christ's *parousia* (coming), the first one and the last one" (βασιλείαν τὴν παρουσίαν αὐτοῦ, τὴν προτέραν καὶ τὴν ἐσχάτην φησίν).[18]

St. Maximus writes quite similarly when talking about the "permanently present grace of the Holy Spirit, which works and performs sacraments in the Church," and about the Holy Spirit, Who will grant us His gifts (eschatological reality) "by the truth itself and in full reality" (κατὰ ἀλήθειαν ἐνυποστάτως, αὐτῷ τῷ πράγματι), when we are liberated

---

[18] St. John Chrysostom, *Homilies on Matthew* 10.2 (PG 57:186).

from corruptibility and mortality, that is, when our true deification is made possible.[19]

In the light of this theological understanding of Orthodox eschatology, it is necessary to say, at last, the following.

The eschatological character of the Church, although expressed and brought to its culmination in the Eucharist, manifests itself also in all other dimensions and activities of the Church's being and life in this world and history.

First of all, the Church itself as community, as the people of God, is not and must not be confined only to historical human society, be it even "religious" and "Christian"; the Church is primarily in history the assembly (synods) and gathering (*synaxis*) of all God's children around the "Firstborn among many brethren" (Rom. 8:29).

Thus, all the ecclesiastical ministries and institutions and structures must be placed and considered always within the eschatological dimension of the Church, because only in this way may the ministries and their *diakonia*, and the mission of the Church in the world not be determined by simple, secular categories (for example, sociological perceptions of "love" as the "implementation of the Kingdom of God in the world with peace, justice, and equality," or as so-called liberation theology, etc.).

Orthodox eschatology is neither "catastrophic eschatology," a Montanist escape from the world and from the mission of the Church in the world, nor is it an "optimistic eschatology" of secular humanism, which considers the socializing and civilizing process to be the "new creation."[20]

Orthodoxy does not preach a "perfect society" on earth or an endless progress of civilization in history, because such an understanding ignores the disastrous presence of sin and evil, and, most importantly, of death in the world and history.

Orthodoxy witnesses by its ecclesial being and life, and especially by its eschatology, to the final liberation of all creation, of humanity

---

[19] St. Maximus the Confessor, *Mystagogy*, 24 (PG 91:704–5). See also the Troparion of the *Paschalion* hymnology in the Liturgy of St. John Chrysostom: "O Christ, great and most Holy Pascha! O Wisdom, Word, and Power of God! Vouchsafe that we may more perfectly partake of Thee in the days which know no evening of Thy Kingdom."

[20] See John Meyendorff, *Orthodoxy in the Contemporary World* (New York, 1981), in Russian.

and of the world from all "principalities and powers and dominions" in the history of this world. This final liberation is confirmed by the historically real Resurrection of Christ. It is confirmed in Christ by our sacramental rebirth through the "new-creative and life-creating" (καινοποιοῦντος καὶ ζωοποιοῦντος) Holy Spirit; and then, in the *Parousia* and the universal Last Judgment, it is confirmed in Christ and by the Holy Spirit through the bodily resurrection of the human race and the transformation of all creation, whereupon a new heaven and a new earth will begin.

10

The Eschata in Our Daily Life[1]

In Greek, we call the first things *protologia,* and the last things *eschatologia.* Neither term can be directly translated into English. The technical term for the latter is "eschatology," that which concerns the end of time, the last things. But *protologia* I do not think has even a technical translation in English. It concerns what is at the beginning of time, or before the beginning of time. I could speak in simpler terms of a prologue and an epilogue to a book. The reality of our lives is not a book, however, even if that book is the Bible.

A short while ago Milton's famous *Paradise Lost* was translated into Serbian. I was present at the presentation of the book, and although I could not say anything about it as a poet, I could say something about Milton's theological approach to the whole issue. I would like to begin by comparing the approach to this matter by Milton on the one hand and by the Orthodox Christian Tradition on the other.

Milton's approach is protological, which means that he looks at the Bible with the emphasis on the beginning of time—on creation, and on its initial state—whereas I would like to see the Bible eschatologically, with the emphasis on the end of time and the final state. To put it in different and simpler language, according to Milton, something happened in the past, and that which happened in the past determines what has happened ever since. In contrast, the attitude of Orthodox Christian theology is that, whatever may have happened in the past is one thing; what is to happen in the future is far more important.

When this matter came up with my theological students at the seminary where I teach, I tried to give them a metaphor from a world which Europeans know well, namely football. Allow me to pursue the

[1] A lecture given at the Hellenic Cultural Center, London, 1992.

145

same metaphor now. Take the attitude in a football game of Maradonna, Linneker or Stoykovich. Their opponents put in a goal or two in the first half, and that of course to some degree determines the style of play of their team. Maradonna, or whoever, has not yet shown what a good player he is. At some point, however, he suddenly, with great flair, puts in a first and then a second goal, and at half time they are equal. People then say that if Maradonna can do that in just two simple shots in the first half, what on earth will he do if he actually starts to play hard in the second half?

The Bible is the playground of the wonder and the miracles of God, and yet the most important thing in the Bible is not the wonders of God, the creation, the saving of the people of Israel and so forth, but rather that it is turned towards the last times, towards what will be done by God—by Him Who with so little effort has already done such great things in past history.

So what God did at the beginning is less important as far as the Bible is concerned, than what He will do in the future—at the end of time. That beautiful book, the Song of Songs, is a book about two people in love, in which the beloved leaves, and yet still draws his lover to himself. This is indeed like our relationship with God, only we are still in the first half; God is drawing us after him into a deeper communion.

Understanding Time

I will now turn to the understanding of time, both in antiquity, and according to the biblical revelation. Antiquity in general—except for the people of Israel, to whom the biblical revelation was given—looks on the past as better than the present, and as the determinant of the future. There was once a paradise which was gradually spoilt: our desire is to return to that paradise. So it is, for instance, with Odysseus. He too wishes to return to his paradise lost, his island, rather in the same way that Milton looks on it. The end must return to the beginning in a circular movement.

But the biblical understanding is exactly the opposite. Our nostalgia—unlike that of Odysseus, which is the nostalgia of all human beings—is for the future, for what is to come. It is turned not towards the past, but to what is ahead of us. Paradise is not behind us but in front of us. We seek for the person whom Adam lost in Paradise, and that person—in the fullness of his glory—we shall find ahead of us.

Take the example of the Prodigal Son, who having departed from the house of his father, and having failed miserably in life, one day has the nostalgic longing to return to his father's house. On his return, he is met by his father who has already left the house in order to meet his son. My question is, was it the nostalgia to return to the past that drew the son back, or the understanding that his father would come out to meet him? Both must be true. But from the biblical point of view, it is the movement of the father towards the Prodigal Son which is the most significant. This then is what I mean by the eschatological attitude of the Orthodox Church.

This attitude is illustrated by icons in the Orthodox Christian Tradition, where there is no perspective as in Western art, going into the picture. Instead, the perspective is from the person in the picture toward the viewer. This might be called the "reverse perspective" of Orthodox iconography, and no doubt for those artists who have gone through schools of fine art it may seem a very naive sort of perspective. But the thing to grasp is that God and the saints come out to greet us as if heaven is already here to enrich our everyday lives.

The ancient view, which we have already discussed in relation to regaining paradise, depended on a recollection of some event in the past. The Orthodox attitude is to a greater extent dependent on calling on the Holy Spirit, Who comes to us from the future. The Orthodox liturgical Tradition unites the recollection of the past, the *anamnesis*, with the *epiclesis*, that is, the calling on the Holy Spirit. Recollection, the past and history are not abolished, but are rather redefined by the *epiclesis*, which we must always understand eschatologically.

The end of time, to recapitulate, determines the beginning, and not the beginning the end. In the book of Revelation, this is summed up in the famous phrase: "I am the Alpha and the Omega, the Beginning and the End" (Rev. 21:6). St. Maximus the Confessor, who wrote in the seventh century, said that when we make the plan of a house, it is not the first drawings which determine the house. Instead, it is the vision of the architect of how the house will be at the end which determines the beginning, that is, the drawings.

What St. Maximus said—although I am simplifying his sophisticated philosophical language—is that the mystery of the Incarnation of Christ possesses the power to explain the enigmas of the Bible and also to explain and help us understand creation. He who has known the mystery of the Cross and the Tomb will have reached this point of understanding. However, he who has entered the mystical power of the Resurrection will have understood the very purpose of God in his creation and in the revelation of the Bible.

The whole experience of revelation, of the Incarnation, did in fact give a great thrust forward to the concept of historical movement and the process of historical change. Before the Bible, and in particular the New Testament, we do not have the same sense of historical time or of development in history. The ancient and the Greek world feared history in this sense. They were afraid of what was new and unexpected, and accepted the past as a stable certainty. That is why what was most important to them was the cosmos, the beautiful stability and perfection of the world, which the ancient Greeks explored.

The great Indian civilization also had a very similar attitude in avoiding historical development. For Gautama Buddha, the whole process of becoming is something to be escaped from, and it is in escaping from it that we can reach nirvana. Whether nirvana is being or non-being is not the important point. The important point is that it was crucial for the Buddha that we leave the process of history, the process of becoming.

For the Bible, history is one of God's great blessings. It is the result of creation and it is what gives meaning to the life and drama of man. But although the Old and New Testaments gave this impulse and encouraged the idea of progress and the creativity of man in history, they could not and did not stop at that point. Without eschatology, history would merely be a succession of events which would have no meaning and no conclusion. The significance and importance of history are not disputed, but we do not stop with the concept of history. If the Prodigal Son had gone back home and his father had not come out to meet him, then the return would have been in vain.

The Incarnation of Christ in history is an affirmation of history. Simultaneously, however, with the eschatological reality of the Resurrection, we are freed from the bonds of a historical record which is always moving on, always evolving. That is why St. Maximus, in the passage already quoted, said that it is the Resurrection which gives meaning to creation, and it is the Resurrection which gives meaning to the Incarnation itself.

Eschatology in our daily life means to believe in the Resurrection, to believe in the eternity of life. By this I do not mean an eternal life of the soul or of the world. In the language of the Gospel, it means something more than that, namely an *anakephaleosis*, a life for all, in a summing up of all history. It is the Holy Spirit Who, by coming to the Church and entering into our daily lives, brings to us this eschatological sense.

The Holy Spirit and the World to Come

However great a painter, a poet, or a footballer like Maradonna may be, however much they may have developed their talents, such gifted people usually understand that what they do at a particularly crucial moment is the result of inspiration. It is not the direct result of any talent or gift, or of any training or study that they have made in the development of their talents. It is a universal human experience that truly great works and truly great achievements are the result of inspiration.

However, this does not mean that we do not have to prepare, study or develop our talents. It means that the inspiration which refers to the *eschaton*, to the end of time, is something more than all that. That "something more" in our daily life is the presence of the Holy Spirit.

If we celebrate a Liturgy and the Holy Spirit is not present, then what we do is a mere ritual. Even an important event such as a martyrdom, as in the case of St. Polycarp of Smyrna, would be little more than the passion and death of any man, if the Holy Spirit were not there to bless it. In Dostoyevsky's *The Brothers Karamazov,* Alyosha the monk says to Dimitri (the sinner, in effect) that they are very much the same. Alyosha may be a monk, and one or two steps up the ladder ahead of Dimitri, but it's all very much the same. There is very little difference between them.

I believe that modern European civilization, which has progressed so far, and which is so wonderful in many respects, is only a very short distance away from our backward Balkan life. Where there is an absence of the oil of mercy, where there is an absence of the salt of faith, where there is an absence of the charisms and fruits of the Holy Spirit, where there is not the still, small voice in the breeze, as with Elijah, then all our achievements are as nothing. The basic hunger and thirst of human existence remain unfulfilled.

Even if man does not sin or fall into evil, he remains a prisoner of being, a prisoner of nature, a prisoner even, if you wish, of the whole universe—for that is still nature, and without the Holy Spirit, man would remain its prisoner. Eschatology means that man is not in prison either in the circle of time or in the unfolding of events, because Christ came from beyond time, from the eschaton, in order to break the chains of time and history. The Holy Spirit continually keeps open the gate to the coming world, to Paradise.

Christ, in his Incarnation, brought the Kingdom of God to man, and in His Resurrection He raised the human body next to God's throne. That is a matter of history, a historical event, and it is the greatest affirmation of human history. And yet, if the Holy Spirit had not been sent as a second Comforter, to keep the heavens open, and also the place at the right hand of the Father open to us, then the event of Christ becoming man would remain an event imprisoned in history, in the historical records. Or, at most, there would have been a process of making history eternal. The Orthodox Christian experience of the end of time, however, is not an experience of making history eternal. This would be an eternity of the same thing, an exhaustion of spirit.

A Marxist whom I know in Belgrade, and who has not yet become a Christian, said: "You speak to me about Christian mysticism, and that reminds me of a cat who is sitting in the sun and is just bored with life." I replied to him that what he thought of as Christianity is not Christianity. It is the joy of the game, the joy of meeting, the joy of the embrace. It is the taste of love, which however much you may enjoy it leaves you unsated. You do not ever feel sated, but you feel as if you want to pass through your own physical limitations. God, by His eschatological action, has freed Himself for us, so that we should not be shut up in Him.

The experience of true love is an eschatological experience. The experience of hope is also an eschatological experience, an experience of the end of time. The same is true with the experience of expectation, and this comes from the fact that man is not what he appears to be, but what he shall be. Man is by his very nature an eschatological creature. If we do not accept this, and it is our privilege as free creatures not to accept it, then we condemn man to imprisonment, even if the boundaries of the prison are huge, even if they are the galaxies, even if they are eternity. Love wants man to be free, to be unbounded, to be an eschatological creature turning to the end of time.

Two experiences of the disappointment of human love can be seen in Dostoyevsky and Marcuse. Dostoyevsky says that if you love man, you feel it with all your being; but all the time you feel that, even if you love man, so long as you cannot love God you are impotent to achieve what you wish to achieve. The love of God keeps open the eschatological dimension of the love of man. That is why the two loves, for God and man, symbolically form the cross. These two loves, toward man and God, are not merely ethical commands, they are the ontological foundations of man, and yet also a cross for man. If we remove either the vertical or the horizontal segments of the cross, all that we are left with is a beam. If we separate the love of man from the love of God, we do not find the eschatological dimension which love itself demands, while the love of God is indeed impossible without the love of man.

Herbert Marcuse—a German Marxist who lived in America and tried to combine Marx and Freud—has one of his heroes say in a prayer to God: "O God, save me from myself." With Christ's becoming man, God came out of Himself in a movement of love. He is the ecstatic God—and this word "ecstatic" literally means "moving out of oneself" in the Greek. This is a God Who moves out of Himself, an ecstatic God, as Dionysius the Areopagite says, Who comes out of Himself to meet us going out of ourselves to meet Him.

That is why I say that love is an eschatological experience, an eschatological type of life. When I speak of love in this sense, however, I mean a crucified love. That is why for us Christians, love experienced eschatologically in our everyday life means a cross.

A Christian must be a restless spirit, a revolutionary spirit, a man who is continually living on the chance, on the impulse. So that is why I say that man is not only *homo faber,* man the craftsman, or *homo sapiens,* man the thinker, but also *homo ludens,* man the player. Not even *homo religiosus,* the religious man that Eliade talks about, but *homo ludens,* the player, who is at the same time a person giving and seeking love: a man of communion. In the Greek, "communion" and "society" are very similar words. Thus a man of communion should also be a social being who is interconnected with others.

Communion means, in the strictest sense, at least two people permanently open to each other, and that forever without end. If we believe that communion ends, and thus loses its eschatological sense of reaching to the end of time, then communion starts to be debased, even if it is not totally destroyed. God in His being is the eternal communion. This is what the Holy Trinity means, the one communion of three beloved persons among themselves.

The creation of the world is a calling to us to come into that communion. History is a movement, a journey, towards that very end. If we have had an eschatological foretaste of the true God Who loves us, we can only keep it if we also love our fellow human beings. Then we understand that communion, or society in this sense of "communion," will not cease—that of all things under the sun, the only truly new thing is this communion of love which is also everlasting, because it comes from the end, the eschaton, and is God's communion.

Paradoxically, from this fact of communion I would draw the inference that as Orthodox Christians we are always in a tragic position in our relation to the world. This is as true for our contemporary situation as it was in former times. Our history, even when it is successful, is always a crucified history in this world. But the Christian sense of a crucified history or tragedy is not the same as that of ancient Greece. Without tragedy, human beings cannot come out of themselves. But God came into this tragedy and was crucified, and in that way we have indeed come out of the tragedy. The tragedy of the Cross became the Resurrection. The Resurrection does not abolish the reality of the Cross, but the Crucifixion is not deified in itself. It can never be, for it is not the end, but the gateway to the Resurrection, which is the end realized in history—although history still has to run its natural course.

This knowledge is the knowledge which is given to us by the Holy Spirit. That is why Christians in such early Christian texts as the *Teaching of the Apostles,* said, "May the Holy Spirit come and this world pass." It did not mean that they were against the world, it meant that they were not prepared to be enclosed within the world, even a world created by God. "I am wounded by your love," says the beloved in the Song of Songs, and he or she who is wounded by love is without consolation. However, this being without consolation is a blessing.

Let me give you an example. When I was growing up under Communism, the Communists told us what a wonderful world they were creating: that it was the kingdom of God on earth. These promises, this vision, troubled us. Fortunately, the same happened much earlier to Dostoyevsky. In fact, the first victim of Communism was the first man, Adam. When Satan whispered to him that he could become the equal of God, why did Adam fall into the trap? Because in one sense, man *is* created to be equal to God. The lie of the Devil and the lie of Communism were persuasive because they struck a true chord in human beings. They use this to try to fill humans with something that is wrong.

That is why St. John Damascene said that Adam fell into sin through stretching out in a mistaken way towards God. And indeed, speaking as a Serbian Orthodox Christian, my personal experience tells me that the devil is a very powerful agent, with a dynamic capacity to draw us. All of this, however, pales into insignificance when compared with the vision of meeting the God Who comes out to meet us. When, with bitter tears for my sins, I had that experience—which was indeed an experience of bitter dissatisfaction even with my success—then I realized that the devil is in fact very weak, and that man is stronger than both the devil and the archangel. And because Christians were living in a regime that imposed itself, not only with force but also with a very attractive ideology, I understood then why the devil is so aggressive in our lives. He is aggressive because he is by no means certain that he can win man over.

By contrast, God is not aggressive toward us. Sometimes He even withdraws, because He is so sure that man is drawn towards him. Love is not aggressive, and neither is truth or eschatology. When we accept these realities, we live in the certainty that everyday life is eternal. We do not wish to lose that certainty given to us by the anchor of faith, which, as St. Paul says, we have thrown into the third heaven. Yet we have in fact been tormented not just as individuals, nor as peoples—Greeks, Serbs, Russians—but we have been tormented through seeking the anchor of historical certainty, the certainty of success and of effectiveness.

Living in Eschatological Time

In the last resort, we understand that God shows His love for us in that we are not successful and He does not permit us to be so. The love of God wants us to be free, free from every idol. Even God can be our idol, and the worst idol of all is ourselves. As St. Andrew of Crete said, in his Great Canon at the beginning of Lent: "I have become an idol to myself." St. John ends his epistle by saying: "Little children, preserve yourselves from idols."

The Orthodox Christian eschatological stance toward life, which is simultaneously liturgical and ascetic, is a stance of crucified love that leads to the resurrection. The resurrection does not come if we do not pass through the experience of crucifixion. That is why the eschata in our daily life are not feelings of happiness in a church service, which leave us feeling satisfied and secure. In fact, religion in itself is a dangerous phenomenon. It can be an excuse for wrongdoing, an alibi against unbelief, a substitute for crucified love. This is so because it is possible for man, with the great abysses which lurk inside him, to return inside himself and look on himself as the final end or purpose of his life. In doing that he will lose the fact of the loving and suffering God.

We can replace Christ in our daily life as we can replace God with all number of "gods." Our eschatological experience, however, is that Mary in the Gospels was right: only one thing is needful for the experience of Christ, and that is to follow Him, as in the book of Revelation the martyrs followed Christ. This does not mean that we stand back and become inactive in history. It does not mean sloth, but expectation. It means an expectation of continual crusade—not with power, but with God-given weakness.

In all our weakness we should remember that the Holy Spirit is with us and in us, calling, "Abba, Father" (Gal. 4:6). In this *epicletic* attitude—that is, calling on the Holy Spirit—in this situation which is both liturgical and ascetic, it does not make a great difference who are the saints and who are the sinners; who are the virtuous and who are the fallen; who is higher up the ladder and who is lower down. In what way were the thieves on the right and on the left of the crucified Christ so different? The difference was that while both had sinned and both saw the end staring them in the face, only one thief saw it as personal and salvific. He cried out, in a true moment of repentance—of eschatological *epiclesis*—"Remember me, O Lord, in Thy kingdom."

Here then is the cross between commemoration and *epiclesis*, a biblical dialectic between history and eschatology. But it is not a dialectic for dialectic's sake—not a dialectic for some evolution or some revolutionary change—but a dialectic of crucifixion and resurrection, a dialectic of love and faith.

I end with the thoughts of St. Mark the Ascetic, which can be summed up in this way: The eschatological perspective is a continual light on our lives. God will not send us to hell because we are sinners and have done particular sinful deeds, nor will He send us to Paradise because we have done good deeds, but because of faith, which exists because of love. He will judge us, or rather we will judge ourselves, from our response to love: love coming out to meet us, love shining through from the end, which is God Himself.

This stance, this open response to love, can be described as eschatology present in our daily lives. It is hard for us to act like this. Many times even as Christians we prefer certainty, control and safety, but these are illusions and barriers to eschatological presence. As St. John Chrysostom, one of the greatest of the Fathers, said: "When you are uncertain, when you have nowhere to lean or to stand firm, then indeed you are paradoxically more certain because it is only God Who is your support and your strength." This is not a stance of hopelessness, nor is it angst. It is more like the openness that a child will have toward another child, or a child will have to its parents, knowing that it is loved because it also loves.

For many children, of course, this love simply fills them. It gives them sweetness and joy, and as these children become adults, this love will inevitably meet the experience of the cross. If they are faithful in their love, and if they come through the cruel experience of the cross to resurrection, then they will return to a childlike openness. They will be living in eschatological time.

The Holy Trinity,
icon by St. Andrei Rublev, 15th century.

Part IV

11
Between the "Nicaeans" and "Easterners": The "Catholic" Confession of St. Basil

There is no doubt that the fourth century has a special place in the history of the Church's Trinitarian theology, that is, the theological expression and formulation of the faith in the Holy Trinity: Father, Son, and Holy Spirit. This was the century of the greatest anti-Trinitarian heresies. The Fathers of the fourth century were engaged in an extremely difficult theological and ecclesiastical struggle with the most dangerous Trinitarian heresy of antiquity, Arianism, and with its subsidiary development of "Pneumatomachianism." These heresies, which were theologically and ecclesiastically overcome at the councils of Nicaea and Constantinople, were condemned because they denied the divinely revealed truth found in the Church's Scriptures and Tradition, that the Christian God *is* the Holy Trinity, and that the three holy and irreplaceable names of this revelation—Father, Son, and Holy Spirit—are in reality the three distinct but inseparable divine hypostases ("persons"), as particularly specified in the work of St. Basil.[1] The final destruction of Arianism and Pneumatomachianism, however, as well as their condemnation and rejection, was a difficult task and no easy accomplishment.

As is now apparent, the Arian and Pneumatomachian rejection of faith in the Holy Trinity as Christian orthodoxy was done in a manner completely at odds with the Trinitarian heresy that preceded them, Monarchianism, whose main proponents were Sabellius in the West and Paul of Samosata in the East. The third-century Monarchian heresy, under the influence of a Judaistic, narrow, monolithic understanding of God, denied the faith in the Holy Trinity by fusing all three divine hypostases into one. By this, in fact, the existence of the Son and

---

[1] St. Basil insisted on this especially in his work *Against Eunomius* (1.5.16; 2.6–8.28, etc.); cf. also *On Faith* 4 (PG 31:685–88).

the Holy Spirit as separate divine hypostases was denied, and they were regarded as merely different forms of God's appearance (*modus* according to Sabellian "modalism"), or as different powers of God's activity in the world (*dynameis* according to the "dynamism" of Paul of Samosata). In opposition to the Monarchian "fusion," the Arians, mainly under the influence of Greek religio-philosophical thought (which, in the same way as Jewish thought, could not accept the Christian revelation of God as Trinity), denied the Holy Trinity by division, that is, degrading the Son and the Holy Spirit by separating them from the divine essence of the Father. It appears that, although Sabellianism and Arianism were mutually opposed, in the end they arrived at the same point: the denial of the Church's faith in the Holy Trinity. These opposing heresies were described by St. Basil with the following names: Monarchianism—"the Judaizing heresy" (because of its sterile monotheism); Arianism and Pneumatomachianism—"Greek polytheism" (because of the division of one divinity into three gods).[2] The Trinitarian theology of the Church of the fourth century stood between these two extreme and unbalanced positions. For the Fathers of the fourth century, and especially for the great Cappadocians led by St. Basil the Great, who bore the brunt of the struggle against the aforementioned heresies, the path of the Church's Trinitarian theology passed exactly in the middle of these two extremes. The reason for this was not, however, because the truth always rests "in the middle," as a compromise between extremes, but because, as St. Basil's most intimate friend and coworker in theology St. Gregory the Theologian thought, in *this* case the middle path was the truth itself. That is, the middle path coincided with the Church's confession of faith in the Holy Trinity, which was originally accepted from Christ by the Church through the Holy Apostles and which, as the apostolic confession, was transmitted and preserved in Holy Baptism (Matt. 28:19).[3] For St. Gregory the Theologian and St. Basil the Great, avoidance of the Monarchian and Arian heretical extremes

---

[2] *On the Holy Spirit* 18:44–45 and 77; *Letter* 210.3; cf. also St. Gregory the Theologian, *Sermon* 20.5–6 and 8.1 (PG 35:792, 1072).

[3] St. Basil often invokes the tradition of Baptism in relation to the Trinitarian faith: *Against Eunomius* 1.5; 2.22, 3.2, 5; *On the Holy Spirit* 12.28; *Letter* 105 and 259.2; *Homily* 24.5, etc.

meant "maintaining the boundaries of the true worship of God" (ἐν ὅροις ἵστασθαι τῆς θεοσεβείας).[4]

In order to understand better these "boundaries of the true worship of God"—that is, the true Church's faith in the Holy Trinity and the correct (i.e., orthodox) thought about it, on which St. Basil especially insisted—it is necessary to consider the history of the Monarchian and Ario-Pneumatomachian heresies and the reaction to them in the East and in the West. At the end of the second century and the beginning of the third, the Monarchian heresy arose in the East and then was transmitted to the West, even to Rome itself. In the East it was successfully opposed by the learned Alexandrian theologian Origen. It was also opposed by a series of Eastern Church councils, especially that of Antioch, which very energetically condemned the Monarchian heresy as based on the Jewish understanding of monotheism, and professed the traditional faith of the Orthodox East in the tri-hypostatic God. Also in the West, Monarchianism was vaguely condemned in the person of Sabellius. Two of the best Western theologians, Tertullian and St. Hippolytus, very clearly unveiled the lie and falsehood of Monarchianism in their theological treatises. Neither in their own time nor later, however, do Tertullian and especially St. Hippolytus seem to have had the final word in Western Trinitarian theology. On the basis of the personal testimony of St. Hippolytus himself, in the third century the Roman bishops Zephyrinus and particularly Callistus (217–222) were themselves infected with some sort of Monarchian heresy, a kind of modified Sabellianism.[5] In general, there was a certain tendency in western theological thought toward Unitarianism: an underlying, one-sided emphasis on the unity of God. Western theological thought, in its approach to the mystery of the Being of God, started from the unity of the nature of God, the one essence (*una substantia*) of God, and dealt only secondarily with the three persons (*tres personae*) as persons, which was neither adequate nor sufficient. (This different perspective in approach to the Holy Trinity is already demonstrated by the character

---

[4] St. Gregory the Theologian, *Sermon* 20.5–6 (PG 35:1072). Cf. also St. Gregory of Nyssa, *Against Arius and Sabellius* (PG 45:1281).

[5] Cf. St. Hippolytus, *Philosophumena* 9–10. Cf. also Theodoret, *History of Heresies* 3.3 (PG 83:405).

of the mid-third-century dispute between Dionysius of Rome and St. Dionysius of Alexandria.)

Seen from this perspective, it becomes far more understandable why in the period after the First Ecumenical Council the Roman bishops and almost the whole West so firmly stood for the Nicene expression "homoousios" (ὁμοούσιος), overlooking the fact that under the mantle of Nicene "consubstantiality" Marcellus of Ancyra professed pure Sabellianism. Rome and the West remained deaf and insensitive to all Eastern protests that under "consubstantiality" Marcellus actually professed a Monarchian heresy of the Sabellian type, denying the hypostasis of the Son. For this reason, St. Basil wrote to St. Athanasius that "Even until now those from the West in all their letters to us never cease mercilessly to anathematize and excommunicate the notorious Arius, while at the same time they never criticize Marcellus of Ancyra, who spreads an opposite heresy and impiously denies even the existence of the divinity of the Only Begotten, wrongly interpreting the name 'Logos.'"[6] This silent sympathy of the Western "Nicaeans" for Marcellus, or at least their theological insensitivity to the danger of his heresy, is by itself important. It could hardly be explained and justified as a policy of protecting the authority of the Nicene Council, of which Marcellus was a fiery adherent, because it was precisely from this kind of "Nicaeans" that St. Basil and the other great Cappadocians had to protect and defend the Nicene faith in the consubstantiality of the Son with the Father, interpreting in a non-Monarchian manner (that is, correctly and in the orthodox way) the Nicene expression "consubstantial."[7]

The existence in the West in the pre- and post-Nicene period of this tendency toward perceiving and emphasizing first of all the one God, the one divine essence (because of which all the dangers of the Monarchian "fusion" of the persons of the Holy Trinity will remain for a long time insufficiently understood) represented a danger for a balanced and orthodox faith in the Holy Trinity, though undoubtedly this orthodox faith existed in the West. The examples of Dionysius of Rome in the third century, or even better yet, of St. Hilary of Poitiers

---

[6] *Letter* 69.2.

[7] Concerning the *correct* interpretation of "homoousios," St. Basil speaks already in *Letter* 9.3 (written in 361–362).

in the fourth century are proof of this. They correctly believed in the Holy Trinity. True, St. Hilary was in part influenced by the East, but precisely the fact that he understood and accepted Eastern Trinitarian theology indicates that the West was not alien to the Church's apostolic faith in the Holy Trinity.

In textbooks of Church history, especially those produced by Western scholars, it is usually maintained that after the First Ecumenical Council the whole East was Arian or semi-Arian. This was not, however, the opinion of St. Basil the Great. (In any case, St. Basil did not allow for such an opinion about his bishop, Dianius of Caesarea, the successor of Eulalius, who had endorsed the Creed at the Council of Nicaea. Dianius, however, belonged to the camp of the "Easterners.")[8] Although Arianism undoubtedly originated and spread mainly in the East, it was also in the East that this heresy was definitively conquered and destroyed. The struggle against Arianism was not waged in the East in the same way as it was in the West. Instead of a one-sided, persistent, and formal adherence to the Nicene Council, anathematizing all those who did not accept the term "homoousios," in the East the struggle with the heresy had a far broader and more complex scope. It is true that the East was reserved toward the expression "consubstantial" for a long time after the Nicene Council, but this silence should be understood correctly, for in many cases it had no Arian or heretical connotation.

We have seen how the Monarchian heresy was energetically condemned everywhere in the East. At the great Antiochian council in 268, even the term "homoousios," which was used by Paul of Samosata precisely in a Monarchian sense, was condemned. (St. Athanasius, St. Basil the Great and St. Hilary testify to this.) Taking into consideration the earlier condemnation of this expression and particularly the openly Sabellian interpretation of it in the fourth century by Marcellus of Ancyra, it is easy to see why it was not easy for the Eastern fathers to accept the expression "consubstantial," even though the Nicene Council stood behind it. Indeed, if considered by itself, "homoousios" undoubtedly implied certain dangers and allowed various interpretations. With St. Basil, therefore, we encounter constant emphasis on the need for the *correct*

---

8 Cf. *Letter* 51.12.

and *sound* understanding and interpretation of the Nicene expression "consubstantial," in the context of all other expressions and names used by the Nicene Creed concerning the Son of Man.[9] In other words, as Fr. Florovsky rightly maintains,[10] the Nicene definition could only be understood and interpreted in the light of the entire belief and confession of the Trinitarian Christian faith. This interpretation was worked out by St. Basil and his fellow Cappadocians. In addition, it is good to have in mind that, against the Arian "division," the Nicene Council spoke more about the "unity" and "indivisibility" of the Divine Being, whereas the Eastern bishops placed the emphasis on three hypostases, that is, the Church's traditional faith in the Trinity: Father, Son and Holy Spirit. That is why St. Dionysius of Alexandria in his own time, without any hesitation or concession, replied to the Monarchians: "If they [the Sabellians] see division in the fact that there are three hypostases, let them know that they are three anyway, even if they do not like it; otherwise, they would deny the Holy Trinity itself."[11] The confession of the three divine hypostases was for the East the precious traditional faith of the Church, which it could never abandon. St. Basil the Great constantly and clearly speaks of this in his works: "If the beginning of my life is Baptism, and the first of all the days of my life is regeneration [in Baptism], then it is obvious that precisely those words which are pronounced in the grace of adoption [i.e., the words of Baptism, 'in the name of the Father, and of the Son, and of the Holy Spirit'] are more precious and meaningful than all others."[12]

It should be noted, however, that St. Dionysius of Alexandria and many other bishops of the East were disciples of Origen. Together with

[9] There are numerous occasions on which St. Basil feels the need to emphasize the correct understanding of the Nicene "homoousios": cf. *Letters* 52.1–3; 159.1; 226.3; 125.1–3; 214.3–4; 361. In this endeavor, St. Basil had before him the example of St. Athanasius the Great, who in his treatise *Concerning the Councils* (33–36) tries to explain and interpret the main expression of the Nicene Creed: ἐκ τῆς οὐσίας τοῦ Πατρὸς and ὁμοούσιος.

[10] G. Florovsky, *Vostochnye ottsy IV-go veka* (Paris, 1931), p. 15.

[11] As quoted by St. Basil in his work *On the Holy Spirit* (72), in which he also quotes the testimonies of other pre-Nicene fathers concerning the traditional faith in the divinity of the Holy Spirit and, consequently, the divinity of the Holy Trinity (PG 32:201).

[12] *On the Holy Spirit* 26.

the precious teaching of the three divine hypostases they also inherited that characteristic weakness of Origen's theology: subordinationism. This weak point of Origen's theology was skillfully exploited by the Arians. They claimed St. Dionysius of Alexandria as a fellow Arian, and it was left to St. Athanasius to defend his predecessor. In this defense, it is again the teaching of the Trinity that is emphasized. St. Athanasius writes: "Accordingly, says Dionysius, we undividedly extend God into a Trinity, and again a Trinity undiminished we reduce into One." By this Trinitarian confession, according to St. Athanasius, Sabellius is silenced and the Arian heresy is conquered;[13] that is, by such a Trinitarian confession both Monarchian "fusion" and Arian "division" of the Divinity are refuted.

The traditional Eastern teaching about the three divine hypostases was the strongest weapon against all Monarchian "fusion," because by this teaching the real existence of the three unconfused divine hypostases—Father, Son and Holy Spirit—was expressed. In the East, the starting point in the doctrine of the Trinity was the hypostasis of the Father, thus making the whole theological perspective Trinitarian, tri-hypostatic. It is a biblical, personal perspective, where the foundation of both the Church's faith and theology is the *personal* revelation of God, a personal-hypostatic-revelation of the Son of God in the flesh, as in John 1:14, 18. This revelation is possible only if the Only Begotten Son—the "Logos"—is a hypostasis distinct from the Father, i.e., a separate person, who as such testifies about the Father. Many theologians have noted that in its Trinitarian theology the East always began by the confession of the three divine hypostases and only then affirmed their indivisible unity.[14] Here lies one of the essential differences between the Church's theology and Neoplatonic philosophy, with which the Fathers were acquainted very well. The Church's theology as expressed by the Fathers begins with the

---

[13] St. Athanasius, *Concerning Dionysius of Alexandria,* 17ff (PG 25b:504ff).

[14] Cf. Th. de Régnon, *Etudes de théologie positive sur la Sainte Trinité* (Paris, 1892), I, p. 433; G. Florovsky, *Vostochnye ottsy* (Paris, 1931), pp. 75–76; G. L. Prestige, *God in Patristic Thought* (London, 1952), pp. 233–41; V. Lossky, *The Mystical Theology of the Eastern Church* (New York, 1976), pp. 56–58; J. Meyendorff, "La procession du Saint-Esprit chez les Pères Orientaux," in *Russie et Chrétienté,* 3–4 (1950), pp. 159–60, and also *A Study of Gregory Palamas* (London-New York, 1974), pp. 228–29; P. C. Chrestou, "L'enseignement de Saint Basile sur le Saint-Esprit," *Verbum Caro,* 89 (1969), p. 92; K. Rahner, *The Trinity* (London, 1970), p. 58; and others.

ever-existing and personal Trinitarian God, Father, Son and Holy Spirit: the truly existing three divine names given to us in revelation, and not with some unlimited, undefined and impersonal "One" (τὸ ἕν) which has nothing in common with the living God of the Bible revealed as Trinity.[15] With the appearance of the Arian heresy, which did not "fuse" but precisely "divided" the Divinity, many in the East incorrectly assessed the situation and thus strayed into an obvious heresy. This occurred because many of the theologians in the East did not sufficiently emphasize or adequately express the unity of the three divine hypostases; they often spoke of the "unity of will" or the "unity of consent" between the divine hypostases,[16] using expressions which were too weak and insufficient to radically exclude the Arian idea of "division."

From what has been said thus far concerning the East, it is clear why Nicaea had to use such strong language as "begotten of the Father," that is, "from the essence of the Father," and "consubstantial with the Father." Only such terms would eliminate any kind of Arian perversion, and would instead emphasize the substantial numerical unity and the equal divine dignity of the Son with God the Father. This is why our great Cappadocian St. Basil, as before him St. Athanasius in Alexandria, upholding the substantial unity in the Holy Trinity, accepted from the very beginning the Nicene faith and called the Nicene Creed "the great doctrine of the true faith, τὸ μέγα τῆς εὐσεβείας κήρυγμα."[17] Thus, the term "homoousios," which did not allow the least doubt in the substantial unity of the divinity of the Father and the Son, was accepted into the Creed primarily through the efforts (after St. Athanasius' death) of St. Basil the Great and the Cappadocian Fathers.

The process of this acceptance of the Nicene formula, however, was not the same in the East as in the West. The difference resulted from a different spiritual sensitivity towards a subtle but crucial theological problem. It was not a question of mere "Greek triviality"; rather, the theological thought and feeling of the Eastern theologians, as Pres-

---

[15] G. Florovsky, *Vostochnye ottsy*, p. 76.

[16] Cf. the so-called "Lucian's Creed" (second Antiochene formula) in 341 (in St. Athanasius, *Concerning the Councils* 23.6).

[17] Cf. *Letters* 52.1; 140.2; 159.1.

tige rightly maintains,[18] was far more subtle and deep than the theological thought of the Latin West. In the East, as we have said, the most important question was that of the acceptance of the real and distinct existence of the hypostases of the Son and Spirit, not confused with the essence of the Father (and not reduced to mere "powers" or "attributes" of that essence), although united with the Father by nature. To those in the East, rejection of the three hypostases signified the abandonment of the inherited apostolic faith and the acceptance of the Sabellian heresy, the danger of which was pointed out often by St. Basil. According to him, it was insufficient to employ only the Nicene expression "homoousios," because taken in itself this term could be used to veil the hypostatic distinctions within the Trinity. Therefore, it was necessary while confessing the unity of the Trinity by *nature* (τὸ ὁμοούσιον) to confess also the personal-hypostatic *distinctions of the three hypostases*, i.e., their real existence (τὸ κοινὸν τῆς οὐσίας καὶ τὸ ἰδιάζον τῶν ὑποστάσεων).[19] The West, on the other hand, as we have seen, avoided speaking about the three hypostases. This was not simply due to the "poverty" of the Latin language; in fact all of the Western and many of the Eastern "Nicaeans" spoke of "three hypostases" (*personae*, πρόσωπα). However, to St. Basil this alone was never enough, because the term "hypostasis" was used even by Sabellius.[20]

Viewing the matter from this perspective, we can easily understand why the well-known attempt at reunion between the Eastern and the Western Fathers at the Council of Sardica in 343 failed. In the "extended" exposition of the Nicene faith, which some of the Western Fathers (St. Hosius of Cordova and Protogenus of Sardica) tried to present at the council, it was maintained that "the hypostases of the Father and the Son are one," μίαν εἶναι ὑπόστασιν.[21] This was rejected by both St.

---

[18] G. L. Prestige, *God in Patristic Thought* (London, 1952), pp. 6, 201.

[19] *Letter* 210.4–5; cf. *Letters* 214.3–4 and 236.6.

[20] Cf. *Letter* 210.5: "For it is not enough merely to indicate the differences between the persons, but it is necessary to confess that every person exists in a true hypostasis, because even Sabellius spoke about the existence of persons without hypostases (that is, without real personal existence)."

[21] Theodoret, *Ecclesiastical History* 2.8. Cf. also Sozomen, 3.12; and St. Photius, *Homily* 16.6. Disapproval of the "extended" exposition of the Nicene faith attempted in Sardica is also found in St. Athanasius, *Tome to the People of Antioch* 5.

Athanasius and the other Eastern Fathers as being absolutely unaccept-
able, even if the word "hypostasis" in the West was identified with the
word οὐσία, "essence." St. Basil the Great commented on this with
these words: "Those who say that 'ousia' (essence) and 'hypostasis' are
the same are compelled to confess only different 'persons' (πρόσωπα),
and by avoiding the use of the word 'three hypostases' they do not succeed in escaping the Sabellian evil."[22] Such dangerous omissions were
both impermissible and unforgivable in the East, and they could not be
covered over even by the authority of the Council of Nicaea. When a
little later the same thing happened in Antioch with the "Eustathi-
ans"—i.e., the strict "Nicaeans" headed by Paulinus—St. Basil the
Great did not hesitate to characterize it as "Marcellus' sickness," the
Sabellian heresy.[23]

The same perspective allows a better understanding of the "Homoiousians" in the East, a movement gathered mainly around Basil of
Ancyra and with which St. Basil obviously had some connection (cf. the
Council of Constantinople in 360 and further history). Basil of Ancyra
ascended to that city's episcopal chair after the dethronement of Marcellus, who was a "Nicaean." No doubt Basil of Ancyra was more Orthodox than Marcellus. He was an extraordinarily subtle theologian, both
anti-Monarchian and anti-Arian. Later, St. Photius will praise him and
commend his theology and faith. Also even St. Athanasius himself, the
"Father of Orthodoxy" and the "true Nicaean," will recognize him as
fully orthodox and call him a "brother in faith."[24] The Homoiousians
accepted the Nicene faith in all respects, except for the term "homoou-

[22] *Letter* 236.6.
[23] See *Letters* 214.3; 210.3; 125.1; 129.1.
[24] St. Photius, *Homily* 16.6. St. Athanasius, in his *Letter concerning the Synods of Ariminum and Seleucia* (41.1–2), which was written in 359, says: "Toward those who accept everything that is written in Nicaea but hesitate only at the expression τὸ ὁμοούσιον, we should not act as enemies. Because we speak with them not as with Ari-ans, nor as with those who oppose the fathers, but rather as with brothers who think as we do, except that they doubt the word *homoousios*. By confessing that the Son is from the essence of the Father and not from some other hypostasis, and that the Son is not a creature, but that He is the true Son by nature (γέννημα), and that, as the Lo-gos and Wisdom, He is coeternal with the Father, they are not far from accepting the word *homoousios*. Such was exactly Basil of Ancyra, who wrote about the faith."

sios," an expression not only formerly condemned in the East but also currently compromised by Marcellus. They used the term "homoiousios" (ὁμοιούσιος) instead of the Nicene expression since they thought it better showed the real existence of the hypostasis of the Son, as distinct from the hypostasis of the Father.[25] Basil of Ancyra, while opposing the Arian heresy (as is seen in the councils of Ancyra, 358, and Seleucia, 359), did not forget the Sabellian error (the "fusion" of the hypostases), and so always emphasized the real existence of the three hypostases. St. Basil the Great, however, did not use the term "homoiousios" but rather the Nicene formula "homoousios," although he insisted that even this term had to be understood in terms of what has been said above. To this great Cappadocian, the true theologian of the holy and saving Trinity, the expression "homoousios" signified primarily an incomprehensible, ineffable, *natural*, indivisible and existential "unity" and "communion" of the divine hypostases of the Holy Trinity: "οἰκεία καὶ συμφυὴς καὶ ἀχώριστος κοινωνία."[26] Consubstantiality, the unity of the Trinitarian divinity, was contemplated and understood as an ineffable and inexpressible "communion according to the essence," κοινωνία κατ᾽ οὐσίαν, and "communion according to the nature," κοινωνία κατὰ φύσιν.[27] The Only Begotten Son is consubstantial with His Father, but He is also the truly existing Son, as a distinct divine hypostasis, even as the Father is a distinct divine hypostasis. In the same way, the Holy Spirit who is "from God the Father" is also consubstantial according to nature, συνουσιωμένως κατὰ φύσιν, with the Father and the Son, but He is also a unique and distinct divine hypostasis.[28]

As St. Basil tells us, the Eastern bishops did not consider it sufficient to recognize "three persons," τρία πρόσωπα, or as in the language

---

[25] A clear exposition of faith by the leader of the Homoiousians, Basil of Ancyra, is contained in his general epistle *On the Holy Trinity* (in St. Epiphanius, PG 42:425–44). Concerning this work, V. Bolotov, A. Spassky and others rightly consider that it contains the same teaching as that of St. Athanasius.

[26] *On the Holy Spirit* 63; *Against Eunomius* 2.12.28; *Homily* 24.35; *Letter* 52.2–3; and also the whole *Letter* 38, which, although written by St. Gregory of Nyssa, expresses the theology of St. Basil.

[27] *Homily* 15.2–3 (Περὶ πίστεως). Cf. also G. Florovsky, *Vostochnye ottsy*, pp. 83–84.

[28] *Homily* 15.3; *Letters* 159.2; 125.3.

of the Latin West *tres personae,* because even under the word "person" lurked the shadow of Sabellianism. A clear and unambiguous confession of three hypostases was needed,[29] showing them to be three concretely existing persons, where the hypostasis is understood as a crucial personal seal and the bearer of the unique personal existence, as a personal τρόπος ὑπάρξεως which cannot be reduced to anything else, neither essence nor nature nor any attribute of the divine nature, because a real person is irreducible to anything else, even to its own nature or essence. In his Trinitarian theology St. Basil the Great always combined the two terms "hypostasis" and "homoousios," in order to express more correctly the ineffable mystery of the Trinitarian being, life and communion, κοινωνία, of God;[30] that is, the mystery of the consubstantial and life-creating Trinity: the Father, the Son Who is begotten of Him, and the Holy Spirit Who proceeds from Him.

"Homoiousian" theology was continuing firmly in the sound Eastern theological tradition, with its primarily personal Trinitarian perspective, but this theology taken in itself had its own weaknesses. St. Athanasius suggested in a brotherly way to the holders of this theology that they should replace ὁμοιούσιος with the stronger term ὁμοούσιος, and should also extend this teaching of the consubstantiality of the Father and the Son to include the Holy Spirit. A great theological struggle awaited the Cappadocians headed by St. Basil, through which they persevered with honor. For the holy Cappadocian Fathers, having become embroiled in the contest between the "Nicaeans" and the "Easterners," succeeded in winning a real victory for the cause of Nicene consubstantiality and the true faith in the Holy Spirit. They did this in such a way as not to sacrifice anything of the sound Eastern Triadological tradition. The name "Neo-Nicaeans," later given to them, signifies precisely that.[31]

---

[29] *Letters* 210.5 and 236.6. This last letter of St. Basil was written in 376, while in that same year Jerome was writing from the East to Pope Damasus in Rome (*Letter* 15.3–4) saying that he regarded the expression "three hypostases" to be Arian!

[30] Concerning this idea of the Cappadocian Triadology see an interesting article by J. Zizioulas, "Vérité et Communion dans la perspective de la pensée patristique grecque," *Irénikon* 4 (1977), pp. 469–73 and 492.

[31] There is an interesting article by J. Lebon, "Le sort du 'consubstantiel' Nicéen," *Revue d'histoire ecclésiastique* (Louvain), 47–48 (1952–1953), which is directed against the term "Neo-Nicean" and, in general, against the Eastern Triadological tra-

So it should not be forgotten that St. Basil and the other Cappadocians were firmly rooted in the general *Eastern* dogmatic tradition, and not particularly in that of "homoiousianism." And, of course, St. Basil learned from St. Athanasius, but not from him alone. While fighting for the Nicene faith, the Cappadocian Fathers preserved the traditional theological vision of the East and all the good elements of the pre-Nicene Eastern theological tradition of the Holy Trinity. Yet such is the inner logic of the faith and life of the Church in the Holy Spirit that the one and true dogmatic tradition of the Church cannot be completely expressed, even by an ecumenical council. It should be said also that the Cappadocian Fathers theologically overcame the weaknesses that had plagued the pre-Nicene Eastern Triadological tradition, e.g., the subordinationism of Origen, the so-called cosmological aspect of the Logos, and the mingling of the "economic" aspects in the revelation of the Trinity with the *theology* of the Holy Trinity. Thus they truly manifested the "theological mind" and "theological language" through which the catholic (ecumenical) Church of Christ in the whole universe found the true and God-befitting expression of its traditional apostolic and evangelical faith. St. Basil no doubt made the greatest contribution to the finding of the correct theological terminology, the words which were adequate to the Orthodox faith in the holy and life-creating Trinity. His Triadology and that of the other Cappadocians, his brothers in spirit and body, has become therefore the universal and catholic Triadology of the Church, without which all further theology is inconceivable.

One of the most important and fundamental elements in the Trinitarian theology of the East, inherited from the Church's biblical, apostolic Tradition, is the teaching of the monarchy of *the Father.* This teaching about the divine monarchy, about the one divine origin—or,

dition. Mgr. Lebon one-sidedly insists on "la doctrine de la simplicité divine et du monothéisme rigoureux" (p. 488) and "la rigueur de la foi monothéiste" (p. 528), by referring particularly to J. Tixeront (*Histoire des dogmes,* II, 76–89). It is strange how this well-known Roman Catholic theologian and historian "presses" some texts of St. Basil beyond their intended meaning. His approach to the question of the Eastern Triadology of the fourth century is typically Western, starting first with the essence of God. This is the weakness of this otherwise interesting article.

stated more precisely, the faith of the Church in "one God the Father," a faith which dominates the entire Holy Scripture and the Church's apostolic Tradition, testified in all of the ancient creeds, in the baptismal formula, and in the liturgical anaphoras of the ancient apostolic Church—this faith is the starting point of Eastern Trinitarian theology. This theology is not simply a theology of the "one God," but precisely the Christian Trinitarian theology about "one God the Father," Who has an Only Begotten Son born from Him, and a Divine Spirit proceeding from Him. In the words of St. Cyril of Jerusalem—one of the bishops from the camp of the Easterners, but undoubtedly far more orthodox than many formal "Nicaeans"—the "reality of the monarchy" of the Christian God consists precisely in the identifying of the monarchy with the dignity of the Father: "For it is necessary to believe not only that there is one God, but also that He is the Father of the Only Begotten Son,"[32] "the timeless beginning (ἀρχὴ) and the fountainhead (πηγὴ)"[33] of the divinity of the Son and the Holy Spirit. These words of St. Cyril concerning the monarchy of the Father will be almost literally repeated by St. Basil the Great many times in his works *Against Eunomius* (1.20, 24, 25; 2.12; 3.6); *On the Holy Spirit*, ch. 18, which is dedicated to the theme "How to preserve in the confession of the three hypostases the precious dogma of the monarchy"; and Sermon 24, "Against the Sabellians, Arians and Eunomians." The understanding of the monarchy of the Father is present also in the liturgical anaphora of St. Basil. The famous and very important words of St. Basil from his aforementioned Sermon 24: "Εἷς Θεὸς ὅτι καὶ πατήρ," "God is one because He is the Father,"[34] will be frequently repeated by St. Gregory the Theologian and St. Gregory of Nyssa.[35] They contain what was dear to the Cappadocians and to the whole Orthodox East in general, namely, that the source and foundation of the unity of God's being consists in the mystery of the hypostasis of God the Father, from Whom the Son

---

[32] St. Cyril of Jerusalem, *Catechesis* 7.1.
[33] St. Cyril of Jerusalem, *Catechesis* 11.20.
[34] St. Basil the Great, *Homily* 24.3 (PG 31:605A).
[35] St. Gregory the Theologian, *Sermon* 20.6–7; 42.15 and others; St. Gregory of Nyssa, *Against Eunomius* II (PG 45:476); *Tractatus Adversus Graecos Ex Communibus* (PG 45:180).

is begotten and the Holy Spirit proceeds. For the mystery of the Christian God consists in the mystery of *God the Father,* and only subsequently the *one essence* of the Divinity, which in fact is the essence of God the *Father.* Therefore St. Basil, when writing against Eunomius, concentrates on the name *Father,* Πατήρ, as the most important and meaningful Christian name for God, which is given to us in the divine revelation by the Holy Spirit. St. Basil insisted on that biblical name for God, for only through that name—together with the other unique, unrepeatable and irreplaceable biblical names of the Holy Trinity—can "adequate doxology" be offered.[36]

The Church's apostolic faith in the monarchy of God the Father, from Whom the Son is born and the Holy Spirit proceeds, has been confessed in the East ever since, but in pre-Nicene theology it did not always find its expression in adequate terms or concepts. Therefore in many pre-Nicene theologians, who mingle the plane of the *economic* or Trinitarian manifestation with the *theological* plane, which refers to the being of the Holy Trinity itself, we encounter the teaching of the *subordination* (*subordinatio*) of the Son and the Holy Spirit to God the Father, so that the Son and the Spirit are regarded at some degree lower than God the Father. This was the case with Origen and his disciples. As far as Origen is concerned, however, it should be indicated that his Trinitarian perspective, developed in the struggle against Monarchianism, was basically correct, and did not lead inevitably into Arian heresy, as is often thought. Origen himself deserves credit for the theological defense of the Trinitarian dogma of the Church. He was the one who first used the expression "three hypostases" for the Holy Trinity.[37] However, when in the struggle against Monarchianism he emphasized primarily the tri-hypostasity of the Christian God, a point which was denied by the Monarchians, in his desire to preserve also the Christian theology about *one* God he sought refuge in the idea of subordination of the Son to the Father, and the Holy Spirit to the Father and the Son. The intention of Origen—to preserve the single principle in God and by this to preserve Christian monotheism—was correct and could be interpreted

---

[36] *Against Eunomius,* 1.5.16; 2.6–7.
[37] *Exegesis of the Gospel of St. John* 5.2.6.

as such if Origen had maintained only the personal, *hypostatical* monarchy of the Father, on the level of hypostases, where the first hypostasis of
the Holy Trinity is God the Father as the ἀρχή ("origin") and πηγή
("fountainhead") of the Son and the Spirit, and as such is "greater" than
they (cf. John 14:28). The fundamental weakness and fallacy of Origen
was that he spoke also of the *substantial* subordination of the Son to the
Father, and of the Spirit to the Father and the Son; that the Son of God
by *nature, power* and *honor* is subordinated to the Father and is lower
than the Father, and the Holy Spirit is lower than both of them. This
same weakness of Origen was perpetuated by his disciple St. Dionysius
of Alexandria, for which he was criticized by St. Basil, who excused him
with the explanation that St. Dionysius did this "not out of an evil intention, but from a desire ably to oppose Sabellius" and to show him that
"the Father and the Son are not the same hypostasis."[38]

Despite the respect which Origen enjoyed in the East, his sub-
ordinationist understanding of the mystery of the Holy Trinity was condemned and rejected by that same East, and Origenism was overcome in
the East together with Arianism. This happened not only at the Fifth
Ecumenical Council (A.D. 553), but also much earlier, at the time of
the Cappadocian Fathers. Indeed, Origenism was not simply rejected,
but was precisely overcome and conquered.[39] Neither the authority nor
the philosophical-theological learning of the great Alexandrian would
change the apostolic Tradition of Trinitarian faith which reached St.
Basil the Great and found its most adequate expression in "Cappadocian" theology. However, these great Fathers, having rejected the theological mistakes of Origen and of other Easterners, did not discard or
abandon that correct Eastern Triadological perspective, for which the
"much learned and diligent" Origen struggled according to his abilities,
as St. Athanasius recognized.[40] St. Basil the Great and his Cappadocian
disciples did not abandon the traditional apostolic faith of the Church

---

[38] *Letter* 9.2.
[39] Cf. G. Florovsky, *Vostochnye ottsy*, 12. J. Gribomont, in his well-known article
L'Origénisme de Saint Basile, underestimates the independence of St. Basil from Origen, especially in his understanding of the Holy Trinity.
[40] St. Athanasius, in his work *On the Nicene Council* (27), tried to defend Origen
and to show that he was not Arian, but Orthodox.

in the monarchy of God the Father, but understood it as being proper to God, and expressed it in the "God-befitting words" of their theology.[41] Starting with the monarchy of the Father as the origin, principle and fountainhead of the Son, St. Basil distinguishes and explains the hypostasis of the Son, and from these holy and irreducible names concludes that they are ὁμοούσιοι καὶ ὁμότιμοι, "consubstantial and equal in honor." This also holds for the hypostasis of the Holy Spirit, Who is of the same divine honor (ὁμότιμος),[42] glory and dignity as the Father and the Son, and therefore equally belongs to the Holy Trinity. Thus the teaching about the *threeness* (or, more precisely, the *tri-hypostasity*) and the *consubstantiality* of God, understood inseparably and unconfusedly, is held together in the divinely wise and God-inspired theology of the Holy Trinity of the Cappadocian Fathers. This theological *distinction* and *discrimination,* διάκρισις, binds together what is *common* in the Trinity, τὸ κοινὸν τῆς οὐσίας, ἡ θεότης, and that which is *separate and distinct,* τὸ τῶν προσώπων ἰδιάζον, τρεῖς ὑποστάσεις,[43] but without intermingling or separation. This was the work of the Cappadocian Fathers, for which they have been so widely recognized and glorified in the universal Church throughout the centuries.

The theological greatness of St. Basil and the other Cappadocian Fathers consists precisely in the fact that they showed that when theologizing about the greatest mystery of the Christian faith, the Holy Trinity, one ought not to stray into heretical extremes, nor into any kind of human philosophy or religious theory; but one should rather progress in the royal and balanced path of the truth of God, the path of the true Church's faith. That is the reason why, in fact, only the holy Cappadocians successfully waged the battle of the Church's theology against the heretical teachings of Arianism and Monarchianism. The Church as a whole achieved this victory at the Second Ecumenical

---

[41] The correct and *Orthodox* understanding of the *monarchy* of the Father is that the hypostasis of the Father is the cause and fountainhead of the hypostasis of the Son and the hypostasis of the Holy Spirit, and is regarded in this way as "greater" (μείζων). This view is given by St. Basil the Great (*Against Eunomius* 1.20.25; 2.12) and St. Gregory the Theologian (*Sermon* 40.43).

[42] St. Basil the Great, *De Fide* 4 (PG 31:688); *Against Eunomius* 3.2–3; *On the Holy Spirit* 18.45; *Letter* 90.2; *Homily* 24.5.

[43] *Against Eunomius* 1.19; 2.28–29; *Letter* 210.4–5; 214.3–4; 236.6.

Council in Constantinople in 381. Without the theological work of the Cappadocians and the Second Ecumenical Council—which was mainly prepared by St. Basil, but which he did not live to see—even the Council of Nicaea would not have been enough.

The theological character of the Holy Cappadocians in the East clearly indicates that the "whole East" was not Arian or "semi-Arian," as many Western historians dealing with that period assert. On the contrary, the orthodoxy of the East was recognized by St. Athanasius the Great himself, although he personally suffered more than others from many Eastern bishops and was often the prey of their Arian schemes. At the Council of Alexandria in 362 the holy and truly great Athanasius recognized the Eastern Triadology as fully orthodox, to which testifies his *Tomos to the Antiochians,* probably offered by St. Athanasius personally to St. Basil when he became a bishop. St. Athanasius while he was alive recognized and approved all the great theological and ecclesiastical work of St. Basil the Great,[44] even though those in the West still were suspicious of Eastern Triadology and even suspected Basil the Great himself of being an Arian or semi-Arian. The great theological spirit of the Alexandrian "Father of Orthodoxy" was far more open-minded and subtle, and he himself was far more of an "Easterner" than were many of the one-sided formal defenders of the Nicene "consubstantiality" in the West. Contrary to St. Athanasius, certain "Nicaeans" living in the West and in the East, instead of cooperating with Basil and the other Eastern bishops gathered around him, supported the notorious Sabellian Marcellus of Ancyra and other semi-Sabellians, like Paulus and Apollinaris, whom St. Basil and St. Gregory the Theologian attacked openly.[45]

---

[44] This is attested to in the correspondence of St. Basil with St. Athanasius and the "Letter to John of Antioch" by St. Athanasius. From the letter to the Neocaesareans by St. Basil the Great (*Letter* 204.6), it could be concluded that St. Athanasius had passed on the decisions of the Council of Alexandria to St. Basil.

[45] *Letters* 52.4; 129.1; 131.2; 214.3–4; 226.3–4; St. Gregory the Theologian, *Letter* 104 (PG 37:185–92). It is characteristic of the correspondence of St. Basil with Apollinaris, which has been preserved and is now regarded as authentic, that St. Basil from the beginning disagreed with the teaching of the "Nicene" Apollinaris concerning the Holy Trinity, and his interpretation of the Nicene *homoousios* (see *Letters* 361–63).

From what has been said above, we would call attention to the fact that the theological work of St. Basil the Great and his brothers in spirit and flesh, particularly the two Gregories, was a truly, universal, "catholic" act of the Church. For, indeed, when we speak of the Triadology of the holy Cappadocian Fathers we are referring not to the "theology" of a particular school, but rather to a theological confession of the catholic and universal Church of Christ. For this reason St. Basil, although a metropolitan of the relatively small city of Caesarea in Cappadocia, could boldly say that those not in communion with him were separated from the Church herself, whereas those who were in communion with him were in communion with the Church.[46] It is characteristic also of the Cappadocian Fathers that they did not belong to any of the famous "theological schools," but were really "universal teachers," οἰκουμενικοὶ διδάσκαλοι, of the Church, because they themselves were humble disciples of the faith and tradition of the universal and apostolic Church. Their theology of the Holy Trinity was universally accepted as the true criterion of the Church's faith in the holy, life-creating, and saving Trinity, consubstantial and undivided. Their theology, therefore, cannot be placed on the same level as the theology of just any theologian (like Origen, St. Augustine, or someone else), or any theological school (be it Alexandrian, Antiochian, or some Western school), as some Roman Catholic theologians would prefer to do.[47]

It should also be said that Cappadocian Trinitarian theology and its Triadological terminology provided a foundation for the entire subsequent *Christological* confession of the Church, especially since the Council of Chalcedon. The Trinitarian formula of Cappadocian theology, μία φύσις—τρεῖς ὑποστάσεις, "one nature—three hypostases," which was mostly the product of the work of St. Basil the Great, became the basis for the Christological formula μία ὑπόστασις—δύο φύσεις, "one hypostasis—two natures." This term had been employed already by St. Gregory the Theologian in his *Letter to Cledonius* against the Christological heresy of the "Nicaean" Apollinaris. The foundation

---

[46] *Letter* 204, to the Neocaesareans.
[47] Cf. M. J. Le Guillou in *Istina* 3–4 (1972), pp. 457–64; and in his books *L'Esprit Saint et l'Eglise* (Paris, 1969), 195–234, and *Le mystère du Père* (Paris, 1973), pp. 87–130.

of Christological theology and its terminology on the Triadological theology of St. Basil and the holy Cappadocians is obvious in all the later orthodox Fathers.[48] On the theology of St. Basil and the holy Cappadocians was founded all the subsequent theology of the Holy Fathers in the East up to and including St. Gregory Palamas. This theology is even today the fundamental confession of the Orthodox Church.

St. John Damascene,
fresco in the Studenica Monastery, 1208.

---

[48] Concerning this see J. Meyendorff, *Christ in Eastern Christian Thought*, second edition (Crestwood, N. Y.: St. Vladimir's Seminary Press, 1975), pp. 76–77, 145–47, 209–13.

12

Icon and Incarnation
in the Holy Fathers and St. John Damascene
Constantinople, 1987[1]

1.

From the very beginnings of the debate over holy icons, Christological dogma has been at the very center of the theological question of
icons. Orthodox theology even before St. John Damascene, but especially after him, has emphasized the importance of the dogma of the
Incarnation for Orthodox iconography and iconology. The question of
icons, and first of all the icon of Christ, was posed as the question of
whether it was possible to generally describe God Who is by nature
indescribable (ἀπερίγραπτος). But for Orthodox theology, that question was answered with the mystery-fact of the divine *Incarnation*, for
it resolves the dual theological problem of the indescribability (τὸ
ἀπερίγραπτον—limitlessness, immenseness) and the describability (τὸ
περιγραπτόν—comprehension, limitation) of God, Who according to
the nature of His being is endless and limitless.

In this sense, it should be noted that St. John Damascene started
his great theological work, his Dogmatic Theology (*Exact Exposition of
the Orthodox Faith*), with the words of St. John the Evangelist: "No
man has seen God at any time; the Only Begotten Son, Who is in the
bosom of the Father, He has declared him" (ἐξηγήσατο—has brought
to the public, has shown, has revealed) (John 1:18). This evangelical
truth, contained in these words about the mystery of God and the Incarnation, simultaneously demonstrates the dual theological question
and its solution: the possibility and reality of the Incarnation of God,

---

[1] A lecture delivered in the Greek language in Constantinople on the occasion of
the 1200th anniversary of the Seventh Ecumenical Council, November 1987.

the Invisible and Limitless, and, along with that, the possibility of Christian iconography, iconology and icon veneration.

On the one hand, then, it is impossible to create any kind of picture or description ("sketch") of God, because He is Invisible and Ineffable (indescribable, unportrayable), and "No one has ever seen God" as such (cf. John 5:37: "You have neither heard His voice at any time, nor seen His form"; and Deut. 4:12). On the other hand, the Only Begotten Son of God, "Who is the Image of the Invisible God" (Col. 1:15), by His Incarnation revealed the Invisible God in a human form, as St. Damascene said by paraphrasing the words of the forefather Jacob: "For I have seen the human face of God, 'and my life is preserved'" (Gen. 32:30).[2] Therefore, when we talk about the Incarnation and the veneration of icons, it is necessary to always bear in mind this dual truth of Orthodox theology: the essential invisibility and indescribability of the Godhead, and the fact of the Incarnation of the Logos—the Son of God—through which God in Christ has become visible to mankind in reality.

It is precisely because of this that the Person of the God-man Christ—One Hypostasis in two natures—is the foundation and key for solving the question of the icon as a *"topos (locus)* of theology." This then tightly connects the theme of iconography, iconology, and icon veneration with the theme and the fact of the Incarnation. In addition, this connection was clearly expressed by the Seventh Ecumenical Council in Nicaea, 787, in its dogmatic *horos* (statement), with these words: "He who venerates an icon venerates the person (τὴν ὑπόστασιν) of him who is depicted on it."[3] This view of the problem, that is, the tight connection between the icon and Incarnation, was stated by St. John Damascene, and he was not the only one.

2.

Before St. Damascene, the Patriarch of Constantinople, St. Germanus (715–730), theologically placed the veneration of the holy icons on a Christological foundation. It could have been that St. Germanus had a personal reason. It is known that as the Bishop of Cyzicus, in the

---

[2] *On the Divine Images* 1.2 (PG 94:1256). For the works of St. John Damascene we quote from Migne and from the new critical edition of B. Kotter, 1975.
[3] Mansi, *Collectio Conciliorum*, 13.377.

year 712, he took part in a delayed condemnation of the Sixth Ecumenical Council, but soon after that, in the year 715, when he was already the Patriarch of Constantinople, he convened a council of around
one hundred bishops that reestablished and confirmed the Sixth Ecumenical Council (680–681)—the last great Council to have dealt with
Christological dogmas.

About ten years later, when the iconoclastic controversy occurred,
headed by three bishops from his Patriarchate, St. Germanus tried peace-
fully to discuss the question of the meaning of icons and the legitimacy
of the veneration of icons. On this occasion, in his Letter to John of Sinai, he wrote the following lines that clearly demonstrate the Christological foundation of Orthodox iconography and the veneration of
icons: "We do not depict an image or a picture or a shape or some form
of the Invisible Godhead.... But, since the Only Begotten Son of God,
Who is in the Father's bosom, calling back (saving) His creatures from
the sentence of death, deigned to become man by the kindness of the
Father and the Holy Spirit, we therefore depict His human image and
appearance according to His human body, and not His incomprehensible and invisible Divinity; and with this we attempt to present our
faith (clearly, visibly), showing that He is not a fantasy and has not taken
our nature to Himself as a shadow, ... but in reality and in truth (αὐτῷ
πράγματι καὶ ἀληθείᾳ) He became a perfect man in everything."[4]

St. Germanus of Constantinople wrote similarly in his Letter to
another iconoclast, Bishop Thomas of Claudiopolis: "It is necessary to
depict in icons characteristics of the Lord's image (ἰδέας—appearance)
according to the flesh in order to contradict heretics who slander that
He did not truly become man but was only a fantasy, and in order to
give certain guidance (χειραγωγίαν δέ τινα) for those who cannot easily
ascend the heights of spiritual understanding.... [It is necessary] so that
the mystery will be impressed (in their minds and hearts) through observation—that God manifested Himself in the flesh and was believed
in throughout the world (cf. I Tim. 3:16); so that this will be seen as
sanctifying and salvific for all of us; so that what is written in the evangelical sermons about His life in the flesh on earth among us humans

---

[4] PG 98:157C.

will permanently be inscribed in people's memory (through icons); and so that His Glory and Holiness which we preach and venerate will be more clear."[5] From this cited example of Patriarch St. Germanus, as well as the previous one, it is obvious, above all, that the truth of the Incarnation of Christ is the theological basis for creating His icon, and that iconography and icon veneration are in their own way a public and visual teaching and preaching of the salvific Christian mystery of God's Incarnation.

To cite one more text of St. Germanus, from his well-known writing *About Heresies and Councils:* "We have received (through Holy Tradition) that when we paint (write) on wood our Lord Jesus Christ according to the human image—that is, according to His visible Theophany (κατὰ τὴν ὁρατὴν αὐτοῦ Θεοφάνειαν)—we do so as a constant reminder of His life in the flesh, His suffering and salvific death, and the resulting redemption of the world, and through this we understand the height of dispassion of God the Logos."[6]

From all these quoted texts of St. Germanus of Constantinople (the end of the last one is based on Canon 82 of the Council in Trullo held in 692), it is clear that Orthodox church iconography and icon veneration is founded on the central event of the Christian faith: the Incarnation of God the Logos. The Incarnation of Christ is a revelation and manifestation of the Hidden and Unseen and Uncircumscribable God. The Incarnation is, according to the words of St. Germanus, a true and full *Theophany*—"His visible Theophany."

This word *Theophany* introduces us to the center of the whole divine revelation, which was witnessed and written about in the Old and New Testaments. It is well known that the Holy Fathers of the East saw, in the biblical pronouncements and in the Revelation of the mystery of the Incarnation, the mystery of *describing* in words the God Who is of an Indescribable nature. From this description of Theophany in *words,* the transition to describing God as Christ, *by means of pictures,* drawings and colors (i.e., icons) is normal. In this way the Holy Fathers and, as we saw, St. Germanus, made the connection between logography

5 PG 98:173BC.
6 PG 98:80A.

(the written word) and iconography (the writing of images), and connected both of these methods with *Theophany*—the *Theophanies* of God—as they were experienced in the general context of God's Revelation and manifestations in the Old and New Testaments. This distinctly biblical theme of *theophanies* will appear later in the noted Synodicon of Orthodoxy (849), where it is said that "even before the Incarnation of the Logos" the prophetic visions of God in the Old Testament were already "the revealed iconography (of the prophets)."[7]

But there is a clear difference in the degree of fullness between the Old Testament *Theophanies* and the unique New Testament *Theophany* of the personal Incarnation and becoming human of Christ. That is why the noted 82nd canon of the Quinisext Council in Trullo (691) (upon which St. Germanus draws textually), by placing church iconography and Orthodox icon veneration on a clear Christological foundation, even before St. Germanus and St. John Damascene did, emphasized the precedence of New Testament *realities* of Truth above the *shadow* of the Old Testament. That is why they decided that real *iconography* should be practiced in the Church instead of mere symbolical portrayal, so that in the future Christ would not be depicted symbolically "as Lamb," but realistically "as true Man"—the Incarnate God. Here is the full text of that holy Canon formulated before the emergence of the iconoclastic heresy:

"In some pictures of the venerable icons, a lamb is painted to which the Forerunner (John) points his finger, which is received as a type of grace, indicating beforehand through the (Old Testament) Law, our true Lamb, Christ our God. Embracing therefore the ancient types and shadows as symbols of the truth, and patterns given to the Church, we prefer 'grace and truth,' receiving it as the fulfillment of the Law (cf. John 1:17). In order therefore that 'that which is Perfect' may be delineated to the eyes of all, at least in colored expression, we decree that the figure in human form of the Lamb who takes away the sin of the world, Christ our God, be henceforth exhibited in images, instead of the ancient lamb, so that all may understand by means of it the depths of the humiliation

---

[7] See the critical edition: J. Gouillard, *Le Synodikon de l'Orthodoxie*, in Travaux et Mémoires, 2 (Paris, 1967).

of the Word of God, and that we may recall to our memory His life in the flesh, His passion and salvific death, and His redemption which was wrought for the whole world."[8]

It is obvious, from this text of the 82nd Canon of Trullo, that Orthodox church iconography and icon veneration were theologically founded on Christology even before the iconoclastic controversy; that is, they were founded on the New Testament reality of the Incarnation as a true and full Theophany.[9]

3.

This Christological context, in which the question of holy icons is immediately placed, was not foreign to the theological tradition of the Orthodox East. This is because, in the East, all the theological problems before the iconoclastic controversy, including those of Triadology (Trinitarian theology), had their beginning and final resolution in the question of Christ's Person. Christology was the starting point for the theological thought of the Eastern Church Fathers. It should be emphasized, however, that the Christology of the great Fathers of the East meant far more than just a simple question or just one chapter from Christian dogmatic theology, since for the Eastern Fathers Christology was always tightly connected with all the "branches" of Christian theology: with Triadology, Pneumatology, Soteriology, Ecclesiology, Cosmology, Anthropology, and Eschatology. In short, using words from the Holy Fathers, Christology tightly connects Theology *par excellence* (Triadology) with the Theanthropic Economy (the salvation and dispensation) of the world and man, and holds them in a close unity, but without confusion or commingling.

---

[8] Mansi 11.977–80. Cf. *The Seven Ecumenical Councils*, The Nicene and Post-Nicene Fathers, Second Series, vol. 14, p. 401. See also the text with commentary by Zonaras and Balsamon in Ralis-Potlis, *Syntagma*, vol. 2, pp. 492–93; cf. Bishop Nikodim Milaš, *Pravila Pravoslavne Crkve sa Tumačenjima*, vol. 1, p. 570.

[9] Cf. the treatise of G. Ostrogorsky, "Povezivanje pitanja o ikonama sa hristološkom dogmatikom u spisima apologeta iz ranog perioda ikonoborstva" ("Connecting the question of icons with Christological dogmatics in the writings of apologists from the early period of iconoclasm"), in *Collected Works*, vol. 5 (Belgrade, 1970), pp. 148–63.

In the same way, with regard to the question of the use and veneration of the holy icons in Church, Christology includes many other elements from Christian theology, belief, and grace-filled experience.
Thus, the controversy about the holy icons showed that the issue was
not just about a secondary question concerning "pictures," nor was it
about incidental "helpful" or "didactic" tools for the "illiterate"—a
view which reduces Orthodox iconology to one-sided religious didac-
tics, and the icon itself to illustration.[10]

The great value and multidimensionality of the Church *icon* was
emphatically shown by St. John Damascene in his well-known work
Three Apologies on the Divine Images. (On this occasion we will not
delve into many texts of St. John Damascene that address the question
of icons, but instead we will only cite certain parts that are important
for our theme.)

This great systematic theologian talks firstly about God's icon—
the living and natural icon of God the Father, which is His Only Begotten Son: "The Son is the living, essential, and identical (ἀπαράλλακτος)
image of the Invisible God, bearing the entire Father within Himself,
being identical (ταυτότητα = identity) to Him in all things, differing
only in that He is caused (τῷ αἰτιατῷ)"—i.e., differing only according to
hypostasis.[11] After speaking of this divine level of the icon, St. Damascene adds the anthropological level: that a man is also an icon, for in
the beginning he was created "after His own image (κατ' εἰκόνα) and
likeness."[12] But this Godlike icon in man, after man's fall, was darkened
and tarnished, because with the fall the relationship and the first communion with God was broken; and as a result, man has become incapable of seeing his *Prototype*—the Son of God, according to Whose
"image" he was created. The Incarnation of the Son of God—the natural *Icon* of God and the *Proto-image* of man, took place so that salvation
would be made possible and secured, i.e., so that there would be a reinstatement (restoration) and final deification of the created Godlike
icon in man and mankind.[13]

---

[10] Cf. Leonid Ouspensky, *La Théologie de l'Icône dans l'Eglise Orthodoxe* (Paris,
1980), especially chapter 60: "Le sens et le contenu de l'icone," pp. 133–75.

[11] *On the Divine Images* 1.9 (PG 94:1240).

[12] Ibid., 3.26.

[13] Ibid., 1.4 and 1.21.

It is clear that St. John Damascene creates the context of an integral and profound theology of the icon, which we can rightly call *Christological iconology*, using at the same time theological, anthropological, and soteriological elements, that is, all the basic elements of Christian theology.

4.

Precisely out of this *Christological iconology*—or, we could even say, this *theological ontology*, expressed through the language of icons—there arises in the Church the holy and unbroken tradition of Orthodox iconography and icon veneration, the tradition on which St. John Damascene bases his inspired treatises *On the Divine Images*.[14] The Seventh Ecumenical Council also invoked the same Church tradition of icons when it concluded that "The depiction and painting of images is the part of the tradition of the Church (τῆς εἰκονικῆς ἀναζωγραφίσεως ἐκτύπωσις), which conforms to the preaching of the Gospel and has as its aim the confirmation of the true, and not imagined, Incarnation of God the Logos as a man."[15] The Seventh Ecumenical Council in Nicaea followed not only this affirmation, but also everything in St. John Damascene's theology of the icon. That is why St. John Damascene was celebrated by this council together with St. Germanus of Constantinople and St. Gregory of Cyprus.[16]

As we have already mentioned, St. John Damascene based his theology of the icon on a Christological foundation, which can clearly be seen from his three treatises on icons. From the abundance of teaching contained in these treatises, we will cite as proof only a small part:

"When you see that the Bodiless has become man for you, then make an image (icon) of His human form. When the Invisible has become visible in flesh, paint in an icon the likeness of Him Whom you have seen. When the Bodiless and Incomprehensible ... Who exists (eternally) in the form of God (ἐν μορφῇ Θεοῦ), and took on Himself the form of a servant (μορφὴ δούλου), and condescended (*kenosis*—to the limits of human nature), ...when He has put on human form, then

---

[14] Ibid., 1.1–2, 23; 2.16, etc.
[15] Mansi, 13.377.
[16] Ibid., 13.357, 400, 413.

depict in an icon the image of Him Who was willing to show Himself visibly, and show this icon before the eyes of all. Depict His indescribable condescension, birth from the Virgin, baptism in the Jordan, transfiguration on Mount Tabor, saving death on the Cross, burial, Resurrection, and Ascension into heaven. All this describe with words (in letters) and with colors (in icons)." [17]

"We paint in icons the invisible God, not as invisible, but as having become visible for our sakes by partaking of flesh and blood (i.e., with the Incarnation—cf. Heb. 2:14). We do not depict in icons the Invisible Divinity, but rather God's visible body." [18]

"In antiquity God, Who is bodiless and without form (ἀσχημάτιστος—indescribable), was not depicted; but now that God has appeared in the flesh and dwelled among men (cf. Baruch 3:37), we depict that which is visible in God. We do not bow to matter, but rather to the Creator of matter, Who for my sake became matter, accepted to dwell in matter, and Who through matter brought about my salvation. I do not venerate it as God—in no way! However, the body of God is God through the hypostatic union (with the Divine), having become unchangeably the Logos Who anointed it (ὅπερ τὸ χρῖσαν), and also remaining what it is by nature: flesh animated with a soul both rational and noetic—created, and not uncreated. So indeed I respect and give honor to the rest of matter, through which my salvation has come, because it is filled with divine energy and grace." [19]

"If we attempted to make an image (icon) of the invisible God, this would be sinful indeed.... But we do not do such a thing; rather, when God incarnated and appeared on earth in the flesh and out of His unspeakable goodness dwelled among people (cf. Baruch 3:37), and took on Himself the nature, corporeality, form, and color of the flesh, then we, making an image (icon) of Him, do not err, because we eagerly wish to see His appearance (τὸν χαρακτῆρα—the drawing of His image)." [20]

---

[17] *On Divine Images* 1.8
[18] Ibid., 1.4.
[19] Ibid., 1.16.
[20] Ibid., 2.5.

5.

In all the above-cited quotations, as well as in many others that we have omitted because of space limitations, St. John Damascene and other Orthodox venerators of icons emphasize the essential change that took place between God and the visible world through the event and during the event of Christ's Incarnation. With the Incarnation of God the Logos, a new order of things began—*a new relationship* between God and people. "Willingly God took upon Himself a material existence (as a man, as a psychosomatic being); He became visible, and with this He gave matter a new function and a new value."[21]

According to St. John Damascene, following St. Gregory the Theologian and St. Maximus the Confessor, this *new relationship* of God with the created world, which came about with the Incarnation, is called the *second communion*—δευτέρα κοινωνία, that is, a new and last community of God and man in Christ.[22] From this new community— this Christ-centered (or God-man-centered, as Fr. Justin Popovich would say) community, which is actually the *Church* as the House of God, Christ's *Body*, the *Community* of the Holy Spirit (II Cor. 13:14; Eph. 1:17–23, 2:19–22)—arise immense salvific consequences for the world and man, for the entire creation, spiritual and material. These are the gifts of divine grace, *gifts* of the Holy Spirit given to us in the Church, which constitute the fullness of the new life in Christ for the sons of man adopted by God in the Incarnated Son of God. In the visual and tangible world, this is seen in the glory and beauty of the Church of God, whose exceptional and spiritually artistic expressions are the holy icons.

The holy icons of the Orthodox Church—above all the icon of Christ as the Icon *par excellence*—confirm this new relationship between God and the created world: the new *covenant* (*alliance*) of God with mankind, a new divine-human community of eternal life pro-

---

[21] Jean Meyendorff, *Initiation à la théologie byzantine* (Paris, 1975), p. 64.
[22] The words of St. John Damascene in the Sermon on the Transfiguration 4; cf. also St. Gregory the Theologian, PG 36:636; St. Maximus the Confessor, PG 90:520. The same Christological and soteriological-anthropological theme of the theology of the icon is found in St. Damascene's poetry, most especially in the Canon for the Feast of the Transfiguration.

claimed and experienced in the community of those faithful who have been called and have answered that call—brothers of Christ, gathered in the Holy Eucharist of the Church. This is why the holy icons in the Orthodox Church have a *liturgical* character. Moreover, this is how the holy icons, in the words of Fr. Georges Florovsky, became not only works of Christian art, but also theological documents and facts, and dogmatic and liturgical records.[23] The icon becomes exactly the same as the Gospel in the Church of Christ. In the words of St. Theodore the Studite, the holy icon is the visual Gospel: "In His visible, bodily form (i.e., Christ's image, icon) on a wood panel, it is possible to understand that which is in the God-inspired Gospels."[24] Something similar was expressed by the Church in the *Synodicon of Orthodoxy:* "The greatness of the economy of Christ is perceived by the faithful through sermons and through iconographic depictions."[25] In the words of Fr. John Meyendorff: "The joyous news about God Who became man, about the presence among people of a venerated and deified human nature—firstly in Christ, and then, through Him and the Holy Spirit, in the Mary the Theotokos and in the saints—all this *adornment of the Church* was now expressed through the Christian art of Byzantium."[26]

6.

We do not intend here to spend more time on Byzantine iconography as the authentic expression of Christian art, nor on the development of the Orthodox theology of the icon. Therefore, in the context of this lecture, we will not quote the texts of other Orthodox theologians on the holy icons: texts like those of the Patriarchs of Constantinople St. Tarasius and St. Nicephorus, or of St. Theodore the Studite. Also, we will not consider the dogmatic pronouncements of the Seventh Ecumenical Council about icons and icon veneration.

---

[23] G. Florovsky, *Byzantine Fathers of the Fifth to the Eighth Centuries* (Paris, 1993), pp. 247–54. See also the article in English in *Church History,* vol. 19, no. 2 (1950), pp. 77–96.

[24] PG 99:340.

[25] In the new critical edition of the *Synodikon:* J. Gouillard, *Le Synodikon de l'Orthodoxie* (Travaux et Mémoires, 2) (Paris, 1967), p. 47.

[26] *Initiation à la théologie byzantine,* p. 73.

189

We wish to look into the great theme of the Incarnation, not only as the foundation of Orthodox iconography and icon veneration, but also as the general foundation of the *theology of the icon*, according to the way that the theme of the *icon* was seen in biblical and patristic tradition.

In the times that preceded the emergence of the iconoclastic controversy and the Seventh Ecumenical Council, the great theologians of the Church in the East extensively occupied themselves with the biblical—above all Pauline—theme of the *icon*. The biblical theme of the *icon* was taken up most especially by the great Cappadocian Fathers, by St. Athanasius the Great, and before them by St. Irenaeus of Lyons, whose theology is a direct continuation of the icon-theology of the Holy Apostles Paul and John.

Let us take, as an example, a well-known quotation from the work of St. Irenaeus *Against Heresies* (5.16.2), in which this great theologian of early Christianity recapitulates the biblical Christological-anthropological theme of man as an *icon of God*, in a protological and eschatological manner—beginning with the creation of man "according to the *image* of God," and ending with the final fulfillment of "the *likeness* of God" in each man and in mankind, that is, with God's economy of salvation and the recapitulation (ἀνακεφαλαίωσις) of everyone and everything in the incarnated Christ.

Explaining the biblical narrative about the creation of man "according to the image of God" (Gen. 1:26), St. Irenaeus writes: "The truth of this was demonstrated when the Logos of God became man (with the Incarnation), conforming Himself to man and man to Himself, so that through the conforming of man to the Son of God, man became dear to God. In ancient times it was said that man was made according to the *image* of God, but that was not shown (i.e., it was not seen) because the Logos had not yet become visible: the Logos according to Whose image man was made. This is why he (man) easily lost the likeness (τὴν ὁμοίωσιν). When the Logos of God became man, He confirmed both: because He showed the true image (icon—τὴν εἰκόνα), having become that which His image was (that is, man), and also having reaffirmed the *likeness*, conforming man to the Invisible God through the visible Logos."[27]

---

[27] This part of St. Irenaeus' writing (*Against Heresies* 5.6.2) is preserved in the Greek original in St. John Damascene's *Sacra Parallela*. (Here we use the critical edition of St. Irenaeus' writings, *Sources Chrétiennes*, vol. 5, 153 [Paris, 1969], p. 217.)

To this connection between the anthropological meaning of the *icon* and the Incarnation—which binds God's "image and likeness" to man on a *Christological* basis in such a way that it includes protology and eschatology—St. Irenaeus added a *Pneumatological* dimension. It is known that the Christology and anthropology of St. Irenaeus are permeated and closely connected with Pneumatology, for only in this way are they a complete expression of the true Catholic (that is, Orthodox) Faith and theology of the Church. Hence, the teaching of St. Irenaeus' anthropology is only one chapter of Christology and Pneumatology.

Here is how that truth, in the context of the theme of the *icon*, is set forth by the holy bishop of Lyons: "Now God shall be glorified in His handiwork (man), fitting it so as to be conformable to, and modeled after, His own Son (cf. Rom. 8:29). For by the hands of the Father, that is, by the Son and the Holy Spirit, man, and not merely a part of man, was made in the image and likeness of God. Now the soul and the spirit are certainly a *part* of the man, but certainly not the (whole) man; for the perfect man consists in the commingling and the union of the soul receiving the spirit of the Father, and the admixture of the fleshly nature which was molded after the image of God. For this reason does the Apostle declare, 'We speak wisdom among them that are perfect,' (I Cor. 2:6), ... whom also the Apostle terms 'spiritual,' they being spiritual because they partake of the Spirit, and not because their flesh has been stripped off and taken away (cf. I Cor. 2:15, 3:1). ... But when the Spirit of God, united with man's soul, is united with the flesh created (by God), then man is rendered *spiritual* and *perfect* because of the outpouring of the Spirit, and this is he who was made in *the image and likeness of God.*"[28]

7.

From this passage of St. Irenaeus, as well as elsewhere in his writings and in the entire theology of the Holy Fathers of the East, it is evident that Christian anthropology and of course Christology were always supplemented, and even conditioned, by Pneumatology.[29] Because this is

---

[28] *Against Heresies* 5.6.1.
[29] See for example, Jean Zizioulas, *Implications ecclésiologiques de deux types de Pneumatologie,* "Communio Sanctorum"—Mélanges à J.-J. von Allmen (Geneva, 1982), pp. 141–54.

so—and because Orthodox anthropology, which is an openly Christo-centric anthropology, is always understood and comprehended only in the context of a complete and proper Christology, which is closely con-nected with and mutually influences Pneumatology—it is clear that Pneumatology also enters into the anthropological theme of the icon, i.e., the image and likeness of God in man. This is why St. Irenaeus explic-itly emphasizes that without Christ—that is, without the incarnate Son of God Who is anointed by the Holy Spirit—it is not possible to speak about the true image (icon) and likeness of God in man. In fact, St. Ire-naeus affirms that this means the following: The full, perfect, incorrupt-ible, and unalterable fulfillment and perfection of the *image and likeness* of God in man, and therefore in the Church, is not possible without the presence and mediation (*energy*) of the Holy Spirit: "Where the Spirit of the Father is, there is a living man, ... there is the flesh possessed by the Spirit, forgetful indeed of what belongs to it, and adopting the quality of the Spirit, being made conformable to the Word of God."[30]

St. Irenaeus then adds the following truth of Orthodox Christo-logical-Pneumatological anthropology: "The fruit of the activity of the Holy Spirit is the salvation of the body. For what else could be the vis-ible fruit of the invisible Spirit, but that the flesh is made perfect and able to receive incorruption."[31]

This same thought in the theological testimony of St. Irenaeus is repeated by St. Athanasius the Great in his well-known work *On the Incarnation* (chapter 8): "God the Logos (with His Incarnation) gave us the first-fruit of the Holy Spirit, so that we could become the sons of God in the image of the Son of God."[32]

St. Cyril of Alexandria also explores the anthropological theme of the *icon*—the theological question of the *image and likeness* of God in man. He also, of course, bases everything on the Christological founda-tion of the Incarnation: "Man's image (form, appearance) does not al-

---

[30] *Against Heresies* 5.9.3.
[31] Ibid., 5.12.4.
[32] PG 26:997A. This same thought was developed in the theology of the icon by the great Cappadocian Fathers. See, for example, their commentary on Genesis 1:26–27 in the well-known *Homilies on the Creation of Man,* which are ascribed to St. Basil and St. Gregory of Nyssa (in the critical edition of *Sources Chrétiennes* 160 [Paris, 1970]).

low us to see God, except in the exceptional circumstance when the *Logos became man like us* while remaining the true Son of God by nature: in Him, since He is God, this can be seen in a mysterious way."[33] St. Cyril expounds this thought further, as has been done before him by many Holy Fathers, who understood the truth about the *image and likeness* of God in man Triadologically, that is, in the sense that man was created according to *image* of the Holy Trinity. But St. Cyril immediately adds that placing the theme of the *icon* on a Triadological foundation does not change the matter significantly, because in the patristic tradition Christology and Triadology are inseparable from each other. It follows that the anthropological theme of the icon is closely connected with both, and with Pneumatology, as we have already seen earlier in the writings of Sts. Irenaeus and Athanasius.

Here is one distinctive passage from the writings of St. Cyril that demonstrates our point: "Even if it is said that man was made in the image of the Son of God, then he is in that case in the image of God. For in him shine all the characteristics (οἱ χαρακτῆρες) of the consubstantial Trinity, since the Divinity is one in nature in the Father, Son, and Holy Spirit. ... Thus, it is enough that we believe with simplicity that we are created in the divine image (icon), receiving our natural likeness to God. If it is needful to add something not quite impossible (then we shall): it was necessary that we, who are called sons of God, be created according to the image of the Son of God, so that our features of sonship would befit us better (be more suitable for us)."[34]

From this citation of St. Cyril of Alexandria it becomes clear to us how the great theological theme of the *icon*, in its theological and anthropological aspects, combines—through the mystery of the Incarnation and of *Christ becoming man*—into one unique mystery of our salvation and deification, and our adoption by God through Christ in the grace of the Holy Spirit.

It is the same with the theological theme of Orthodox painting and of the veneration of the holy *icon* as an artistic *image*. The foundation and justification of Christian church iconography and icon veneration is the divine-human icon of Christ the Incarnate God, and the

---

[33] PG 75:1329.
[34] *De dogmatum solutione* 4; ed. P.E. Pusey (Oxford, 1872), p. 558.

icon is thus, according to the same belief and grace of salvation, the meaning and justification of the holy icons of the Most Holy Theotokos and the holy people of God in the Church.

8.

We will conclude this talk by quoting, without further comments, three characteristic texts which are at the same time biblical and patristic, and which clearly summarize our whole theme.

First, the words of St. Theodore the Studite: "The fact that God created man according to His image and His likeness shows that the act of making icons (εἰκονουργίας—*iconography*) is a divine thing."[35]

The second text is from St. Diadochus of Photiki (fifth century). Explaining what is beauty and the glory of God, St. Diadochus interprets verse 15 of the Prophet David's Psalm 16: "In righteousness shall I appear before Thy face; I shall be filled when Thy glory is made manifest to me." St. Diadochus writes: "Divine nature is not in some image or form. The words of the Psalm mean that in the face and glory of the Son of God our Invisible Father will be made manifest to us. God in His kindness allowed His Logos to take visible form in His Incarnation into human nature, so that man, after looking at the density of the form (image) of His glorious body—since one image sees the other—after much purification could see the magnificence of the resurrection as he sees it in God Himself. So will the Father mysteriously appear (κρυφοφανεῖ) before the righteous ones, in the manner in which He appears to the angels, while the Son will appear openly because of His body. It is truly meet that those over whom God will rule as King in eternity see Him recognizably (γνωστῶς), which would be impossible if the Logos of God did not take upon Himself the visible image through His Incarnation and becoming human."[36]

Finally, we conclude with the words of the forefather Jacob (Gen. 32:30), the words that St. John Damascene quoted but saw only in reference to the time after the Incarnation of Christ: "I have seen the human face of God, 'and my life is preserved.'"[37]

---

[35] *Antirrhitique* 3 (PG 99:420A).

[36] *The Vision* 21. *Oeuvres spirituelles, Sources Chrétiennes*, no. 5 (Paris, 1966), pp. 175–76.

[37] *On the Divine Images* 1.22; PG 94:1256.

13

The Teaching of St. John Damascene on the Most Holy Theotokos: *Orthodox Theotokology*[1]

"It is with justice and truth that we call holy Mary the Mother of God; for this name embraces the whole mystery of the Economy of salvation."[2]

St. John Damascene

From my mother, and then from my spiritual father, I learned a biblical truth—that it is necessary to "set a watch" (Ps. 140:3) over one's mouth when talking about the *mysteries of God.* How much more so must we do this when we speak of the divine Mystery, of the theanthropic *Mystery above all mysteries*—of Christ incarnate and become man, and of His Mother, the Most Holy and Most Blessed Theotokos and Ever-virgin Mary. If Moses the God-seer stood with fear and trembling before the bush on Mt. Sinai, which "burned with fire, and was not consumed" (Ex. 3:2), and which was only "a shadow of the truth"— a vision of the Theotokos, the True Inconsumable Bush—then what

---

[1] This article was written as an introduction to our new critical edition of the Greek text *Homilies of St. John Damascene on the Most Holy Theotokos*, printed in Athens under the title: Ἡ Θεοτόκος (Athens, 1970). The critical edition of these homilies (based on the twelve oldest manuscripts) was prepared because the Greek text in the 1712 edition of M. Lequien (republished in Migne, PG 96:661–80 and 700–61, and also repeated in the series *Sources Chrétiennes*, no. 80: P. Voulet, *St. Jean Damascène, Homélies sur la Nativité et la Dormition* [Paris, 1961]), contains many errors that often change the meaning of the text, including the dogmatic meanings. Our Athenian edition, apart from this introduction, is accompanied by many theological scholia, which offer in detail many other aspects of the theological teaching of St. John Damascene about the Most Holy Theotokos.

[2] *Exact Exposition of the Orthodox Faith* 3.12. For the Greek text, see Migne, PG 94:789–1228; Kotter, vol. 2.

should we, undeserving sinners, do when speaking of Christ and the Holy Theotokos? We can only pray together in the fullness of the Church of Christ, following our hymnodists and canonarchs—the holy poets of the Church—among whom is the "gold-pourer" (ὁ χρυσο-ρρόας), St. John Damascene:

Guard my mind, O my Savior,
For the Guardian of the world I wish to praise:
Thy Most Holy Mother.
With the fortress of words strengthen me,
And with the depth of conception fortify me.
Grant me, therefore, language and speech,
And unashamed thought.
For every gift of enlightenment
Is from Thee, the Light-giver,
Who dwelt within the Ever-virgin womb.
(Ikos from the Dormition of the Theotokos)

It is without doubt that a theophany—some divine mystery that included St. Damascene, Christ, and the Theotokos—took place in the soul of St. John Damascene, which renewed him and made him forever dedicated and devoted to the twofold *Mystery* of Christ and the Theotokos. He was united with the theanthropic mystery and reality of the Church of Christ, whose living personification is the *Ark*—the Most Holy Theotokos. Since that time his right hand and his organs of speech, his ascetically multiplied God-given talents—and above all his heart and mind—were in the service of the *Only Begotten* and *Firstborn* Son of God and Son of the Virgin, and of His dearest Virgin Mother, the Theotokos—first in Jerusalem, the *Mother of all Churches,* and then in the entire catholic Church throughout the centuries. Thus, all his works—theological and apologetic, homiletic, and poetical—are inspired and filled with Christology and "Theotokology," and with praise of Christ and the Theotokos.

All of his theology, homilies and poetry can be condensed into these few words of his: "Hence it is with justice and truth that we call holy Mary the Theotokos, for this name embraces the whole mystery of the Economy of salvation. For if She who bore Him is the Theotokos, then assuredly He Who was born of her is God as well as man.... And thus it is that the Holy Virgin is thought of and spoken of as the Theotokos—not only because of the nature of the Logos (Who entered her), but also because of the deification of man's nature (taken from her).... For the Theotokos, in some supernatural manner, was the means for the fashioning of the Fashioner of all things and of the becoming man of the God and Creator of all, Who deified the nature that He assumed, while the Hypostatic (Personal) union preserved those things (the divine and human natures) that were united, just as they were.... God (Christ), being perfect, becomes perfect man, and the only *new thing under the sun* (Eccl. [cf. pp. 9, 38]), by which God's boundless power is manifested. For what can be greater than God's becoming man? *And the Word was made flesh* (John 1:14) from the Holy Spirit and the Most Holy Virgin Mary and Theotokos, and became the Mediator between God and man, and the Only Lover of mankind."[3]

St. John Damascene writes in his greatest dogmatic work, *An Exact Exposition of the Orthodox Faith,* as well as in his *Homilies on Christ and the Theotokos,* concerning the theanthropic *Mystery* of Christ and the Theotokos, and concerning the supreme mystery of the Church as the theanthropic community of the Holy Trinity and humanity.

Close to the end of his monastic life St. John Damascene wrote his main theological work, *An Exact Exposition of the Orthodox Faith,* in which he emphasized the holy and divine *Tradition* of the Orthodox Catholic Church. Everything that he wrote about God, the Holy Trinity, Christ, and the Most Holy Theotokos, he took from "the divine Tradition" which God has revealed to us in the Economy of salvation in Christ. "All that the Law and Prophets, Apostles and Evangelists have handed down to us, we receive, acknowledge and respect, and we seek nothing more than this.... We are obliged to receive this and abide in it, without shifting the eternal boundaries or violating divine Tradition."[4] St. Damascene wrote the same thing earlier in his well-known

---

[3] *Exact Exposition* 3.12.
[4] *Exact Exposition* 1.1.

Treatises on the Divine Images: "Therefore, brethren, let us stand upon the rock of our faith and the Tradition of the Church, without moving the boundaries that our Holy Fathers have set, without allowing room to those who wish to introduce innovations and tear down the edifice of the Holy, Catholic, and Apostolic Church of God."[5] For St. John Damascene the divine Tradition is, above all, that entire *edifice* and *body* of the Orthodox Catholic and Apostolic Church,[6] which is built upon the *"Foundation,"* i.e., the *"Cornerstone"* (I Cor. 3:11; Eph. 2:20) of the Apostle Paul, and upon "the Rock of theology" (Matt. 16:18) of the Apostle Peter—and that *"Rock"* (I Cor. 10:4) is Christ.[7]

St. Damascene's faithfulness to the Tradition of the Church consists, above all, in his *Christology*. As do the Bible and the texts of the Holy Fathers, so too does St. Damascene observe and interpret everything *Christologically*. Christ the Savior, One of the Trinity, born of the Holy Virgin—*God* and *man*—is the central theme of the Holy Bible and Holy Tradition,[8] and therefore also the central theme of St. Damascene's theology. Christology occupies the greatest part of his works—not only of his dogmatic work, *An Exact Exposition of the Orthodox Faith* (where two out of four books are dedicated to Christology), but also of his homilies about the Most Holy Theotokos. His teaching about the Theotokos is within the structure of Christology and the theology of Christ the God-man. It never becomes a separate teaching, like Roman Catholic "Mariology," or an "anthropological" teaching based on the Virgin Mary. The Orthodox theology of St. Damascene is not "anthropology" or "Mariology"; rather it is, above all, Christology—

---

[5] *On the Divine Images* 3.41 (PG 94:1356).

[6] Without further exposition of Damascene's ecclesiology, we point out only a few elements of his teaching on this topic. Cf. *On the Dormition of the Theotokos* 2.4, and *Confession of the Faith*.

[7] See *On the Transfiguration* 6 and footnote 49; *On the Great and Holy Saturday* 30; and *On the Divine Images* I (PG 94:1284). Cf. also the Canons of St. Damascene to Apostles Peter and Paul, June 29, ode 3.

[8] Cf. St. Athanasius the Great, *Against the Arians* 3.29 (PG 26:385): "The entire goal and character of the Holy Bible consists of demonstrating the twofold promise concerning the Savior: first, that from eternity He was God and Son, Logos, the Brightness and Wisdom of the Father; and second, that He later, because of us, took flesh from the Virgin Mary Theotokos and became man."

—which in itself, of course, includes anthropology and *Theotokology*.[9] This approach derives from the fact that Christ is at the same time the true and perfect God and the first true and perfect Man, while still remaining *One and the Same Christ the God-man.*[10]

This is why the Holy Virgin who gave birth to Christ the God-man is called Theotokos—Θεοτόκος. The name itself and the dignity of Christ as God Who "took flesh and became man" is given to His Mother in the flesh with the name *Theotokos*—the name which "embraces the whole mystery of the Economy of salvation."[11] For the name "Theotokos" (she who gave birth to God) confirms that He Who was born of her is true *God* and *man*, as St. Damascene says: "If she who gave birth is the Theotokos, then He who was born of her is undoubtedly *God*, and also undoubtedly *man*."[12]

Being faithful to the Tradition of the Orthodox Apostolic Church and the tradition of the great Fathers—the defenders of Orthodox doctrine that the Holy Virgin is truly the Theotokos—St. Damascene unambiguously confesses her to be the true *Theotokos*. Together with his "divinely wise father," St. Gregory the Theologian, St. Damascene repeats: "If someone does not confess the Holy Virgin as the Theotokos, he is a stranger to the Godhead"[13]—a stranger to God. At the same time, St. Damascene does not overstep the boundaries of true *Orthodox*

---

9 Western Scholastic categorizations and partitioning of theology created the so-called "Mariology" (there even exists a "Josephology"). We purposely do not use the term "Mariology," because the term "Theotokology," in the opinion of Fr. Justin Popovich, directly points to the connection between the teaching about the Most Holy Theotokos and the doctrine of the Incarnation (i.e., Christology), and to the dependence of the former on the latter.

10 Cf. *On the Dormition* 1.4: "One Christ, one Son, the same God and man; at once perfect God and perfect man; fully God and fully man, one hypostasis combined from two perfect natures—Divinity and humanity, and in the two perfect natures—Divine and human; not only God or only man, but rather one and the same Son of God and God incarnate; at once the same God and man." See also the Dogmatikon in the eighth tone (written by St. Damascene): "He is the only Son, twofold in nature, but not twofold in Persons (Hypostasis). By confessing Him truly as perfect God and perfect man, we confess Christ our God."

11 *Exact Exposition* 3.12.

12 Ibid.

13 *On the Nativity of the Theotokos* 4.

faith in the Theotokos and remains faithful to the tradition of the Holy Fathers.[14] Hence he says: "We bow down only to the True God," while "honoring and respecting the Mother of God.... Knowing the Holy Virgin as the Mother of God, we in no way think of her as a goddess (such myths are appropriate only to Hellenic foolishness), for we believe in her mortality. But we know her as Mother of God, since God took flesh from her."[15] From these words of St. Damascene we can clearly see that the Most Holy Theotokos of our Orthodox Faith is not an end or goal on her own. This can be seen more clearly in the *Homily on the Nativity of the Theotokos*, in which St. Damascene addresses her: "You lived not for yourself, for you were not born for yourself; but you lived for God, for Whom you came into life to become a vessel for the salvation of the world, so that the ancient Counsel of *God,* concerning the Incarnation of the Logos and our deification, would come to be fulfilled through you."[16]

The teaching of St. Damascene about the Most Holy Theotokos is to be found in connection with the "ancient and true *Counsel*"[17] of God concerning "the Incarnation of the Logos and the deification of man." That is to say, in "the unfathomable depths of God's love for mankind,"[18]

[14] Above all he is faithful to the teachings of St. Cyril of Alexandria, who more than anyone else fought to defend the Orthodox faith in the Theotokos, but who still said: "We have never considered anyone among those created to be divine, because we were taught to respect as God only Him Who is true God by nature, while the Blessed Mary we know as human, similar to us" (*Against Nestorius* 1.10, PG 76:57).

[15] *On the Dormition* 2.15.

[16] *On the Nativity of the Theotokos* 9. We Orthodox theologians need to have in mind these clear Christological words of St. Damascene—not only in relation to the Protestants, who deny any veneration of the Theotokos, or in relation to the Roman Catholics, who with their new "dogmas" and their autonomous "Mariology" spoil the true and authentic image of the Virgin Theotokos, but also in relation to those Orthodox theologians who want to present their doctrine about the Theotokos outside the Christological context, bringing it into the non-Orthodox, non-Traditional terrain of the so called "sophiology" of S. Bulgakov for example, or of some sort of independent "anthropology," etc. The true belief and Tradition of the Orthodox Catholic Church of Christ proclaimed the Theotokos as the "scepter of Orthodoxy" through the mouth of St. Cyril of Alexandria during the Third Ecumenical Council (cf. Mansi 4:1253), St. Cyril being one of the most Christological of all Church Fathers.

[17] *On the Dormition* 1.1.

[18] *On the Dormition* 1.10.

the Divine and Life-giving Trinity in Unity, our God, "having gathered Himself together in council,[19] by the united counsel of His will," before all the ages determined the Incarnation and becoming man of God the Logos, and the deification of man. This preeternally "predestined Counsel"[20] of God reveals to us "the endless abundance of God's goodness,"[21] and this is precisely revealed through the Most Holy Theotokos, for "she revealed the inexpressible abundance of God's love for mankind."[22] God the Father, Who, according to the words of St. John Damascene, "benevolently willed" "the fulfillment of the eternally ordained mystery"[23] of the Incarnation to take place within the Theotokos and through her, in His *foreknowledge*, had preordained her to be the Mother of His Only Begotten Son—Who is without beginning and bodiless—and Who took flesh from her *for us and our salvation*."[24] Understandably, God's "preordination" of the Holy Virgin is incomprehensible to us, but in God it corresponds to and is identified with His pre-eternal *foreknowledge* of the personal *freedom*, personal *free will*, personal *worth*, and personal *sanctity* of the Holy Virgin Mary.[25] Having this in mind, St. Damascene utters these words to the Virgin Mary in his *Homily on the Nativity of the Theotokos:* "God saw you in advance as *worthy*, and grew to love you; and, loving you, He predestined you, and in latter times brought you into being, and made you the Theotokos, Mother and Nourisher of His Son, the Word."[26] St. Damascene's words

---

[19] This term, which is most important and almost impossible to translate, belongs to St. Photius of Constantinople; cf. *Homily on the Nativity of the Theotokos* 9, published in *The Homilies of Photius* by V. Laurdas (Thessalonica, 1959), p. 96.

[20] *On the Nativity of the Theotokos* 7.

[21] · *On Holy Saturday* 1; cf. *On the Dormition* 2.7.

[22] *On the Dormition* 2.16.

[23] *On the Nativity of the Theotokos* 10.

[24] *On the Dormition* 2.15.

[25] According to St. Damascene, "Predetermination is the work of the divine command based on foreknowledge" (*Exact Exposition* 2.30); for "He knows beforehand those things that are in our power, but He does not predetermine them" (ibid.). God's foreknowledge and foreseeing of the future are not prescribed for anyone; it is simply foresight, as the Holy Fathers say. For "God does not wish that He alone should be just, but that all should, so far as possible, be made like unto Him" (*Exact Exposition* 4.19).

[26] *On the Nativity of the Theotokos* 7.

"brought you into being" mean that God brought her into the world by means of her parents, and He foresaw and knew in advance not only the worthiness of the Holy Virgin Mary,[27] her virtues[28] and her "most-pure virginity,"[29] but He also foresaw her righteousness,[30] and the wisdom and virtuous life[31] of her *parents*. For this reason He bestowed upon them this great gift—a daughter who would give birth to God, making them the grandparents of God. Characteristic are the following words of St. Damascene from the *First Homily on the Dormition*: "Truly you have found grace—you who were worthy of grace."[32] These words of the Savior show the principle of *cooperation* between God and man, a principal of *cooperation* or "*synergy*" between God and man's free will in the entire history of God's salvific Economy concerning mankind. But let us examine this question a little more closely.

After our forbears in Paradise accepted "the false promise of divinization,"[33] they fell away from God through *disobedience*,[34] whereupon they found themselves naked (i.e., they were left without the grace of the Holy Spirit).[35] Then they were clothed in the "skin garments of mortality,"[36] in corruptibility and coarse physicality,[37] and through their fall into sin they became subject to death and decay.[38] After them all of us, their descendants, "born from Adam and therefore like unto him, have inherited the curse and corruptibility,"[39] and found ourselves naked, outside of Paradise, i.e., without the grace of the Holy Spirit. Since that time the man-loving God began to "pedagogically" prepare, organize and "Economize" the providential plan of our salvation.[40] But since

[27] Ibid.
[28] *On the Nativity of the Theotokos* 9.
[29] *On the Nativity of the Theotokos* 5; *On the Dormition* 2.2.
[30] *On the Nativity of the Theotokos* 9.
[31] *On the Nativity of the Theotokos* 5–6; *On the Dormition* 1.6.
[32] *On the Dormition* 1.8.
[33] *On the Dormition* 2.2.
[34] *On the Dormition* 2.3.
[35] *On the Dormition* 2.2.
[36] *On the Nativity of the Theotokos* 4; *On the Dormition* 2.2.
[37] *Exact Exposition* 3.1. Cf. also *On the Withered Fig Tree* 3, and *On Holy Saturday* 24.
[38] *Exact Exposition* 4.13.
[39] Ibid.
[40] *Exact Exposition* 3.1.

we had fallen freely and by our own will, in order that "good be neither forced nor extorted,"[41] it was necessary that we again *freely* and voluntarily receive and accept the God-created ("Economized") plan of our salvation and the healing from the fall and decay, i.e., to freely *cooperate* and *collaborate* in God's Economy for our salvation.

Terms such as "collaboration," "cooperation," etc. designate above all that man on his own was not capable of "doing" or "accomplishing," of "working out" or "creating" his own salvation—because, in the words of David, repeated by the Apostle Paul, "they have all turned aside; they have together become unprofitable; there is none who does good, no, not one" (Ps. 13:4; Rom. 3:12).[42] The salvation of man could only be accomplished by God, Who is "the cause and beginning of every good," and Who "works all in all" (I Cor. 12:6).[43] However, it was necessary for man to *collaborate* and *cooperate* with God, the Creator and Perfecter of our salvation; for, "according to the Holy Fathers, salvation is given to those who desire it and not to those who are forced."[44] The entire meaning of the history of the Economy of salvation is contained in God's activity and man's collaboration, to which God *invites* and *calls* man. People freely and voluntarily accept this *invitation* and *call* throughout history—perhaps in small numbers, but even these few become God's *"elect"* (Rom. 11:5, 7), in the words of Apostle Paul, and through these *"elect"* God prepares the salvation of other people. In this way, throughout the history of fallen mankind, the salvific Providence of God, the salvific and untiring grace of God, has always found "reliable points of support"—or, in the words of the holy Apostle Paul, "vessels of mercy" (Rom. 9:23)—through which the sanctified history of the salvation of man has taken place and has been fulfilled, but always on the basis of the free *collaboration*, the free *synergism* and *cooperation* of God and *man.*[45] This is how, throughout the entire history of the Old Testament, through

---

[41] *Exact Exposition* 4.19. "What is done out of necessity is not virtue" (*Exact Exposition* 2.12).

[42] *On the Dormition* 1.6.

[43] *Exact Exposition* 2.3.

[44] See St. Maximus the Confessor, *To Thalassius* 54 (PG 90:528).

[45] According to the Holy Fathers, "Destroying one's freedom is the same as destroying the man" (see St. Nicholas Cabasilas, PG 150:638, and his *Three Homilies on the Theotokos* in the new edition by P. Nellas [Athens, 1968], with very interesting scholia).

God's elect and voluntary collaborators, the plan for mankind's salvation, i.e., the gradual preparation of mankind for the arrival of Christ the Savior, was progressively being fulfilled.

According to the same divine teaching, the Economy of salvation reached its climax and conclusion in the Most Holy Virgin Mary, who is most surely included among "the elect,"[46] as one *worthy* and, by her own volition, *obedient* unto God.[47] In this sense, she has served the Most Holy Trinity more than anyone else,[48] and has cooperated with the Economy of salvation more than all people together since the beginning of the ages. Thus, St. John Damascene, and in general all the Holy Fathers of the Church, view the entire Old Testament as God's general preparatory "calling" and "election," which encompassed all generations up to the Most Holy Virgin Mary.[49] In other words, the Holy Fathers, and with them St. Damascene, view the Old Testament as a *genealogy* of the Most Holy Theotokos, who gives birth to Christ, the Savior of the world.[50] He is the Savior of those people who comprise this *genealogy* and ultimately of the Most Holy Virgin herself;[51] and through her He is the Savior of mankind.

[46] *On the Dormition* 1.3.
[47] *On the Dormition* 1.8; 2.3.
[48] *On the Nativity of the Theotokos* 7–9; 5.
[49] Cf. Romans 11:7, 5. Especially interesting and profound is the interpretation of Romans 11:5 and 7 given by St. Symeon the New Theologian. In his *Ethical Discourse* 2, he Christologically interprets the entire history of mankind, which, according to him, begins from the "rib" of the first Adam and is carried out by the Old Testament "elect," and concludes through the Theotokos in the God-man—the second Adam—as the Church, which in actuality is "Christ Himself" (see *Sources Chrétiennes* 122, pp. 326–38).
[50] *Exact Exposition* 4.14; *On the Dormition* 1.3.
[51] Concerning her salvation through Christ, the only Savior, the Theotokos herself confirmed and confessed soon after the Annunciation: "And my spirit has rejoiced in God my Savior" (Luke 1:47). In one sticheron before the Feast of the Nativity of our Lord, it is said: "The Lord has manifested Himself through the Virgin Mother. And His Mother has bowed down to Him as a servant, and she said to Him Whom she held in her arms: How didst Thou descend into me, and how wert Thou conceived in me, my Redeemer and my God?" Cf. what the presbyter of Jerusalem Chrysippus (fifth century) writes about how Christ saved the Holy Virgin from "the fall in which her descent from her proto-mother Eve placed her" (*Homily on Mary Theotokos*, in *Patrologia Orientalis*, vol. 19, p. 338).

In this way, according to St. Damascene, and generally according to the Holy Fathers of the Church, the Most Holy Virgin Mary represents the culmination and conclusion of the entire Old Testament, and all of the prototypes and prophecies of the Old Testament refer to her.[52] She is the culmination and the fruit of the entire Old Testament "pedagogical" preparation of mankind for the reception of the incarnate God the Savior. Because of all this it is neither possible nor necessary to separate the Virgin Mary from her race, or to separate her origin from Adam and mankind. According to the words of St. Damascene, Adam is her *ancestor* in the same measure that he is of all other people, and she is "a daughter of Adam"[53] and the daughter of David "the forefather and ancestor of God,"[54] from whose root she was born "according to the promise" of God,[55] uniting in herself the priestly and royal lineage.[56]

The birth of the Most Holy Virgin Mary from the "root of Jesse,"[57] and hence from David, took place in the context of the miraculous cure of her mother Anna's barrenness.[58] According to St. Damascene, this does not give reason enough for an unnatural separation of the Most Holy Theotokos from her human lineage—from her "forefathers and God-fathers." This is why she is called "the daughter of David"[59] and "the daughter of Adam."[60] Conversely, the Holy Virgin, as "the daughter of old Adam" is, along with all the other descendants of Adam, under *"the liability of her father,"*[61] i.e., under "the *blame* of the old fallen Adam" as regards the question of her own conception and birth from

---

[52] *On the Dormition* 1.9–10.
[53] *On the Nativity of the Theotokos* 6; *On the Dormition* 2.2.
[54] *On the Dormition* 2.2.
[55] *On the Dormition* 1.7; *Exact Exposition* 4.14.
[56] *On the Nativity of the Theotokos* 6.
[57] *On the Nativity of the Theotokos* 3.
[58] *On the Nativity of the Theotokos* 2; *On the Dormition* 1.6–7. Similar miracles were performed by God in the Old Testament. God bestowed a similar miracle upon Anna (Hannah), the mother of Prophet Samuel (I Kings [I Sam.] 1:19), and upon Elizabeth, mother of St. John the Baptist, whom God consecrated even in his mother's womb (Luke 1:15), like the Prophet Jeremiah (Jer. 1:5). Despite this no one has ever thought that these Holy Prophets were born exempt from the ancestral sin.
[59] *On the Nativity of the Theotokos* 9.
[60] *On the Nativity of the Theotokos* 6; *On the Dormition* 2.2.
[61] *On the Dormition* 2.2.

her parents, and as regards her own death—which was the consequence of the ancestral transgression. Therefore the Virgin Mary is conceived from the seed of Joachim[62] in the womb of Anna—in other words, from the natural *marital relationship*[63] of Joachim and Anna,[64] and as such "she has her being from earth,"[65] and "she inherits a corruptible body from Adam."[66] The same relates to her death: The Most Holy Virgin died a human *death*.[67] As "the daughter of Adam," she "gave her body to the earth because of Adam,"[68] and her most pure and blessed soul "natu-

---

[62] *On the Nativity of the Theotokos* 2.

[63] According to St. Damascene, "We know that all mortals after the first parents of the race are the offspring of marriage" (*Exact Exposition* 4.24). Christ was the only one that was not born from the natural relationship of a man and woman (i.e., not from marriage), because He was conceived in the immaculate womb of the Virgin, not from relations with a husband, nor out of passion, but of the Holy Spirit" (*On the Nativity of the Theotokos* 3; *Exact Exposition* 3.1). According to the teaching of the Holy Fathers, marriage was established so that "mankind would not be extinguished and destroyed by death" (*Exact Exposition* 4.24), and the ability to inherit ancestral sin is connected to the seed of fallen Adam (cf. St. Symeon the New Theologian, *Ethical Discourse* 13, in *Sources Chrétiennes* 129, p. 408). This is why the Lord and Savior Jesus Christ was not conceived from this seed of Adam, for according to St. Gregory Palamas, "Had the Lord been conceived by the seed (of man), He would neither have been a new man nor without sin, nor the Savior of those who sin" (PG 151:169). St. Maximus the Confessor speaks more clearly about this: "All those born of Adam are conceived in transgression (Ps. 50:5), being under the sentence of the forefather.... After the fall, human nature has, as the beginning of its coming into existence, passionate conception from seed and birth, and, as the end, a painful death through decay. The Lord Jesus Christ, not having such a beginning with His birth, was not subject to such an end, i.e., death" (PG 90:788 and 1325). See St. Epiphanius of Cyprus on the birth of the Virgin Mary from her parents: "She was not born in any other way than according to human nature, as are others—from the seed of the husband and from her mother's womb" (PG 42:748). Also see St. Tarasius of Constantinople, *Homily on the Entrance of the Theotokos* (PG 98:1485).

[64] *On the Nativity of the Theotokos* 2; *Exact Exposition* 4.14.

[65] *On the Nativity of the Theotokos* 3.

[66] *On the Dormition* 2.8.

[67] *On the Dormition* 2.15. Cf. St. Andrew of Crete, *On the Dormition* 1 (PG 97:1052): "If the truth must be told, she too was touched by natural death." St. Damascene in his writings about the Most Holy Theotokos often follows St. Andrew of Crete, who was originally from Jerusalem, and therefore a witness of the tradition of Jerusalem.

[68] *On the Dormition* 2.4.

rally separated" from her unblemished and most pure body, and her body "was committed to burial, as custom required."[69]

All that has been said thus far clearly and unambiguously demonstrates that the Most Holy Virgin, as well as all of mankind, inherited from the forefather Adam the *inheritability of the ancestral sin,*[70] with the *responsibility* (in the words of Damascene) and *consequences* of that sin. This is why St. Damascene speaks very clearly and conclusively about the *purification* and *sanctification* of the Holy Virgin by the Holy Spirit at the time of the Annunciation, when, by the power of the grace-bestowing arrival of the Holy Spirit the Virgin was *purified* and *sanctified*. Only then did the conception of the Only Begotten Son of God by the Holy Spirit take place within her. St. Damascene writes: "God the Father predestined her, the prophets prophesied about her by the Holy Spirit, and the sanctifying power of the Holy Spirit which came to her *purified* and *sanctified* her, and, so to speak, nourished her; and then Thou, O Word of God, didst indescribably make Thy home in her."[71]

All that has been said thus far, of course, does not mean that St. John Damascene does not recognize or emphasize the great *holiness* of the Most Holy Theotokos. Quite the contrary. Together with the whole Orthodox Church, St. Damascene recognizes, emphasizes, praises and celebrates the great *personal holiness* of the Theotokos, as we shall soon see in more detail. Here we only wanted to set forth St. Damascene's authentic Orthodox teaching. His teaching clearly shows how distant this Orthodox Father of the Church is from any new "cacodoxy" [*cacos* = bad] of the Latin Western Church about the so-called "immaculate conception" of the Most Holy Virgin, that is, about her supposed exemption from the inheritability of the ancestral sin from her very conception in her moth-

---

[69] *On the Dormition* 1.10.

[70] Cf. St. Athanasius the Great (PG 26:1061): "Mary is our sister, for we are all from Adam." Cf. St. Augustine, *Against Julian* 4–5 (Migne, PL 45).

[71] *On the Dormition* 1.4; *Exact Exposition* 3.2. On the purification of the Most Holy Virgin see also Damascene's work *Against the Nestorian Heresy* 43 (PG 95:221–24); also his Annunciation Canon (odes 7 and 8) and many other of his church hymns. See about this also in the writings of Sts. Gregory the Theologian (PG 36:633 and 37:462); Cyril of Jerusalem (PG 33:976); Sophronius of Jerusalem (PG 87c:3245–48); Andrew of Crete (PG 97:817); etc.

er's womb.[72] This Western innovation about the Most Holy Theotokos, dogmatized by the "infallible" Vatican[73] (even though this teaching is totally foreign to the Holy Scriptures and Holy Tradition), separates the Virgin Theotokos from her ancestors—her forefathers and parents—and from the human race with which she is ontologically connected (even though this connection is the reason why she is a *real representative* of mankind). By this teaching they also deny the meaning of the preparation for the Economy that occurred in the history of the Old Testament, concerning which we have already spoken. This erroneous teaching about the "immaculate conception" of the Virgin devalues her real worthiness and her personal choice of holiness. But above all, this unfounded Roman "dogma" undermines the reality and genuineness of our salvation, because this pseudo-dogma denies the unity of mankind and the unity of human nature, and also brings into question the reality of the truly *salvific Incarnation* of Christ—His birth from one actual representative of fallen mankind.[74]

[72] Without taking into account the authentic teaching of St. Damascene about the Holy Virgin, and the dogmatic basis and consequences of his teaching, some Roman Catholic theologians seek to include under his name the concept of *Immaculata Conceptio*. For example, M. Jugie, "St. Jean Damascène et l'Immaculée Conception," in *Bessarione* (1923), pp. 1–7; Chevalier, "La Mariologie de St. Jean Damascène," in *Orientalia Christiana Analecta* 109 (1936), pp. 140ff; V. Grumel, "La Mariologie de St. J. Damascène," in *Échos d'Orient* 40 (1937), p. 318; and P. Voulet, in the abovementioned *Homilies* of St. Damascene, *Sources Chrétiennes* 80 (Introduction, p. 20). In contrast to these see the following Orthodox theologians: V. Anagnostopoulos, "The Teaching of St. John Damascene on the Theotokos," in *Orthodoxia* (Constantinople, 1956–57), pp. 31–32 (in Greek); A. Lebedev, *Differences between the Eastern and Western Church Teachings on the Virgin Mary the Theotokos* (Warsaw, 1881; in Russian); G. Florovsky, "The Ever-Virgin Mother of God," in *The Mother of God: A Symposium* (London: Members of the Fellowship of St. Alban and St. Sergius, 1949 and 1959), pp. 58–60; cf. S. Bulgakov, *The Unconsumed Bush*, the first three chapters (Paris, 1927); cf. also A. Kniazev, "Immaculata," in *Le Messager Orthodoxe* 7.3 (1959), pp. 22–30.

[73] This teaching about "immaculate conception" of the Virgin Mary was pronounced as a "dogma" of the Roman church by Pius IX with his bull "Ineffabilis Deus," on December 8, 1854. See also the constitution "Lumen Gentium" of the Vatican II council (chapter 8.59). Cf. also R. Laurentin, *Court traité sur la Vierge Marie*, fifth edition (Paris, 1967), p. 114.

[74] See Fr. Justin Popovich, *Dogmatic Theology of the Orthodox Church*, vol. 2 (Belgrade, 1935), pp. 256–57; V. Lossky, "Le Dogme de l'Immaculée Conception" in *Messager de l'Exarchat du Partiarche Russe en Europe Occidentale* 20 (1955); A. Kniazev in the aforementioned article, and also in his article "La Mère de Dieu," in *La Vierge Marie*, in the series *Églises en Dialogue*, no. 8 (Paris: Mame, 1968). The unity of human nature is

But let us examine this question closely and in greater detail. According to St. Damascene, the sinless Word of God took on all of human nature in order to *save* man—to unite him with Himself and thus to divinize him. "But He in His fullness took upon Himself me in my fullness, and was united whole to whole, that He might in His grace bestow salvation on the whole man. For what has not been taken cannot be healed."[75] The Word's "taking upon" Himself human nature, or man's reception into the Hypostasis of God the Word (or, more precisely, the indivisible and seamless unity in Christ of the divine and human natures, or even the hypostasizing of man into the Hypostasis of God the Word[76]) assures once and for all the permanent and indivisible *communion* of God and man, which St. Damascene, following St. Gregory the Theologian, calls "a second communion."[77] This "second communion" between God and man came after Adam had lost the "first communion with God,"[78] so that when Christ came into the world He found man already *fallen* in sin. This is why in His Incarnation Christ takes upon Himself the whole of fallen man, except for sin (since sin is not a part of the original human nature). Indeed, St. Damascene sometimes says that the Lord took upon Himself "the whole of Adam as he was before the fall—free of sin,"[79] that is, "Adam's being"[80] or Adam's human nature without sin.[81]

one of the basic truths of Orthodox anthropology and soteriology, but that truth has been already forgotten in Western Roman Catholic theology. Sergei Bulgakov is correct in his observation that in Roman Catholic theology this is connected with "the general absence of a clear anthropology" (*Unconsumed Bush*, p. 23). We have to note that this separation is also due to the Western separation of anthropology from its real Christological roots, and not, as Bulgakov thinks, because of the lack of "sophiology" in the West.

[75] *Exact Exposition* 3.6.

[76] *Exact Exposition* 3.2, 9, 22.

[77] Cf. his *Oration* 45.9 (PG 36:633–36). See also St. Maximus the Confessor, *To Thalassius* 54 (PG 90:520). This "second communion" is precisely that hypostatic unification with God in Christ the God-man, which, remaining eternal and unbreakable, represents the fulfillment of the preeternal plan of the Great Counsel (*On the Nativity of the Theotokos* 8–9; *Exact Exposition* 4.4; cf. *On the Transfiguration* 4).

[78] *On the Nativity of the Theotokos* 8.

[79] *On the Dormition* 1.4.

[80] *Exact Exposition* 3.1.

[81] St. Damascene writes: "The Redeemer Who was to come had to be sinless and not subject to the power of death through sin, also because it was necessary to strengthen and renew human nature" (*Exact Exposition* 3.1).

At the same time St. Damascene, following other Holy Fathers, and especially St. Maximus the Confessor,[82] talks about "the innocent passions" of our fallen human nature—the passions (or afflictions) that the Savior Jesus Christ took upon Himself. "We confess," says St. Damascene, "that He assumed all the natural and innocent passions of man; for He assumed the whole of man and all of man's attributes save sin.... For the natural and innocent passions are those *which are not in our power, but which have entered into the life of man owing to the condemnation by reason of the transgression,* such as hunger, thirst, weariness, labor, tears, corruption.... He assumed all, then, that He might sanctify all."[83] The Lord took upon Himself from the Virgin Mary (from where else?) such human nature, frail and weak, *corruptible* and *perishable,*[84]

---

[82] See *To Thalassius* 21 and 24 (PG 90:312–16 and 405–08). Cf. also St. Basil the Great, *Letter* 216 (PG 32:972), and St. Cyril of Alexandria, *Letter* 45 (PG 77:236).

[83] *Exact Exposition* 3.2.

[84] Speaking of the *corruptible* or *perishable* human nature, St. Damascene, in his polemic against the heresy of the so-called "aphtharto-docetists," makes a distinction between "corruptibility" or "weariness," and "perishability" or "dissolution into components." Weariness means afflictions like hunger, thirst, tiredness, piercing with nails, death or separation of the soul from the body, and so on. Accordingly, the meaning we give "weariness" is the same as when we say that the body of Jesus Christ was corruptible, for the Lord voluntarily took upon Himself all the aforementioned afflictions. On the other hand, "perishability" means "the complete dissolution of the body into its constituent elements, and its utter disappearance, which is preferably termed by many as 'destruction.' The body of our Lord did not experience this form of corruption" (*Exact Exposition* 3.28). Furthermore, St. Damascene explains: "Therefore, to say, along with the foolish Julianus and Gaianus (aphtharto-docetists), that our Lord's body was incorruptible in the first sense of the word, before His Resurrection, is impious. For if it was incorruptible it was not really, but only apparently, of the same essence as ours, and that which the Gospel tells us occurred—i.e., hunger, thirst, the nails, the wound in His side, and His death—did not actually occur. But if they only apparently (docetically) happened, then the mystery of the Economy is an imposture and a sham, and He became man only in appearance (docetically), and not in actual fact, and we are saved only in appearance, and not in actual fact.... But in the second meaning of the word 'corruption,' we confess that our Lord's body is incorruptible, that is, indestructible, for such is the tradition of the inspired Fathers" (*Exact Exposition* 3.28). From this evangelical and patristic teaching expounded by St. Damascene, we can see that the Lord took upon Himself from the Most Holy Virgin this weary and perishable body in order to save us corrupt and decaying people through His suffering on the Cross. From where else could have our Lord taken such a body? And without this body would it have been some kind of Docetism? Leon-

excluding its sinfulness (because sin "is not natural, nor is it implanted in us by the Creator, but arises voluntarily in our mode of life as the result of a further implantation by the devil,"[85] and hence does not enter into the fabric of human nature). This is why He made Holy Mary to be His Mother even though she, according to nature, was "His handmaiden ... but whom, by the Economy of salvation, He made to be His mother, in the unfathomable ocean of His love for mankind. For He truly became flesh, and did not feign His Incarnation."[86] St. Damascene confirms this same truth in many other places. Addressing the same topic elsewhere, he says: "He, therefore, assumed the whole man, even the most noble part of him, which had become diseased, in order that He might bestow salvation upon the whole."[87]

tius of Byzantium also wrote against the heretical "aphtharto-docetists," who taught that the body of the Most Holy Theotokos at Christ's conception "changed," and that this is why she became "incorrupt" at the arrival of the Holy Spirit. This answer of Leontius of Byzantium is very relevant (with regard to the new "dogma" of the Roman Church). He writes: "By respecting the Holy Virgin more than necessary, they (the aphtharto-docetists) did not anticipate the consequences of that teaching ... namely, that the arrival of the Holy Spirit did not take away from her the ability to give birth nor was this an obstacle to it. On the contrary, in this way she conceived supernaturally. Furthermore, we must note that, according to their opinion, after becoming incorruptible the Virgin would also have become the root of the immortality of mankind, instead of the Divine Bridegroom Who was born of her (that is, Christ the Savior)" (PG 86a:1325–28A). These words of Leontius of Byzantium speak much about the erroneous new Roman "dogma" of "the immaculate conception," and about its repudiation of the Christological and soteriological patristic teaching concerning the Most Holy Theotokos.

[85] *Exact Exposition* 3.20.

[86] *On the Dormition* 1.10. It is not particularly necessary to emphasize that for St. Damascene some terms, such as "by reason of the Economy," or "by the Economy," etc., cannot have any Docetic undertones. This has to do with the distinction that St. Damascene is making between Economy and Theology, which is well known among the Holy Fathers. See note 71 in *On the Withered Fig Tree* 1.

[87] *Exact Exposition* 3.18; *On the Dormition* 1.4. Cf. St. Proclus of Constantinople, *Homily* 1, "In Praise of the Most Holy Theotokos" (PG 65:688–89): "If the Lord had not clothed Himself in me, He would not have saved me; in the Virgin's womb He clothed Himself in him who was condemned." Cf. Theodotus of Ancyra (fifth century), *Homily on the Most Holy Mary Theotokos and on the Nativity of Christ* 13 (*Patrologia Orientalis*, vol. 19, p. 333).

This *illness,* weariness or weakness of human nature—or, according to St. Damascene's words, this "natural and innocent passion of my (human) structure"[88]—and our entire *decay* and *corruptibility* are not sin in themselves, because all this entered human nature after the ancestral sin, as *consequences* of the same (as consequences which have entered human nature from the outside, after Adam's transgression through his free will).[89] This is why it is said that the Lord, after having become man and having taken upon Himself all the "innocent passions" or sufferings of our human nature, has Himself become "sin" and "a curse" instead of us and for us (II Cor. 5:21; Gal. 3:13),[90] although He was not a curse or sin but pure *Holiness* and *Grace.* He took upon Himself our sin and our condemnation in order to save us from the same.[91] The Lord Christ, as the God-man, is perfectly sinless, and therefore He does not have any passions or sufferings. But since He is at the same time the *Savior* of fallen mankind, "He took upon Himself our appearance and ranked Himself as one of us."[92] He actually took upon Himself the whole of human nature and its human passions (sufferings) and sin and damnation, and even death itself,[93] thus fulfilling and enabling our own concrete salvation.[94] This is the precise meaning of the oft-repeated soteriological phrase of the Holy Fathers, "To restore like with like."[95]

So then, the Incarnation and "the purpose of God the Word becoming man was in order that the very same nature which had sinned and fallen and become corrupted, should triumph over the deceiving

[88]   *On the Dormition* 1.4. Cf. *On Holy Saturday* 2.
[89]   Cf. St. Maximus the Confessor, *To Thalassius* 42 and 62 (PG 90:405–8 and 652).
[90]   *Exact Exposition* 3.25.
[91]   See the aforementioned *On Holy Saturday* 20: "The Lord became condemned because of us, even though He is not accursed, but is rather a blessing and a sanctifier; He took upon Himself our condemnation and was crucified, died, and was buried because of us."
[92]   *Exact Exposition* 3.25; 4.18.
[93]   *On the Dormition* 1.10, where St. Damascene said: "The Lord did not refuse to undergo death, because He died in body, and with His death He destroyed death, and with corruptibility grants us incorruptibility, and He makes His own death a spring of resurrection" for us.
[94]   *Exact Exposition* 4.18.
[95]   *Exact Exposition* 3.18.

tyrant and so be freed from corruption."[96] In this way the sinless Christ the Lord, incarnate through the Most Holy Virgin Mary, took upon Himself as the *Savior* of man even those "blameless passions" of our fallen human nature, the "passions" which Adam did not have prior to the ancestral sin. This is the meaning of Christ's "humbling humility,"[97] "exalted abasement," diminishment, and self-emptying (κένωσις).[98] This is why, according to Damascene, the Most Holy Theotokos "gave birth to the *salvation* of the world"[99]—Christ the *Savior*—by becoming a *place* or *workshop* in which was fulfilled this salvific taking and receiving of Adam's human nature upon Himself by the divine Savior and Redeemer. "The sheep who gave birth to the Lamb of God, Who takes away the sin of the world—she, the *workshop* of our salvation, is the one who surpasses the angelic powers—she is the handmaid and Mother of God."[100]

This explains why we, the Orthodox, deny and reject the Roman dogma of the "immaculate conception" of the Most Holy Theotokos, which in effect excludes her from mankind's inheritability of the primordial sin, which in turn undermines, as we have seen, the reality and the *salvific effects* of the Incarnation of Christ the Savior. Besides all that has been said so far, the problem of the repose of the Theotokos remains unresolved in the Western "Mariological" doctrine. If the Most Holy Theotokos was not liable to the inheritance of the ancestral sin, then the question arises as to how and why she died—"since death came into the world through sin" (cf. Rom. 5:12), and the Lord Jesus Christ died, even though He was sinless, even though "He was not subject to death," but "took upon Himself death on our behalf," willingly, for the love of us men, as our Savior and Redeemer, as St. Damascene said.[101] Up to now, Roman Catholic "Mariology" has not provided an answer

---

[96] *Exact Exposition* 3.12. See also *On the Dormition* 3.2: The supra-essential God "descended into the virginal womb, was conceived, took flesh, and through His suffering died voluntarily, and with the earthly body He gains incorruption (immortality) through what is corrupted."

[97] *On the Nativity of the Theotokos* 3.

[98] *On the Dormition* 2.7; cf. Philippians 2:6–10.

[99] *On the Dormition* 1.9.

[100] *On the Dormition* 3.5.

[101] *Exact Exposition* 3.27.

to this question—nor can there be one, since the dogma of the "immaculate conception" prevents and excludes that answer.[102]

[102]   And truly, in the last Vatican dogma concerning the bodily assumption of the Theotokos into heaven (this dogma was pronounced in the bull of Pope Pius XII, "Munificentissimus Deus," on November 1, 1950; cf. the constitution "Lumen Gentium" of the Vatican II council, chapter 8.59), the question of whether or not the Theotokos died was not addressed. (Cf. M. Jugie, "La Définition du Dogme de l'Assomption: Brève analyse et commentaire de la constitution apostolique 'Munificentissimus Deus,'" *Extrait de l'Année Théologique* 2 [1951], where on p. 5 the short definition of this dogma is cited: "*Immaculatam Deiparam Virginem Mariam, expleto terrestris vitae cursu, fuisse corpore et anima ad caelestem Gloriam Assumptam.*") In this second dogma concerning the Theotokos nothing has been said about her death, since the dogma of her immaculate conception denies the possibility of her death. Walking on this path, the "infallible" Vatican is, of course, going against the whole tradition of the ancient Church, and has taken the path of Western medieval pietism. (See R. Laurentin, *Court traité*, pp. 149–150 and 182–85, for more details about the theological blind alley in which the Roman Catholic Church finds herself in her doctrine of "Mariology.")
According to the ancient tradition of the Church, most especially the tradition of the Church of Jerusalem—"the Mother of all Churches" (*On the Dormition* 2.4)—in the tradition that is also expressed by St. Damascene, the Most Holy Theotokos did indeed die, and only after her death and burial did her Son take her body to Himself (*On the Dormition* 1.10–13; 2.2–18), as we shall see from our further text. If the Roman Catholic Church were to take this fact into consideration, then only one possibility would remain: to proclaim the death of the Theotokos to be a "redeeming" death, and the Holy Virgin a "Redeemer," or "Co-Redeemer" (*Co-Redemptrix*), as some Roman Catholic theologians have already written, and which is the direction in which "Mariology" is moving. (Cf. Iakintos, Uniate bishop in Greece, *The Great Catechism I: Dogmatic Theology*, second edition [Athens, 1958], pp. 78–79. For more information see Prof. I. Kalogirou, *Mary the Ever-Virgin and Theotokos in the Orthodox Faith* [Thessalonica, 1957], p. 110 [in Greek], and also his article "Mary" in the *Encyclopedia of Religion and Ethics* [in Greek], vol. 8, pp. 673–76. Cf. also R. Laurentin, *Court traité*, pp. 67–70, 141–45, 193, where one can find an expanded bibliography about "co-redemption," i.e., about the Theotokos as "Co-Redemptrix.") Of course, the movement of Western "Mariology" in this direction means the creation of another new "dogma," which will have no other aim but to defend Papal "infallibility" and to move further away from the faith and tradition of the ancient Church.
In connection with the problem of the so-called "redemptive" implication of the Theotokos' death, we will limit ourselves here to stating St. Damascene's categorical refusal even to think about this. Damascene writes: "We do not call her a goddess, for we proclaim her death" (*On the Dormition* 2.15). From these words it is clear that "to proclaim her death" means precisely that she is not God, and so therefore she cannot be a redeemer (or "an angel or mediator, for only the Lord Himself came and saved us" [*On the Nativity of the Theotokos* 4]). On the other hand, with regard to the

For us Orthodox it is clear that the Mother of God died as a human, as "a daughter of Adam,"[103] as St. Damascene has said along with other Holy Fathers. Therefore we, as in other cases, hold to and confess our faith concerning the Theotokos as it has been handed down to us through the Holy Fathers. False Western "pietism" (about which we will say more later) in relation to the Holy Virgin Mary can never be a measure of real Orthodox faith and Christian truth. This Roman Catholic "pietism," which began in medieval times, and which produced two new Roman "dogmas" concerning the Theotokos in the nineteenth century, was proclaimed as dogma by the Vatican, but is foreign to the Christological foundation of true Theotokology, and as such it separates Roman Catholic "Mariology" from Christology and soteriology.

We will now continue St. Damascene's exposition on the holiness of the Virgin Theotokos. St. Damascene emphasizes, praises and glorifies in his dogmatic theology, in his homilies, and also in his church hymns, the holiness of her person, even though the Most Holy Virgin Mary is an inheritor of the nature of the old Adam, since her conception was under the inherited ancestral sin. This glorification of the personal holiness of the Mother of God by St. Damascene is, as always, faithful to the teachings of other Fathers. This is why many of his songs, hymns, canons, and troparia dedicated to the Most Holy Theotokos are recognized and accepted by the Orthodox Church as an expression of her faith and her knowledge, and for that reason they are frequently used in almost all of our services.

For St. Damascene, the Virgin Mary is truly Holy and Most Holy; she is "more exalted than the angelic powers,"[104] and "more honorable than the Cherubim and more glorious than the Seraphim."[105] "She is

question of the death of Christ the Savior, "To proclaim the death of the Lord"—as the Holy Apostle Paul and St. Damascene say about the Eucharistic proclamation of Christ's death (I Cor. 11:26; *Exact Exposition* 4.13)—means precisely that the Redeemer and Savior Christ is God and that His death is truly redemptive and salvific for us. This can never be said about the death of the Most Holy Theotokos. Finally, is it really necessary at all to discuss whether the death of the Most Holy Virgin is a "redeeming" or "co-redeeming" death?

103 *On the Dormition* 2.8, 15; 3.4.
104 *On the Dormition* 3.5.
105 *On the Nativity of the Theotokos* 9.

truly, after God, the holiest of all beings."[106] Like the holiness of the great prophets of God, Jeremiah and St. John the Baptist—who "in their mothers' wombs" were sanctified and filled with the Holy Spirit (cf. Jer. 1:5; Luke 1:15)—in that same way the holiness of the Most Holy Virgin Mary begins "in her mother's womb." However, her holiness is incomparably greater than the holiness of these prophets, and her holiness reaches its climax not at the time of her birth (as Roman Catholic "Mariology" would have it), but at the moment of the conception of the Only Begotten Son of God by the power of the Holy Spirit. In the course of time the holiness of the Theotokos is transfigured and becomes free of decay and immortal in her Dormition and translation[107] to heaven. If the grace of God was great among the holy prophets, who were only prophesying about Christ's Incarnation, how much greater is the grace of God in her who became the Mother of the incarnate God! Likewise, if, according to the words of the saints—"Grace-filled gifts are given according to the love that one has for God"[108]—so great was the love and the other virtues that the Most Holy Virgin possessed, and so great was her holiness, that she received great grace from God.

That the Holy Virgin was truly "worthy of the Creator"[109] (as St. Damascene says) is confirmed by the fact that among all creatures and beings throughout all the centuries she is the only one who had such great sanctity that she was chosen by God to become the Mother of the Holiest—the Mother of God the Logos—and in this way to serve the "only new mystery under the sun,"[110] that is, the mystery of the Incarnation and becoming man of God the Logos. Of course, her sanctity rests on God's entire Economy of the salvation of the human race, as we elaborated in the beginning when we saw that this preordained and pedagogical (salvific) plan consisted in successive "elections" of the most worthy (Noah, Abraham, Isaac, David)[111] throughout the whole

---

[106] *On the Dormition* 2.16.

[107] The Greek word "μετάστασις" means "presenting"—or "transfer," as it is translated in our Church Slavonic texts.

[108] St. Gregory Palamas, *Homily* 37, "On the Dormition" (PG 151:472).

[109] *On the Nativity of the Theotokos* 2.

[110] Ibid.

[111] Cf. *On Holy Saturday* 25; and also *Exact Exposition* 4.14; *On the Nativity of the Theotokos* 6; *On the Dormition* 1.3.

history of the Old Testament. Besides all this, in St. Damascene's work there is an especially clear emphasis on the personal sanctity of the Most Holy Virgin, which we shall discuss more fully below.

We have seen up to now that for St. Damascene the Virgin Mary is a "daughter of Adam" in her human nature, that is, she is by nature identical with all the descendants of the ancient forefather Adam. However, concerning her free will, her personal actions and her personal virtues, St. Damascene contrasts her to the ancestors Adam and Eve, and demonstrates her personal achievement and attainment of holiness.[112] St. Damascene shows—and this is very important—that the heredity of the ancestral sin in the Holy Virgin was deadened and inoperative (inactive), because her free will and all the powers and energies of her soul and body were "consecrated to her God and Lord,"[113] and therefore she had no personal sins. Because of her personal sanctity, the Most Holy Virgin Mary was "chosen from generations of old"[114] and was born "from the noble and royal root of David,"[115] from "the root of Jesse,"[116] from whose vine descended her holy and righteous parents. The holiness of her Old Testament "ancestors and holy forebears" was concentrated and channeled through successive "elections" and purifications of their "seed"[117] down to her faithful and righteous par-

---

[112] *On the Nativity of the Theotokos* 8; *On the Dormition* 2.2–3.

[113] St. Symeon the Theologian writes that the descendants of Adam "willingly and not by force submitted to the tyranny of the devil, as is clearly demonstrated by those who pleased God both before and at the time of the law, who gave their will to God their Lord, and not to the devil" (*Ethical Discourse* 10, in *Sources Chrétiennes* 129, p. 262). Testifying to the possibility of holiness in the Old Testament is the entire chapter 11 of the Epistle to the Hebrews. See also on this subject the excellent article by V. Lossky, "Panagia," in his book *The Image and Likeness of God* (Crestwood, N.Y.: St. Vladimir's Seminary Press, 1974), pp. 199–202.

[114] *On the Dormition* 1.3; 3.5.

[115] *On the Nativity of the Theotokos* 6.

[116] *On the Nativity of the Theotokos* 3.

[117] St. Gregory Palamas speaks very discerningly and profoundly on the "pre-election" of the descendants of Adam and the ancestors of the Theotokos, and on their "purification," in his homily "On the Sunday of the Forefathers." "The Holy Spirit prepared her (the Virgin's) coming into life in advance, from the beginning choosing and cleansing her lineage. He elected the worthy and excluded the unworthy.... For, even the Holy Virgin is by descent of the body and seed of Adam, and Christ is from her in body, yet in many ways that seed was from the beginning puri-

ents. God had prepared the Holy Virgin to gather and synthesize within herself, and even to multiply, all the sanctity of the Old Covenant. Her righteous and God-pleasing parents[118] gave birth to her in chastity and restraint (for they were "God-loving" and not "pleasure-loving"),[119] so that St. Damascene calls the "seed" of Joachim "the most irreproachable seed."[120]

St. Damascene and the Holy Fathers seriously take into consideration the fact of the birth of the Holy Virgin from her elderly and chaste and righteous parents. St. Damascene emphasizes the great holiness and grace bestowed by God upon Joachim and Anna,[121] and also describes how Saints Joachim and Anna "by supplication and through the promise of God bore the Mother of God."[122] Furthermore, the same Holy Father speaks of how the Holy Virgin, even from childhood, "was brought to and given over to the Temple of God,"[123] and how her life was lived in God's Temple,[124] and how she received grace from God there for her holy and virtuous life. Her holy and God-pleasing conduct and her holy and sinless life on the one hand, and God's abundant grace on the other, were so great and so overshadowed humanity, that St. Damascene correctly says that "one such as her has never before existed, and will never again exist"[125] on earth. She is a gift given to our present life, a greater and choicer gift than all the rest of God's gifts.[126]

fied by the election of the Holy Spirit in the best way possible through the generations" (*Homily* 57 [Athens: S. Oikonomou, 1861], pp. 213–16). On the subject of the election of the parents of the Most Holy Theotokos, St. Palamas says: "This is why, instead of parents who had many children, childless parents were chosen, so that from those who were very virtuous could be born the most virtuous Virgin, and from those who were very chaste the Most Pure; and so that chastity, combined with prayer and spiritual exploits, might bear its fruit—to be the parent of Virginity [that is, of the Holy Virgin]" (*Homily* 42, pp. 10–11).

[118] *On the Nativity of the Theotokos* 5.
[119] Cf. II Timothy 3:4.
[120] *On the Nativity of the Theotokos* 2.
[121] *On the Nativity of the Theotokos* 6.
[122] *Exact Exposition* 4.14.
[123] *On the Dormition* 1.7; *Exact Exposition* 4.14.
[124] *On the Dormition* 1.5.
[125] *On the Dormition* 1.6.
[126] *On the Dormition* 1.5.

In order to better understand the question of the personal sanctity of the Most Holy Virgin Mary, let us again more closely examine some characteristic aspects of this question.

Looking from the perspective of St. Luke's Gospel at the Holy Virgin Mary—the second Eve—who lived not in Paradise as did the first Eve, but in this world which "lies in sin," St. Damascene calls her "a lily which grew among thorns; ... a rose from the Jewish thorn,"[127] who was found worthy of hearing the Lord's greeting from the mouth of the Archangel: "Rejoice, O thou who art full of grace, the Lord is with thee," and: "Be not afraid, Mary, for thou hast found favor with God" (Luke 1:28, 30). Explaining these latter words of the Archangel Gabriel to the Holy Virgin, Damascene says: "Truly, *you have found grace, who are worthy of grace.* You have found grace, who labored in the vineyard of grace and who yearned for the riches born of grace. You have found the sea of grace, who kept whole and undefiled the boat of a twofold virginity—for you kept your soul virgin no less than your body, due to which the virginity of your body was also guarded."[128] These characteristic words of the saint most closely and justly express that relationship which exists between the grace of God and human free will—in this instance, the free will of the Holy Theotokos.

The grace of God is undoubtedly a gift of God, but it is given to those who possess in themselves and manifest voluntary fervor, attentiveness, and purity. For man, in the words of St. Damascene, "due to the fact that he was created rational and free, received the power to unite unceasingly with God through his own free and good will" ("even though we do not all do that which has been given to our nature," he adds).[129] God for His part, St. Damascene says in another place, "gives of His powers (energies) to all according to their capabilities and receptiveness, that is, in accordance with the physical and moral purity" of each of us,[130] so that "to each who chooses good, God cooperates (συνεργεῖ—synergizes) in attaining that good."[131] These latter words of

---

[127] *On the Nativity of the Theotokos* 6.
[128] *On the Dormition* 1.8.
[129] *Exact Exposition* 4.13; 3.14.
[130] *Exact Exposition* 1.13.
[131] *On the Divine Images* 3.33 (PG 94:1352).

St. Damascene again reveal and show to us the indispensability of this principle of the cooperation or synergy of God and man ("theanthropic synergy"), a principle which is crucial in the relationship between God and man, and particularly in the history of the divine Economy of salvation of mankind, which in this regard is important in relation to the Most Holy Theotokos. In this cooperation or "synergy," God for His part gives His grace, or, better to say, He gives Himself, and man for his part gives his free will, or, more precisely, his entire self (cf. Col. 2:9–10; I Cor. 15:10). If, according to this principle, God's grace is given to man for his efforts and labor and love towards God,[132] then by analogy we can imagine and picture "the attentiveness (struggle) and life" of the God-bearing Virgin Mary in the Holy Temple of God,[133] when she was made worthy there of such great blessedness.

St. Damascene justifiably says that her life of struggle (*podvig*) in the temple of God was "better and purer than any other,"[134] including among the "others" even the heavenly angels.[135] For, although in a weak human body, the Holy Virgin, through her "twofold virginity"[136] (which the angels do not have, since they are bodiless by nature) demonstrated holiness greater than the holiness of the Cherubim and Seraphim.[137] That is why her supra-angelic holiness is inextricably connected with her most pure and undefiled virginity, or, more precisely, with her *Ever-Virginity*, her eternal virginity.[138]

In the temple of God, in the Holy of holies, the God-loving Virgin Mary, as "the sacred dove, the pure and innocent soul who was also purified by the Holy Spirit,[139] being at the same time "a virgin and a

[132] "Who, after all, loved God more than the Holy Virgin whom we glorify? Who was more beloved of God than her?"—fittingly and with reason asks St. Gregory Palamas (*Homily* 53, "On the Entrance of the Theotokos into the Temple," op. cit., p. 177).

[133] *On the Dormition* 1.7.

[134] *On the Dormition* 1.7; 2.16.

[135] *On the Dormition* 1.8.

[136] In the words of St. John Chrysostom: "Virginity consists precisely in purity of both body and soul" (*On Virginity* 6, PG 48:537).

[137] *On the Nativity of the Theotokos* 9.

[138] *On the Nativity of the Theotokos* 5–6.

[139] *On the Dormition* 2.2. St. Andrew of Crete says that in the Temple of God, "the protector of the Holy Virgin was the Holy Spirit, until she was made known to Israel" (*Oration* 1, "On the Nativity of the Theotokos," PG 97:820).

lover of virginity,"[140] lives out a perfect life woven from the twofold virginity—virginity of the soul and virginity of the body. The Most Pure Lady[141] "was never touched by earthly passions, but was rather brought up in heavenly thoughts."[142] Because she was "the holiest young Lady, protected from the flaming arrows of the evil demon,"[143] and because of her great love for virginity (for which she is also called "the virginity-loving Virgin"),[144] her life was so changed and transformed into a better and divine life—obviously with the help of the grace of the Holy Spirit[145]—that St. Damascene says of her that "she so desired and loved virginity, that it completely filled her like a most pure fire,"[146] and consequently she became "the abode of the divine fire,"[147] like unto a "holy statue sculpted by the Holy Spirit."[148] Her personal virtues and the grace of the Holy Spirit[149] so adorned the Most Holy Virgin Mary that she, "clothed in the most beautiful splendor of the virtues and adorned by the grace of the Spirit,"[150] became "the splendor of human nature ... which gladdened her Creator, God."[151] Because of all this the Most Pure Virgin became "worthy of God"[152] and as such was chosen "to be the Bride and Mother of God."[153]

St. Damascene describes in detail the holy conduct, way of life, and virtues of the Virgin Mary in the Temple of the Lord[154] and in general all of her "unreserved" and "irrevocable" aspiration towards God, her total obedience to God and her love for God, as well as God's love for

---

[140]   *On the Dormition* 2.19.
[141]   *On the Dormition* 2.2.
[142]   Ibid.
[143]   *On the Nativity of the Theotokos* 7.
[144]   *On the Dormition* 3.5.
[145]   *Exact Exposition* 4.14.
[146]   *On the Dormition* 2.2.
[147]   Ibid.
[148]   *On the Dormition* 3.5.
[149]   Cf. *On the Nativity of the Theotokos* 9: "waves of the gracious gifts of the Spirit."
[150]   Ibid.
[151]   *On the Nativity of the Theotokos* 7 and 9.
[152]   *On the Nativity of the Theotokos* 7.
[153]   Ibid.
[154]   Especially in *On the Nativity of the Theotokos* 9 and 11.

her.[155] Finally, in his *Exact Exposition of the Orthodox Faith*, Damascene summarizes everything he had previously said on the personal holiness of the Virgin Mary with these words: "Planted in the House of God and increased by the Spirit like a fruitful olive tree, she became the home of every virtue, turning her mind away from every earthly and carnal desire, and thereby keeping chaste her soul as well as her body, as was meet for her who was to receive God into her bosom; for as He is holy, He finds rest among the holy. Thus, therefore, she strove after holiness, and was declared a holy and wonderful temple fit for the Most High God."[156] Such was the holiness of the Most Holy Virgin in her life before the Annunciation.

But no matter how great was the holiness, glory, virtue, and grace of the Most Holy Virgin Mary before God's Annunciation to her through the Archangel, nevertheless the pinnacle of her glory, "the beginning, middle, and end" of her treasures beyond understanding,[157] is certainly God's Announcement to her that the Son of God was to take flesh and become incarnate of her. This means that the greatest glory of the Virgin Mary is the fact of the birth from her of the God-man, the Lord Christ. Or, in the words of St. Damascene, the greatest glory of the Holy Virgin in her entire life is "the seedless conception (of the incarnate Word of God in her by the Holy Spirit),[158] and the divine indwelling (of the Hypostasis of the Son of God in her),[159] and the virgin birth (from her of Emmanuel, the divine Infant, the God-man Jesus)."[160] For, again in the words of Damascene, all "the glory of the Theotokos is within her, and this is the Fruit of her womb,"[161] the Son born of her—Christ.

And truly, after the Virgin Mary's stay in the Lord's temple, once the priests surrendered her to the righteous and all-wise Joseph as the

---

[155] Cf. *On the Nativity of the Theotokos* 9: "She unreservedly yearned for God, until the beloved drew the Lover near." Cf. also *On the Nativity of the Theotokos* 7: "the Virgin beloved of God."

[156] *Exact Exposition* 4.14.

[157] *On the Dormition* 1.12.

[158] *On the Nativity of the Theotokos* 3.

[159] *On the Nativity of the Theotokos* 6.

[160] *On the Nativity of the Theotokos* 4.

[161] *On the Nativity of the Theotokos* 9.

protector of her virginity,[162] with the coming of the "fullness of time" she received from the Archangel Gabriel the good news from the Holy Trinity, "Whom she served."[163] At that moment the Virgin was vouchsafed the inconceivable and ungraspable man-loving descent of God, Who made her His abode, and through her took place the Incarnation of the Second Person of the Divine Holy Trinity—the Only Begotten Son of God—Whom she met and accepted within herself with infinite obedience and humility,[164] thereby correcting by her obedience the disobedience of her foremother Eve, and becoming in this manner the true Theotokos, the true Birthgiver of God.

However, the entire mystery of the Most Holy Theotokos, as handed down and taught by the Holy Apostles and Holy Fathers, can be summed up as the "mystery of Christ," and its explanation is based on this. The only rule that is valid here is the answer that St. Proclus of Constantinople gave to a Jew. Namely, to the Jew's question, "What are you telling me, that a woman was able to give birth to God?" St. Proclus of Constantinople replied, "I am not telling you that a woman was able to give birth to God, but I am saying that God was able, through the Incarnation, to be born of a woman, for to Him all is possible."[165] Actually, St. Damascene gives the same answer when he says, "This happened because God willed it; for when God desires something, all is possible, while nothing is possible when He does not want it." From these answers of the Holy Fathers it is evident that God's omnipotence,

---

[162] *On the Dormition* 1.7; *Exact Exposition* 4.14.

[163] *On the Dormition* 3.5; 1.8.

[164] *Exact Exposition* 3.2; *On the Dormition* 1.8 and 2.3; Luke 1:38, 48. If the Holy Fathers characterize patience as "divinely created humility," then that characteristic is, first of all, applied to the Most Holy Theotokos, for with her obedience and humility she "made God the Son of man, and man the son of God" (St. Gregory Palamas, *Homily* 53.40, op. cit., p. 188). (Cf. St. Nicholas Cabasilas, *Homily on the Annunciation* 10 [P. Nellas, p. 158].) The humility of the Most Holy Theotokos and her obedience to God forever resolved the problem and tragedy of human freedom, and through that humility and obedience human freedom manifested itself and showed that it is "according to the image and likeness" of the freedom of God. This is how Fr. Justin Popovich speaks about this, following St. Maximus and St. Damascene (*Exact Exposition* 3.14) and other Fathers. Cf. V. Lossky, *The Mystical Theology of the Eastern Church* (Crestwood, N.Y.: St. Vladimir's Seminary Press, 1976), p. 140.

[165] *Homily* 2, "On the Incarnation of the Lord" (PG 65:697).

of which they speak of here, coincides with His man-loving feelings and immeasurable humility.[166] For it is only as God's humility that we can understand the following mysteries: How is it that the Word of God "condescends without moving from one place to another ... and appears on earth,"[167] and descends to the uplifting *kenosis*? How did the Supra-essential One supra-essentially take on human essence in a woman's womb? How did He as God become man without abandoning His divine essence in the Godhead, and even become a communicant in our body and blood? How did the One Who fills all and Who is above all abide in such a small and narrow place? How did the physical and corruptible body of the Blessed Virgin receive within it the overwhelming flame of the Godhead and remain unhurt and unblemished?[168] How was the Theotokos, even before the birth (of Christ), a Virgin, and an Ever-Virgin?[169] All of these and similar questions—or, even better, all of these divine-human mysteries—are inexplicable by the human mind and ineffable to the human tongue. In the words of Basil of Seleucia: "All of this was a mystery, and up to this time has remained a mystery, and will never cease being a mystery."[170] All of this happened "as the One God knows," and "man should not question the nature of unquestionable and unapproachable things."[171]

Because of this divine and incomprehensible mystery of the Incarnation of God the Word through the Most Holy Virgin, she is the true Theotokos and is rightly so called. St. John Damascene writes: "If from her a Child was born, Who is God, how then is she who gave birth to Him not the Theotokos?"[172] The Virgin Mary is truly the Theotokos because she "did not give birth to a simple man but to the true God;

---

[166] Cf. *On the Nativity of the Theotokos* 2: "The ineffable and humbling Incarnation." The Mystery of Christ is precisely called humbling and a *kenosis* (Phil. 2:6–8). The following phrase of St. Damascene is typical here: "The Incarnation is not an act of nature but the way of God's Economic humility" (*Against the Jacobites* 59, PG 94:1464).

[167] *On the Nativity of the Theotokos* 3.

[168] *On the Dormition* 2.7.

[169] *On the Nativity of the Theotokos* 5.

[170] *Homily* 39, "On the Annunciation" (PG 85:445).

[171] *Dialogue against the Iconoclasts*, ascribed to St. Damascene (PG 96:1356A).

[172] *On the Nativity of the Theotokos* 4.

and not simply to God, but to God incarnate."[173] She gave birth "not to a deified man, but to God Who became man."[174] In other words, the Theotokos gave birth not simply to some God-bearing or deified man, but to God Himself, the Logos, the Only Begotten Son of God, Who "took on flesh by the good will of the Father, supernaturally, without change (to His nature), and not from a natural union, but from the Holy Spirit and the Virgin Mary."[175] "For the Theotokos, in some supernatural manner, was the means for the fashioning of the Fashioner of all things and of the becoming man of the God and Creator of all, Who deified the nature that He assumed, while the Hypostatic (Personal) union preserved those things (the divine and human natures) that were united, just as they were."[176] That is, the ineffable union of the divine and human natures of Christ the God-man preserves both natures unchanged and unchangeable. The above-quoted words of St. Damascene mean that the eternal Hypostasis (Person) of God the Logos, consubstantial with the Father in Divinity, took upon Himself in the womb of the Virgin Mary our humanity, that is, our full human nature, and so Christ became one in essence with the Virgin Mother and with us men, uniting in a most profound manner both natures (divine and human) in one Hypostasis, and in one Person, without even the slightest change or mingling, and without the loss of the essential qualities of either of these natures.[177] Hence Christ is simultaneously both God and man, but still true and perfect God and true and perfect man, the one and unique Christ the God-man. In this hypostatic union with the Divinity in Christ, human nature (taken from the Holy Virgin) is exalted and elevated to deification, and for this reason as well is the Holy Virgin called the Theotokos, "not only because of the divine nature of the Logos, but because of the deification of man."[178] For in the womb of the Virgin Theotokos, human nature, through hypostatic union with Di-

---

[173] *Exact Exposition* 3.12; *On the Dormition* 1.3, 4.
[174] *Exact Exposition* 3.2.
[175] *On the Nativity of the Theotokos* 3.
[176] *Exact Exposition* 3.12.
[177] *On the Dormition* 1.1; *Exact Exposition* 3.3, 6. Cf. *Against the Jacobites* 52 (PG 94:1461).
[178] *Exact Exposition* 3.12. In her "God became man, and man became God" (*On the Dormition* 2.16).

vinity, is elevated "to deification, to its assumption of the Word, and to the utmost heights," and "is said to be deified and to have become equal to God in the Word."[179]

The Most Holy Theotokos is also the Christotokos, for she gave birth to Christ,[180] say the Holy Fathers (what is more, it is possible to call her Christotokos [Birthgiver of Christ], Kyriotokos [Birthgiver of the Lord], and Sotirotokos [Birthgiver of the Savior], as well as Theotokos),[181] but since the word "Christotokos" was abused by the "godless and accursed heretic Nestorius"—since he used "Christotokos" instead of "Theotokos"—for this reason we do not call the Mother of God our Savior "Christotokos," but by the more elevated and correct name: Theotokos, that is, she who gave birth to the incarnate God. For the name "Christ" means "the anointed one," and therefore the name "Christotokos" can also be applied to other mothers of prophets and emperors (that is, "the anointed ones" of God), while only the Most Holy Theotokos Mary is truly Theotokos.[182] This is why the renowned Christological theologian of the East, Leontius of Byzantium, rightfully seals the Tradition of the Holy Fathers regarding that name of the Mother of God with the following words: "Theotokos is the most personal and most apt name for the Holy and Most Pure and ever-glorious Virgin."[183]

From the mystery of the divine Incarnation we know that before the birth of Christ, during His birth, and also after His birth the Most Holy Virgin remained ever-virgin, an eternal Maiden—in the words of St. Damascene, "ever-virgin in mind and soul and body."[184] Her eternal virginity means that she, at the hour of her seedless conception of the Son of God through the power of the Holy Spirit, knew neither husband[185] nor marriage.[186] Likewise, at the time of the birth of Christ, "He Who was

---

[179] *Exact Exposition* 4.18; *On the Dormition* 2.2.
[180] St. John Damascene, *Against the Nestorian Heresy* 24 (PG 95:224). Cf. St. Cyril of Alexandria (PG 76:265): "For if she is Christotokos, then she is surely also the Theotokos; but if she is not the Theotokos, then she is not the Christotokos either."
[181] *Homily on the Nativity of Christ*, ascribed to St. Athanasius the Great (PG 28:965).
[182] *Against the Nestorian Heresy* 24 (PG 95:224), and *Exact Exposition* 3.12.
[183] *Against the Nestorians* 4.47 (PG 86a:1708).
[184] *On the Nativity of the Theotokos* 5.
[185] *On the Nativity of the Theotokos* 6.
[186] *On the Dormition* 1.14.

born preserved her virginity intact, only passing through her and keeping her closed";[187] and "Opening the womb, He did not violate the keys of her virginity."[188] In the words of St. Damascene, "Every maiden loses her virginity in giving birth; but she, who was a virgin before giving birth, remained so during her labors and even after them."[189] This superhuman and salvific miracle occurred because the birth of the God-man Christ from the Holy Virgin was "fitting (to human nature) and beyond (human nature)." It was both salvific and supernatural at the same time.

It was "for our sake," says St. Damascene, "because it was for our salvation. It was like unto us in that He was a man born of a woman after a full period of pregnancy. It was above us because it was not by seed, but by the Holy Spirit and the Holy Virgin Mary, transcending the laws of conception,"[190] and because of the "painless labor" of the Virgin.[191] It is clear that the possibility of giving birth in this way was bestowed upon the Holy Virgin by the Divine Life-giving Spirit, "Who purified her and gave her the power to receive and give birth to the Word of God," [192] Christ. Furthermore, the same possibility and capability were given to the Most Holy Theotokos by her Only Begotten Son, "Who with His birth set free the beginning of our nature and sanctified her virginal womb."[193]

---

[187] *Exact Exposition* 4.14.

[188] *On the Dormition* 1.9.

[189] *On the Dormition* 2.2.

[190] *Exact Exposition* 3.7.

[191] *On the Dormition* 2.13. Cf. the Dogmatikon in the seventh tone, the work of St. Damascene: "Thou, O Theotokos, hast shown thyself to be a mother supernaturally, and thou didst remain virgin in a manner past recounting and understanding; and no tongue can describe the wonder of thy birthgiving. For as the conception [of Christ in thee] is all-glorious, O Most Pure One, so is the manner of thy birthgiving beyond comprehension. For where God so willeth, the order of nature is overruled."

[192] *Exact Exposition* 3.2.

[193] The prayer at the blessing of water at Baptism. In his oration *On the Incarnation of the Word*, St. Athanasius the Great said: "This is why when the Virgin gave birth to Him, He (the Logos) did not suffer, nor was He defiled by being in a body. On the contrary, He had a sanctified body as well" (ch. 17, PG 25b:125C). These words of St. Athanasius mean that the Lord Jesus Christ sanctified the body which He took upon Himself as He did the body of the Theotokos, from whom He took His body. This shows that the birth of the Lord from the Holy Virgin had a soteriological character and meaning for His Mother. Cf. also St. Athanasius, *Against the Arians* 3.61 (PG 26:277).

From the remaining writings of St. Damascene about the life of the Most Holy Theotokos after Christ's birth, we see that she "remained Virgin throughout her whole life," "not having any physical relations with any man (up to her death)."[194] She spent the years of Christ's life together with Him, and at the hour of His Crucifixion and Death on the Cross she "experienced the pain and suffering that she had escaped during His birth, when her maternal pain and anguish brought about trembling and tearing in her womb."[195] Later, after Christ's Resurrection from the tomb, the Most Holy Theotokos with joy "preached about Him as God Who died in the body," and Who also resurrected from the dead and conquered death. At the end, after the Ascension of her Son Christ to heaven, the Theotokos, until her Dormition and translation to heaven, lived among the faithful in the Church of Jerusalem, "in the divine and renowned city of David, in Sion," as St. Damascene said: "Sion, the Mother of all Churches throughout the whole world, was the dwelling place of the Mother of God."[196]

The Most Holy Dormition and miraculous translation of the Mother of God is confessed and preached by St. Damascene following "the ancient and true tradition" of the Church of Jerusalem.[197] In his homilies he aptly describes many miraculous events that took place on the day of the Dormition of the Mother of God (as the reader can see on reading his homilies, especially the *Second Homily on the Dormition*). We will not spend much time listing all the events and details related to the miracles, but will instead consider the question of the death of the Most Holy Theotokos, the burial of her most pure body, and her translation to heaven.

According to St. Damascene, it is indubitable that the Most Holy Theotokos died as a human. Even though she is "the spring of life," as St. Damascene says, "it is through death that she is brought to life" in

---

[194]   *Exact Exposition* 4.28.

[195]   *Exact Exposition* 4.14; *On the Dormition* 2.14. St. Philaret, Metropolitan of Moscow writes: "The depth of her suffering did not bring about a storm or foundering, because the depth of her suffering was always submerged in the immeasurable depth of her patience, tranquility, faith, hope, and total devotion to God" (*Sermons and Homilies*, 1844, vol. 1, p. 442 [in Russian]).

[196]   *On the Dormition* 2.4.

[197]   *On the Dormition* 2.4, 18.

heaven.[198] Furthermore, "She who with the birth (of Christ) overcame the limits of our nature is now under the law of that nature, and her most pure body is subject to death."[199] To remind ourselves of our previous citations: the Most Holy Virgin, as a "daughter of the old Adam," at the time of her death "was subject to the ancestral liability,"[200] and "her holy soul was naturally separated from her immaculate body, which was committed to burial as custom required."[201] Regarding the "burial" of the body of the Most Holy Theotokos, St. Damascene says: "That which was formed of earth had to be returned to the earth"; and there in the earth she shed "corruptibility and perishability,"[202] and put on "incorruptibility," that is, she was transformed into a luminous and spiritual body of immortality.[203]

However, in addition to all St. Damascene says about the natural death of the Most Holy Theotokos, he confesses and says, along with St. Andrew of Crete,[204] that the death of the Theotokos was at the same time "above us," i.e., above nature, supernatural. This miracle of her death

---

[198] *On the Dormition* 1.10.

[199] Ibid.

[200] *On the Dormition* 2.2. In all manuscripts the Greek text in this place is: "τὰς πατρικὰς εὐθύνας ὑπέρχεται." In Migne (PG 96:725C) there is a mistake, whether deliberate or accidental we do not know: instead of the verb "ὑπέρχεται" (undergo, submit oneself, surrender), there is another, unusual verb, "ὑπερέρχεται" (overcome), which obviously changes the meaning of the text (it should be noted that this second verb could be used to argue for the teaching of the "immaculate conception"). The same mistake in the Greek text is repeated in P. Voulet's corrected edition (*Sources Chrétiennes* 80, p. 130), even though in his introduction he states that he consulted some old Greek manuscripts, previously unknown to the publisher. The fact is that in the nine oldest Greek manuscripts (which we used for our Athenian edition) the verb ὑπέρχεται (to go under) is used. This is also necessitated by the text, the context of this Homily, and the entire Theotokology of St. Damascene.

[201] *On the Dormition* 1.10.

[202] *On the Dormition* 1.10; 3.3.

[203] Ibid.; cf. *Exact Exposition* 4.27.

[204] Cf. St. Andrew of Crete's *Homily* 12, "On the Dormition" (PG 97:1053): "If, according to the Holy Scriptures, there is no one that lives and does not see death, then clearly the Most Holy Virgin whom we glorify is both human and above human, since she has fulfilled that law of nature together with us, although not in the same way with us, but rather above us." Earlier we mentioned that St. Damascene and St. Andrew of Crete follow one and the same Jerusalem tradition.

took place because "the infinitely great Goodness of the thearchic weakness (θεαρχικῆς ἀσθένειας)"[205] of her Son Christ "renewed the natures"[206] and "made all things new" (Rev. 21:5)—in other words, He refashioned all things into a new way of existence and life. Of course, it is paradoxical and even apparently contradictory to speak about "thearchic weakness" (because God's "weakness" or "powerlessness" means the same thing as "thearchic omnipotence"). But, this "weakness" of God is what saved the world and man.

God's "weakness" is only an apophatic term by which the Holy Fathers name Christ's salvific kenosis (self-emptying) on our behalf, i.e., Christ's humiliation and humbling for us, His condescending Incarnation for our salvation, His salvific suffering for our sake and His Life-giving Death for us—which, being the death of the God-man, is at the same time because of us and above us. It is precisely thanks to His "thearchic weakness" that Christ destroyed the reign of death and corruption through His Resurrection, and has already clothed mortal human nature in immortality and incorruptibility. "I, who am mortal, have now become immortal, and have stripped off my garment of skin; for I have taken off corruption, and put on the robe of divinity."[207]

All His saints, and above all Christ's "Life-giving Mother,"[208] as living members of the eternally living Christ, are proofs of the fact of man's immortalization after Christ's Death and Resurrection. After all, how would it be possible, after Christ's Resurrection, to say that His saints are "dead," when their Leader and their Origin—Christ the God-man—is alive and Life-giving? This is why St. Damascene rightly says that their

---

[205] *On the Dormition* 2.18. This antinomical and apophatic expression St. Damascene takes from Dionysius the Areopagite (*On the Divine Names* 3.2, PG 3:681–84). Read an excellent explanation of this term in St. Maximus' interpretations (PG 4:236–37). This passage from the Areopagite is also cited by St. Andrew of Crete in his homily "On the Dormition" (PG 97:1061–68). Here again the aforementioned publishers [of St. Damascene's *On the Dormition* 2; see PG 96:752A] have changed the Greek text (there does exist one manuscript with the same text), i.e. instead of the word "ἀσθένειας" (weakness, powerlessness), they put the word "εὐσθένειας" (good-strength). It seems that they did this having no understanding of the apophatic and dynamic meaning of the aforementioned term of the Holy Fathers. See our interpretation in the Athenian edition.

[206] The term belongs to St. Gregory the Theologian (PG 36:348).

[207] *On the Dormition* 2.2.

[208] *On the Dormition* 1.5.

death is no longer death, but rather "a splendid translation which grants them habitation with God."[209] Since this victory over death is given "to all God-bearing servants of God—and we believe that it is granted to them all"[210]—how could it not have been given to God's Mother in even greater measure?[211] The death of "the Life-giving Mother" of our Lord surpasses the idea of "death" to such an extent that her death is no longer called death, but rather "falling asleep" (Dormition), "presentation before God," "translation to God," or "habitation with God."[212] Even if we term the death of the Mother of God as "death," then it is more, as St. Damascene says, "a life-bearing death,"[213]—a death which brings life, a death which is actually "the beginning of a new existence" and new life,[214] an eternal existence and eternal life. As to the question of why God has granted His saints and His own Mother translation and passing into eternal life through death, St. Damascene replies that such are God's rightful "judgments" and "decisions."[215]

However, it is clear and obvious that death no longer has any power over the Theotokos (having power neither over her nor in her), as the divinely inspired St. Damascene says in his *Second Homily on the Dormition:* "Today the Treasury of life and the Abyss of grace is covered by life-creating death, and she who gave birth to the Conqueror of death boldly approaches death, if it is fitting to call her all-sanctifying and life-bearing translation to another life 'death.'" For can she, who gave birth to the Son—the true Life—be susceptible to the power of death?[216] How, asks St. Damascene, can death swallow her who is the Mother of Hypostatic Life—her "who is filled with the energy of the Holy Spirit ... and who gave birth to the Father's Goodness: the Hypostasis of God the Logos, Who fills all things with Himself? How could the realm of hell receive her into itself? How could corruption dare to assault that

---

[209] *On the Dormition* 1.10.

[210] Ibid.

[211] This is especially true since there is "a limitless difference between God's servants and His Mother" (ibid.).

[212] *On the Dormition* 1.10; 3.1.

[213] *On the Dormition* 2.2.

[214] *On the Dormition* 3.4.

[215] Cf. *On the Dormition* 2.2: "and she follows the decisions of her Son."

[216] Ibid.

body, once filled with Life? Of course, all this is foreign to her God-bearing soul and body. Death saw her and was afraid. For he had assaulted her Son, but had learned from that defeat and grown wise from the experience."[217]

From all that has been said thus far, it is obvious that the question of "the life-bearing death" of the Most Pure Theotokos bears an antinomy, a paradoxical mystery, an "Adamochristological" mystery. At the same time it is clear that this theanthropic antinomy should not be rejected and simply resolved by human wit and inventions, nor should we try to solve it in appearance with a pietistic interpretation, as the Roman Catholic Church attempts to do with its new Vatican "dogmas" about the "immaculate conception" and "assumption of the Holy Virgin" (without the event of her bodily death). Here, as everywhere else, we need to hold to the faith of the Holy Apostles and Holy Fathers and the ancient Tradition of the Church of Christ. And this faith and Tradition, as we have seen, consists in this: that the Most Holy Theotokos, as the daughter of the old fallen Adam, has died a real human death, but that she, as the Mother of the New Adam—Christ the God-man—overcomes the limits of common death, and through death crosses (first with her soul and then with her body, as we shall see further on) to the eternal, immortal (incorruptible) life with her Son and God. Death for her was not something unworthy or inglorious, and this is why no false glory is necessary for her (like, for example, the false "immaculate conception" from her parents or "assumption" to heaven without going through death, as taught by the pseudo-pietistic "Mariology").

The Most Holy Theotokos has her immortal glory and eternal blessedness which, in the words of St. Damascene, consists in "the seedless conception and divine dwelling and incorruptible birth" of God's Only Begotten Son—Christ the Savior, the Second Person of the Holy and Life-giving Trinity. The glory, honor and blessedness of the Theotokos cannot be compared to any other glory, virtue, grace, or energy,

---

[217] *On the Dormition* 2.3. This is why St. Damascene applies to the Most Holy Theotokos these words of Scripture that are related to Christ: "Thy soul did not enter hell, nor did thy body undergo corruption (cf. Acts 2:31; Ps. 15:10). Your soul was not left in the earth, nor was your most pure and immaculate body; rather, the Queen and Ruler and Mistress and Mother of God and true Theotokos was translated to the heavenly royal palace" (*On the Dormition* 1.12).

be they divine or human: "For she, the Theotokos, was not only a vessel of God's energy, but truly a vessel of the Hypostasis of the Son of God, i.e., God Himself."[218] This is why her death is not something unworthy of her, something that would supposedly diminish her glory; for her Son had already taken that road of death,[219] and as God and Savior has "conquered death by His death," and "as the forerunner of all of us He has entered into the inmost place behind the curtain," that is, the divine and heavenly "Holies of holies."[220]

Because of all this, after His Death and Resurrection, the Holy Virgin's Son and Savior Christ came at the time of her falling asleep (Dormition)[221] and, as a Son "serving His Most Holy and Divine Mother, He took into His royal hands her holy soul"[222] and, accompanied by all the angels and saints, lifted her up, not only to heaven, but "to His Heavenly and Royal Throne,"[223] within the Heavenly Holy of holies.[224] At the holy burial of "the Life-giving and God-receiving body"[225] of the Mother of God,[226] Christ the new Solomon assembled all His heavenly angelic armies and saints and all His apostles of the New Testament with all the faithful in Jerusalem,[227] and He filially, but divinely and invisibly, participated in the burial of the body of His Holy and God-bearing Mother as it was "laid in the all-glorious and all-miraculous tomb." Only three days later her incorrupt body[228] was taken from this same tomb to the Heavenly Kingdom—to the heavenly, eternal and immortal mansions of her Only Begotten and loving Son and God, the Lord Christ.[229] In this manner St. Damascene tells us this much about the Dormition and Translation to heaven of the Most Holy Theotokos.

---

[218] *On the Nativity of the Theotokos* 6.
[219] *On the Dormition* 3.1.
[220] *On the Dormition* 2.12; cf. Hebrews 6:19–20.
[221] *On the Dormition* 2.10.
[222] *On the Dormition* 1.5.
[223] *On the Dormition* 1.11.
[224] *On the Dormition* 2.12.
[225] *On the Dormition* 1.12.
[226] *On the Dormition* 3.4.
[227] *On the Dormition* 2.12.
[228] *On the Dormition* 1.10.
[229] *On the Dormition* 2.14; 3.2, 4.

We could say much more and cite much more from the Orthodox Theotokology of St. John Damascene, from his theology about the Most Holy Theotokos, having in mind that the richness of the God-given theology and (theanthropology) of the Holy Fathers is inexhaustible, but we plan to limit ourselves to what has been said thus far without further expanding this presentation.

We will limit ourselves to one simple note—that it is possible to speak more about the place that the Holy Theotokos has in the heavenly "Church of the firstborn" (Heb. 12:23),[230] about her intercession for the Church here on earth,[231] and generally about the role of the Holy Mother of God in the entire heavenly-earthly Church, which is the Body of her Son—of Christ the God-man, from Whom His Mother is inseparable and indivisible ("for there is no distance between Mother and Son,"[232] as St. Damascene has said). Further, it would be possible to speak about how the Most Holy Theotokos is "the Benefactress of the whole of human nature" and the entire creation of God,[233] and, in addition, about how in heaven the entire creation bows down to her as "to the Queen and Ruler and Empress and Mother of God and true Theotokos."[234]

Finally, let us just say how much more could be said about her, the Mother of our Lord, from our everyday and eternally flowing life and experience of the Orthodox Church! Truly, in the words of the Mother of God, "Henceforth all generations shall call me blessed." The fact that needs to be acknowledged and confirmed is that the honor, praise, glory, and grace of the Most Holy Theotokos in the Orthodox Catholic Church of Christ throughout the centuries never ceases and is inexhaustible. In the words of St. Damascene, "The honor that is given to her passes and ascends to her Son, Who was born of her."[235]

Along with all this, we can mention in passing that much more could have been cited from the services of our Holy Orthodox Church,

---

[230] *On the Dormition* 3.2.
[231] *On the Dormition* 2.8, 16.
[232] *On the Dormition* 3.5.
[233] *On the Nativity of the Theotokos* 1; *On the Dormition* 1.2; 2.11, 16.
[234] *On the Dormition* 1.12; 2.14.
[235] *Exact Exposition* 4.16; *On the Dormition* 1.14.

in which there are many songs and hymns to the Most Holy Mother of God written by the hand and pen of St. Damascene.[236]

The correct, Orthodox faith (right glorification) and correct, pious esteem with which the Holy Orthodox Church honors the Most Holy Mother of God always has as its center and primary aim the fundamental Christian *great Mystery of godliness* (I Tim. 3:15–16)—the great Mystery of the Incarnation of Christ the Savior from the Virgin Theotokos. Therefore, the Mystery of the Most Holy Theotokos converges upon the "Mystery of Christ"—that salvific divine-human Mystery, "the newest of all new things, the only new thing under the sun."[237]

[236] We will cite only one example from the hymns of St. Damascene to the Most Holy Theotokos, so as to show the richness of these hymns dedicated to the Mother of God. It is the well-known Theotokion from the Octoechos (and from the Liturgy of St. Basil the Great), tone 8:

"In thee rejoiceth, O thou who art full of grace, all creation,
The assembly of the angels and the race of man,
O Sanctified Temple and noetical Paradise,
O Praise of Virgins!
Of thee God was incarnate and became a child,
Even our God, Who is before the ages,
For He made of thy body a throne,
And thy womb did He form more spacious than the heavens.
In thee rejoiceth, O thou who art full of grace, all creation.
Glory to thee!"

[237] *Exact Exposition* 3.1; *On the Nativity of the Theotokos* 2; *On the Dormition* 1.9.

235

Most Holy Theotokos,
icon by St. John Damascene, 8th–13th century, Hilandar Monastery

14
Socialism and the Ecclesial Community[1]

A commentary on a text of Dostoyevsky unknown in Greece,
and thoughts on an interview with K. Zouraris

In this article I wish to comment on an extraordinarily interesting text by F. M. Dostoyevsky, entitled *Winter Notes on Summer Impressions,* which, as far as I can determine, has not been translated in Greece. In so doing, I shall take the opportunity provided by an interview with K. Zouraris, published in Vol. 6 of *Synaxi* under the title "The Real Nature of Authority," and use it as a reference point, for I have found many things in it to have a certain similarity to Dostoyevsky's text, even in the absence of any direct allusion.

Winter Notes on Summer Impressions was written at the end of 1862. It is a rather curious work with strange chapters and headings. Toward the end, in the author's familiar style between literature and reflection, Dostoyevsky formulates certain important truths about the problem of human society, as he had observed it in Europe, and some further thoughts on the subject of socialism, including the Christian socialism that was being talked about at the time.

Dostoyevsky was acquainted with the Christian socialist movements—for example, of Fourier, Saint-Simon, Proudhon, Georges Sand—which offered a utopian dream for a solution to the problem: the "Arcadias." His interest in them was occasioned by the French Revolution, which had coined the slogan, a slogan still more or less in use today to signal a solution to social problems and as an expression of socialism: "Liberty, Equality, Fraternity." Dostoyevsky analyzes this slogan in his book, wishing to show what fraternity—brotherhood among men—actually is, as well as liberty and the equality of all. Zou-

[1] *Synaxi*, vol. 9 (Winter 1984), pp. 29–33.

raris refers often to these, and here we might mention something that could prove useful to him. If he had based himself on Dostoyevsky, he would have seen that the problem is not solved simply by making everyone equal, by achieving a social equality, for equality has deeper roots, as does freedom. Nevertheless, there are many more occasions in Zouraris' text where—in his capacity as a sociopolitical analyst—he displays a thorough understanding of St. Nicholas Cabasilas. If, here and there, he appropriates certain views to himself, this is understandable; and he does Cabasilas no injustice. Cabasilas is not, of course, limited to the use made of him here, but such use is perfectly permissible; so why should he not be seen in this light? If this arouses fear or confusion in some people, those who in my opinion are least to blame are Cabasilas and Zouraris.

In any case, Dostoyevsky, after his experience of the West, proves, or rather shows, that brotherhood, equality and freedom do not lead anywhere in and of themselves, because there is no brotherhood, or equality, or freedom in the absence of certain far more fundamental preconditions. This is why Dostoyevsky reminds us of the other possible outcome of the slogan: Brotherhood, Equality, Freedom, or Death. Either you become brothers, equal and free, or death will follow. But this shows up the mandatory nature of the slogan: you will become brothers whether you want to or not. This is why N. A. Berdyaev correctly pointed out that all socialist movements speak about comrades and not about brothers. If comrades do not acknowledge a common father, they cannot become brothers.

Dostoyevsky, in his *Winter Notes on Summer Impressions,* forcefully demonstrates the unworkability of the slogan of the French Revolution, in the absence of certain preconditions. The most fundamental precondition is love, freely given by a free person, love as an opening-up and a sacrifice, not as something compulsory: the selfless love of a brother who freely sacrifices himself for others, without the others demanding his love, and who accepts the sacrifice of others without demanding it, thus bringing about an increase of love, sacrifice, and jubilation from within. This is what Dostoyevsky writes:

The socialist bases himself on the great idea of Liberty, Equality and Fraternity, and tries to make it reality. We can of course say that liberty is understood as liberty for all, and that whatever you do is done with regard to the bounds of the law. Again, equality is equality before the law. But the great problem is fraternity. This is the most difficult. To this day it is a stumbling block for the West. Western man interprets brotherhood as the motivating force of all mankind. But he does not possess it. In spite of this, Western man, the socialist, decides to create brotherhood at any price. The question that remains is whether or not brotherhood can be made. For in the West, particularly in France, the element of individuality is highly evolved: the individual, the private person, the protection of the rights of the individual, the ego. There the individual has great value. But this is also the problem: how can brotherhood be created when each person is highly defensive of his own ego? What is needed is a movement in reverse: for the individual, the ego, to sacrifice himself for the sake of brotherhood. But Western man does not know about such things.

I believe that only the voluntary sacrifice of ourselves, totally conscious and not forced on us by anyone, for the benefit of all, out of love, constitutes the highest point of development of the personality, the development of its greatest possibilities; and this means the greatest measure of control over ourselves. It constitutes the most impressive evidence of our freedom, the fact that we can sacrifice it for others. And I consider this to be the highest point of development of the personality. The best use that you can make of your personal freedom is to offer it to others.

But how can this be accomplished?

Each and every person, without any inner compulsion, without any self-serving calculation, will say to himself before society: We are strong when we are united. Take all of me, take whatever you want from me, do not think of me, do not think that the laws will affect me, I sacrifice all my rights, I beg of you to make use of me as you wish, for my greatest happiness is to sacrifice everything for you and for this not to be harmful to you. I will sacrifice myself to the point of total depersonalization, in order for brotherhood to blossom and abide. And the brotherhood will respond: No, you offer us too much. We have no right to take what you give us, even if you say that it makes you happy. Happiness for us is when our hearts yearn for your happiness. Take everything from us. We want to take care of your happiness so you can be completely free. We want you to be self-determined and not afraid of any enemy or any natural power or other force. We are all near you, we guarantee your security, because we are your brothers; we will live together and that will make us strong. And we want you to be complete and strong. When, therefore, such a relationship exists between people, when we "love one another," everything else will come of its own accord.

In the light of these extracts, I think it worthwhile to turn again to the interview with Zouraris, which as we saw has an obvious connection with Dostoyevsky. For the latter, as is well known, love for man is not possible without love for God. Dostoyevsky has experience of the fact that love for one's neighbor will become, almost inevitably, hatred for one's neighbor unless it is nurtured by love for God, and more specifically, by love for the Incarnate God, the God-man, as Cabasilas envisaged Him—and as Zouraris himself, to his credit, appreciates. For this reason I would say that the communion of men, the communion of love that is emphasized in the second part of Zouraris' interview, is not simply a democracy or a society of equality, but rather a Christocracy, which means the identification of Christ with all of us, as Cabasilas says and Zouraris quite rightly stresses, and also the identification of all and each of us with Christ.

It is well known that the faith of the Church holds that with the Sacrament of Baptism we all become God's anointed. Because He became what we are, we become what He is. The Church brings forth anointed Christians, and thus there is a multiplication of the one Christ into many and an identification of the many with the One. All who are baptized in Christ are one. The identifying of the Master with the servants in order for the servants to become masters—that is, to become sons of God, precisely because the Son of God identified Himself with the sons of men—is a truth expressed in the writings of Dostoyevsky. This, for Dostoyevsky, is the essence of love. We are not speaking of a humanistic, individualistic type of love. Dostoyevsky shows the futility of this altruistic, merely human love in *The Raw Youth,* in which the youth's stepfather has a dream where he realizes that a burgeoning love for mankind is ultimately just a way of filling a void. Zouraris says the same thing in speaking about the loneliness that contains within itself all the tragedy of mankind.

It is striking, too, that Zouraris acknowledges that authority cannot exist. Every authority, he says, is evil. And there cannot be a real community if a community of love does not exist. Thus, he rejects the State for something else. Without stating it clearly, and perhaps without even intending to, Zouraris points unavoidably to the Church. Dostoyevsky does the same thing in *Winter Notes on Summer Impressions*, as in many of his other writings. I would add, however, that Dostoyevsky attaches great importance to something which Zouraris perhaps does not emphasize enough: the fact that love is a free personal act, not merely a social one. Love is a precondition of communion, but at the same time the communion of love cultivates and nurtures love. Dostoyevsky's roots, I would say, go deeper than those of Zouraris; however, Zouraris is to be commended for approaching such subjects and saying honestly that, as a sociopolitical analyst, he sees an inseparable logical connection between these two realities, that is, the relationship of society with God and of society with itself. It is honorable of him to speak only in his capacity as a sociopolitical analyst, and to leave untouched the theological and spiritual understanding of Cabasilas. Like Dostoyevsky in his text, Zouraris probably does not want to make any kind of personal statement in the sense of an open declaration; instead, he confirms the actual experiences of living people. And let us not forget that Dostoyevsky came from an authoritarian society: the most burdensome aspect of his experience in the prison camp in Siberia was not the hardships of the prisoners but the enforced way of life. It was this that led him to realize that there can be no truly organized society unless it arises out of free personal sacrifice, out of personal love. Freely given love creates a free response, and this is what constitutes a free society. A real society can never be enforced. A society cannot force its citizens to love each other, because love is an act of offering that does not expect something in return. That love is given in return simply witnesses to its true nature.

Christian love, divine love, the love of the Holy Trinity—we finally come to it—constitutes, insofar as it is possible to speak of it, the substance of the Heavenly City, of the polity of the Heavenly Kingdom, which is an image of the love of the Holy Trinity and of the communion of the Holy Trinity. Herein lie the profound implications of Dostoyevsky's writings. But, as I believe was said by Pentzikis, however great Dostoyevsky may be, he does not attain the stature of the great

Fathers of Byzantium, and about this I am in complete agreement. But it is significant that in our century with all its anxieties, Dostoyevsky comes very close to the Orthodox patristic viewpoint and provides an authentic Orthodox witness. It is also a fact that Zouraris comes very close to Dostoyevsky. One could find a whole range of similarities, expressed almost in the same words, in this brief interview. I have noted many likenesses between them in his text. And I say this because Dostoyevsky was a great Orthodox Christian. In speaking about Christian socialism and Russian socialism, he meant the Church of Christ. His observation, "For us socialism is the Church, the Church is our social agenda," was an astonishing thing to say. He meant, of course, the Orthodox Church, not the church administration that Peter the Great attempted to set up according to the Western model. Dostoyevsky's criticism of the influence exercised by Peter the Great during the two previous centuries is well known, as is his insistence that we should return to true Orthodoxy, which for him was to be found in the *Startsi* (Elders), in worship, in the Liturgy, and in the Canon of St. Andrew of Crete (a canon of repentance), because, as he said, in it was contained the whole aim and purpose of Orthodoxy (an extraordinary thing to say about such an ascetic liturgical text). He understood that the fulfillment of Orthodoxy, in all its dimensions—including the social and, if you will, the political (in the Pauline sense of "our city is in heaven")—lies in the great miracle and mystery of Christ. He was acquainted with the patristic tradition regarding the great mystery of Christ and understood that this is a key for the interpretation of everything; that whereas the mystery itself cannot be interpreted, it can interpret everything else.

Dostoyevsky's testimony is thus highly significant for us, but we must not overlook Zouraris', which is, I believe, a sincere testimony about an objective realization. He studies Cabasilas, makes certain discoveries, and testifies to them. It is up to him, of course, what use he will make personally of these discoveries. The teachings of the Fathers are not compulsory. Truth cannot be imposed, as love cannot be imposed; it is offered, that is all, to people of good faith who are able to see it. I believe that *Synaxi* did well to include a text such as this one by Zouraris. Well-intentioned people will see it as a positive contribution. They will see that for this man—and I don't want to flatter him, for he is well enough known—a door has opened through which he can enter. Let us not be so narrow as to close any doors and prevent people from entering from different directions into the great entity that is called the Orthodox Church, and that has many dimensions.

I believe that Byzantium did indeed possess the dimensions described by Zouraris, and that Cabasilas is an authentic Byzantine, as Zouraris rightly says. Moreover, we should keep in mind that studies exist today—sometimes from unexpected quarters such as Soviet Byzantinology—which reveal the social dimensions of Byzantium, and Byzantium itself in all its grandeur. This does not mean, of course, that Byzantium did not have weaknesses; rather, it means that Byzantium had the inspiration of patristic and evangelical principles. Let us not forget that the Bible is a social book *par excellence,* a book about the communion of God with His people. The Church is the people of God, a communion. And the polity of the Church is brotherhood: "your brotherhood in the world" (I Peter 5:9). Christ is the firstborn of many brethren. As St. John Chrysostom says, the Church is the family of the Only Begotten Son of God, that is, of a God with many children, with many sons and daughters of God. If someone sees this only in political terms, if he is so naive as to identify it with worldly government and authority, that is his problem. But we must not conceal these aspects of Byzantium, of patristic teaching, of the Gospel, of the Orthodox Church. We have a duty to study them as well, to proclaim them and imitate them. From this point of view the testimony of Dostoyevsky is valuable, and the attempt of Zouraris is praiseworthy.

Pentecost,
icon in Hilandar Monastery.

15
The Mystery of Touch:
Holy Relics in Serbia—A True Physical Love[1]

An interview

Q.: Are there many relics in Serbia?

A.: Starting from the eighth century, when our people were baptized, many pious nobles and also monks tried to gather up holy relics. So, for instance, King Dragutin brought to Serbia a relic of St. Achilleios, in whose honor Dragutin built a large monastery which became an episcopal seat, and indeed a whole city was named after the saint. Again, fragments of the relics of the Holy Apostle Luke were translated to Smederevo, relics of St. Gregory the Theologian were taken to Bosnia, etc., and in our own days pieces of the relics of St. Nectarios of Aegina. We also have the relics of many Serbian saints, such as St. Basil of Ostrog; St. Peter of Montenegro; St. Stephen the First-Crowned, the King of Serbia who later became a monk under the name of Symeon; the Great Martyr Lazar of Kosovo; St. Uros; and above all the relics of St. Sava, first archbishop of Serbia and founder of the monastery of Hilandar, and of his father St. Symeon, whose relics produce myrrh; as well as relics of many other monastic saints. It is not necessary to mention many names.

It is however important to say a few words about the hundreds of thousands of people martyred in Croatia during the Second World War by the Roman Catholic Croats. The Croat nationalists, using the Germans as cover, tortured and killed a vast number of Orthodox, 86,000 of whom were thrown into a ravine in Jadovno, a "vale of tears" as we might translate the Serbian name for the place. The ravine is fragrant to this day, and people make pilgrimages there. There was a con-

[1] *Synaxi,* vol. 4 (Fall 1982), pp. 45–49.

centration camp like Dachau, Jasenovac, with thousands of Orthodox prisoners, many of whom were slaughtered and thrown into the river Savo, which flows by the camp. To this day one finds bones, which the people venerate as holy relics. The state has put up a monument. But beyond being national heroes, these believers were Orthodox martyrs, because even when the fascist Roman Catholic Croats compelled the Orthodox to convert to Catholicism, they often slaughtered them anyway, regarding their conversion as a sham. It is a shocking and momentous fact, and that is why I referred to it. Martyrs and holy relics are not something belonging to some dim and distant past, but something very close to us, something contemporary and living. That is why the camp of Jasenovac is today a place of pilgrimage for the Serbian people.

Q.: What is the place of holy relics in the piety and faith of the Serbian people?

A.: As is apparent from what I have said already, the people hold holy relics in great honor. They regard them not only as sources of healing but also as their centers of peace and unity. The nobles used to come to the relics of St. Symeon the Myrrh-gusher to make peace. And the people regarded the place as a place of national reconciliation, not only a place of inspiration for spiritual life. The significance of the local saints has many aspects. Again, during the Turkish occupation, when Turkey was at war with Austria, the Serbs would gather around the relics of St. Sava and be strengthened as a nation. That was why the Turks took the relics and brought them to Belgrade, and in 1594 they burnt them in a wide open space (where Vracar Square is today) so that everyone could see them. As a folk poem says, Sinan Pasha thought that in this way he would destroy the saint's memory among the people, but St. Sava's dust was scattered throughout Serbia and thus the saint is celebrated as a martyr after his death.

At the relics of St. Ioanniki of Devich, a marvelous thing happened at the time of the last war. Albanian Muslims came to destroy the monastery of the saint, the church and the side chapel where his relics were. They demolished everything, but when they got to the side chapel where the body of the saint lay and went to demolish that, they froze and were unable to move. They fled in terror, and to this day no one has dared disturb the side chapel. St. Ioanniki works many miracles—he is like St. Gerasimos in Greece. Mostly it is people who are possessed that go and receive healing.

St. Basil of Ostrog is to us in Serbia what St. Nectarios is to the Greeks: an ambassador of heaven upon earth, as someone has put it. There have been very many miracles from his relics, many healings. People who are paralyzed, or blind, or sick find a cure. I will tell you about one incident that took place ten years ago and shows the people's deep piety, as well as the familiarity they have with their saints. A hapless poor man who was unable to make a living in the mountains of Montenegro wanted to go to America, but he had no money for the ticket. So he went to St. Basil and stood in front of the casket containing his body and said, "Holy Father, I'm going to take money from you to pay for the ship to America, and I'll give it back twice over." He put his hand into the case where the money was and took some ...

Q.: He stole the money?
A.: He took it with the agreement of the saint; he promised to return it. The casket is open, and the people leave whatever money they want inside. He took it from the feet of the saint.

Anyway, two years later he sent the money to his *kum,* who knew nothing about it, and wrote to him: "Go and put this money in St. Basil's casket." His *kum* went to put the money in the casket, but as soon as he put it in, half of it fell out. He put it back and it fell out again, and again. He got frightened and told the monk who was there, and the monk said to him, "Something's going on; the saint doesn't want your money." The man explained the situation, and the monk advised him to write to his *kum* in America and ask him what had happened. That was how it came out what had happened, and it seemed that the saint did not want money with interest.

In Kosovo, likewise, there are many holy relics, and the people revere them and honor them highly. The faithful come with candles, with votive offerings, with gifts. In the living family of the Church, the people regard the saints as their elder brothers.

Q.: Could one say that this popular piety is something of a custom? To what extent is there vitality of faith among the people?

A.: The main reason for this respect is undoubtedly faith, but we may certainly say that in some way faith is called forth in man by suffering, troubles and dire need. People usually have recourse to the saints when prompted by their needs. But there are also many people who go to the saint when there is some great event in their life that is not a need; they go to receive the saint's blessing. In this case they go on a pilgrimage out of faith, without some need compelling them. And many others go out of gratitude, to give thanks for some benefaction. The faith of the people has its reasons; it is not folklore or superstition. The reason is the love, the charity of the saints who respond to the needs of the people. Frequently, perhaps mostly, it is need that stirs the people. But there is a faith in the Serbian people, a real faith, bound up with actual everyday life, and even with national life and national needs.

Q.: Are there non-churchgoers who go to visit relics?
A.: Even Muslims go to venerate the holy relics.

Q.: How do you explain that?
A.: It is the compassion of the saints, who offer a hand to everyone. St. Stephen of Dechani Monastery and St. Peter of Korisha Monastery also receive Albanians, even those who are now persecuting the Orthodox Serbs. They too receive help from the saints.

Q.: Do the Communists need the holy relics?
A.: Certainly. You should know that many Communists go to monasteries and shrines where no one knows them, far from where they live, and the saints help them, because they do not make distinctions. We can say this honestly and with certainty. When the saints see someone suffering, they help him; but by the act of coming to the saint, that person has made some opening within himself. Look, in Yugoslavia Communism is at an end as a rigid ideology. It survives principally as a matter of power. Power is of interest of course to those who have it, and there are many others who become Communists in order to escape difficulties or to oil the wheels in certain ways. But among the ordinary people, Communism is a dead letter.

Q.: A different question. How do the bodies and even the clothes of saints come to have this fragrance and this power to work miracles? What does this reveal about them? How do the people understand this, and how do you explain it?

A.: The people are not interested in going into the matter and explaining it. They know that once God has touched these people, He has sanctified them. They are people of God, and consequently filled with grace. Now we theologians try in some way to explain it more intellectually, but it is quite clear. Since the Incarnation of Christ we do not have the polarization of soul and body; the human being is one. Christ sanctified all things, and the Church is the Body of Christ; it is not just the soul of Christ, it is everything.

Nikolai Velimirovich of Zhicha, a great Serbian hierarch popularly regarded as a saint,[2] has written something on the "mystery of touch." The Lord healed by touch, as the Gospels tell us. And the people want touch; as St. Paul put it, speaking on the Areopagus: "To seek after God, in the hope that they might feel after Him and find Him" (Acts 17:27). This is not superstition, nor is it in itself an element of idolatry; it is something natural to man as a psychosomatic being. Man wants to touch, he wants to hold, he wants to taste. There is the wonder of the touching of Christ's body by the Apostle Thomas. There is the mystery of the Divine Eucharist and the surety of the resurrection of our bodies, which is manifested and continued in the bodies of the saints; there is the life of the Church, a life not only of the soul, the mind or the emotions, but of the body as well—a life made whole.

Let me tell you about one incident. There was a house where the father, a pious man, had died, and the mother and son did not go to Church, and had not been going for quite a long time. But one day, they invited the priest to bless the house. When the priest had gone, the mother called her son, a lad of twenty, to come and have lunch. "Come and eat," she says, "You've been working all morning and you're tired and hungry." And the son says, "Leave me alone, Mother, the fragrance from the holy water and the incense is all I want." So you see,

---

[2] He was canonized (entered into the Calendar of Saints) by the Serbian Orthodox Church in 2003.

Orthodox life is something whole, it is not chopped up into fragments, and our brain is not adequate to understand it. Besides, I should tell you that the Serbian people have a wariness about too many "explanations" and "arguments," because they have suffered from brainwashing by ideologies and above all by the ruling atheistic ideology.

Q.: One final question, Fr. Athanasius, which preoccupies modern man. Since the body has this place in spiritual life, man should also develop himself physically in order to attain to union with God. What sort of physical development should we be striving for?

A.: The question is not clear. I could easily answer in a theological fashion, so to speak, but I don't know if that would express what my people feel. Better to answer with an example. A Serbian bishop who lives abroad came recently to a monastery in Serbia. He saw people at the All-night Vigil who were kneeling, their heads down on the ground, resting on the floor of the church, and he said, "You will never see such a thing in the West. Here, people worship God whole-heartedly and whole-bodily."

The participation and "development" of the body in Orthodoxy is expressed in asceticism, which is certainly not a rejection of the body but a development of it in unity with the soul. I remember Fr. Justin [Popovich], who when he was ill and was given medicines, and he would bless them before he took them, saying, "Blessed be those who make these medicines, because they too are serving God." We ought to preserve our health, he would advise us, if by doing so we can serve God better. We should not be enemies of the body.

Q.: Let me make the question more specific. I will pose it as it is put by many young people today, and also by quite a few theologians who are trying to satisfy the longings of modern man. Love, they say, is spiritual, but it is also a physical function. In its physical aspect, it increases and is strengthened through physical contact. And so, they say, physical contact can become, and is called to become, the basis for the development of spiritual love and union. How do you see this?

A.: Formulated in this way, the question tries to elicit the answer the questioners want. One would of course have to say a lot to explain the place of the body in Orthodox anthropology: in other words, how an Orthodox Christian lives in his psychosomatic condition. In summary I would say that this modern exaltation of physical love has one good thing about it: it declares from afar and from an opposite route the great truth that the human body must participate in whatever the soul participates in. This modern exaltation of physical love shows something—it is seeking after some fulfillment—but it has taken a wrong turn. Modern literature and films, and indeed everyday life, show clearly that looking for fulfillment exclusively or primarily through physical contact leads to an impasse. And this is only natural, since the inner structure—the complete structure—of man has been removed or is not taken into account in the view prevailing in our day. Today, as one Athonite says, the spiritual laws do not function, they have been reversed; and so man has become a body-worshipper. But the spiritual laws cannot be repealed, and people suffer because their state is contrary to nature.

In his important work *Against the Pagans* (*Contra Gentes*), St. Athanasius writes that sinful man transfers the whole weight of his existence onto his body, whereas he should be oriented toward God; with every fiber of his being, he should live with love toward God. Then everything can function properly. But since the Fall, St. Athanasius says, the struggle for the flesh has become central; man struggles to preserve it and this keeps eluding him, so that he is now in misery, locked into a vicious circle, like a snake biting its own tail. This is not the fault of love; the fault lies in that we have forgotten that love, including physical love, presupposes all sorts of other things with which it is organically entwined. Today's exaltation and isolation of physical love has deadened it. I would say it has made it into a dead idol, a warped object which has nothing to do with real love. Bergman's films and so many other love stories which appear in the cinemas—are they not a testimony to what we see all the time in everyday life, to the failures of love?

Love is something profoundly creative for humanity, so we cannot blame love for our failures; we should rather blame ourselves for having distorted love. The true structure of love is the Cross. There is the axis of love for God, and that of love for neighbor. Both axes must be present in order to have a cross. A cross means that you have to die. And death from love means resurrection and new life. Distorted love becomes a source of failures and troubles for man. True love is a piece of paradise. I have seen instances of faithful and genuine love in real Christian marriages among our people, and you look at this and rejoice, because it is a ray of light from paradise.

But so often today we see failed love, love that has reached a dead end. This is because we have lost the savor of life, the savor of truth; we live with substitutes, and whatever we take into our hands we distort. Not that there is no hope for us today—there is. And that hope is the saints who are the saints of love; the saints who, as St. Maximus says, have Love, meaning Christ, as their teacher of love; Christ Who is the God of love, God incarnate in a body.

In life the saints were filled with the Holy Spirit, and when they have accomplished their course the grace of the Holy Spirit remains inseparably present in their souls and their bodies in the tomb, in their likenesses and their holy icons, not according to essence but by grace and energy.

St. Gregory the Theologian[3]

[3] See St. John Damascene, *First Apology against Those Who Attack the Divine Images* 19.

List of Sources

The essays in the present volume have been translated from Serbian and Greek, and have been selected and arranged by the editor in consultation with the author. Some of the essays have been previously published in English; other essays appear in English for the first time in this volume.

Chapter 1: "O Gentle Light." Published in Serbian in Bishop Athanasius Yevtich, *Hristos—Alfa i Omega* (Christ—The Alpha and Omega), Vrnjacka Banja, 2004, pp. 31–46. Translated by Sister Michaela.

Chapter 2: "The Holy Fathers and the Holy Scriptures." Published in Serbian in *Svetigora*, no. 1, 1992. Translated by Sister Michaela.

Chapter 3: "Christ—the Land of the Living." Published in Serbian in Bishop Athanasius Yevtich, *Hristos—Alfa i Omega* (Christ—The Alpha and Omega), Vrnjacka Banja, 2004, pp. 243–52. Translated by Sister Anastasija.

Chapter 4: "Christ on Earth—The Land of the Living." Published in Serbian in Bishop Athanasius Yevtich, *Hristos—Alfa i Omega* (Christ—The Alpha and Omega), Vrnjacka Banja, 2004, pp. 11–30. Translated by Fr. Rastko Trbuhovich and Vladimir Maricic.

Chapter 5: "The Anthropology of Hesychasm." Published in Greek in Bishop Athanasius Yevtich, Φῶς Ἱλαρόν, Athens, 1991, pp. 23–33, and in Serbian in Bishop Athanasius Yevtich, *Zagrljaj svetova*, Srbinje, 1996, pp. 21–42. Translated from the Serbian by Jasminka Gabrie and Vladimir Maricic.

Chapter 6: "The Creation of the World and Man." Published in English in Bishop Athanasius Yevtich, *Serbian Orthodox Elementary Reading Book*, Valjevo, Serbia: Foundation "Nikolai Velimirovich and Justin Popovich," 2002. Translated from the Serbian by Peter Sherovich.

Chapter 7: "The Holy Sacrament of Baptism: Entrance into and Living in the Church." Published in Serbian in *Kalendar SPC u SAD i Kanadi 1988*, and in Bishop Athanasius Yevtich, *Traganje za Hristom* (The Search for Christ), Belgrade, 1989, pp. 40–45.

Chapter 8: "Liturgy and Spirituality." Published in English and at in Serbian, in Bishop Athanasius Yevtich, *Hristos—Alfa i Omega* (Christ—The Alpha and Omega), Vrnjacka Banja, Serbia: Brotherhood of St. Symeon the Myrrh-gusher, 2004, pp. 99–127. Translated by Vladimir Maricic.

Chapter 9: "Eschatological Dimensions of the Church." Published in English in *The Greek Orthodox Theological Review*, vol. 38, no. 14, 1993, pp. 91–103.

Chapter 10: "The Eschata in Our Daily Life." Published in English in *Living Orthodoxy in the Modern World: Orthodox Christianity and Society*, Andrew Walker and Costa Carras, eds., London: Society for Promoting Christian Knowledge, 1996, pp. 37–49. Reprint. Crestwood, N.Y.: St. Vladimir's Seminary Press, 2000.

Chapter 11: "Between the 'Nicaeans' and 'Easterners': The 'Catholic' Confession of St. Basil." Published in English in *St. Vladimir's Theological Quarterly*, vol. 24, no. 4 (1980), pp. 235–52. Translated from the Serbian by Fr. Atanasije Rakita.

Chapter 12: "Icon and Incarnation in the Holy Fathers and St. John Damascene." Published in Greek and in Serbian, in Bishop Athanasius Yevtich, *Besede Svetog Jovana Damaskina* (Homilies of St. John Damascene), Belgrade, 2003, pp. 421–39. Translated from the Serbian by Fr. Bratislav Krsic and Vladimir Maricic.

Chapter 13: "The Teaching of St. John Damascene on the Most Holy Theotokos: *Orthodox Theotokology.*" Published in Greek in Russian and in Serbian, in Bishop Athanasius Yevtich, *Besede Svetog Jovana Damaskina* (Homilies of St. John Damascene), Belgrade, 2003, pp. 377–420. Translated from the Serbian by Fr. Bratislav Krsic and Vladimir Maricic.

14: "Socialism and the Ecclesial Community." Published in Greek in *Synaxi*, vol. 9 (Winter 1984), pp. 29–33. Translated by Fr. Peter A. Chamberas, edited by Liadain Sherrard.

15: "The Mystery of Touch: Holy Relics in Serbia—A True Physical Love." Published in Greek in *Synaxi*, vol. 4 (Fall 1982), pp. 45–49. Translated by Elizabeth Theokritoff.

Index

Abraham, Forefather, 37, 47–48, 53, 61, 216

Adam, Forefather, 65, 92, 100, 113, 147, 153, 202, 204n, 205–7, 209, 212–13, 215, 217, 229, 232

Albanians, 246, 248

Andrew of Crete, St., 154, 206n, 207n, 220n, 229, 230n, 242

Aquila, 56

Arianism, 26, 159–76

Aristotle, 63n

Asia Minor, 9n

Athanasius of Sinai, St., 56n, 62–63

Athanasius the Great, St., 19, 55–57, 70n, 116–17, 162–63, 164n, 165–66, 167n, 168–71, 174, 176, 190, 192–93, 198n, 207n, 226n, 227n, 251

Athenogenes, Hieromartyr, 10

Augustine, St., 177, 207n

Barlaam of Calabria, 60, 82–83, 121–22

Basil of Ancyra, 168–69

Basil of Ostrog, St., 247

Basil of Seleucia, 224

Basil the Great, St., 9–10, 19n, 22n, 39, 63n, 70, 100, 106, 108, 110–13, 116n, 117, 122, 159–64, 166–78, 192n, 210n

Berdyaev, N. A., 238

Bogomilism, 119

Böhme, Jakob, 76

Buddha, Gautama, 76, 81, 148

Bulgakov, Fr. Sergei, 200n, 208n, 209n

Callistus of Rome, 161

Calvinism, 26–27, 30

Cappadocia, 9–10, 177

Chora Monastery, 41

Chrestou, Panagiotes, 18n, 20n, 122n, 165n

Christology, 15n, 17–22, 30–31, 35, 56–59, 75, 78–79, 114, 116, 118, 123, 134, 137, 177–93, 196–200, 204n, 209n, 211n, 215, 226, 232

Chrysippus of Jerusalem, 204n

Clement of Alexandria, St., 11n

Communism, see Marxism

Constantinople, 41, 73, 159, 168, 171, 179

Cosmas of Maiuma, St., 56–57

Croats, 245–46

Cyprian of Carthage, St., 117

Cyril of Alexandria, St., 39, 192–93, 200n, 210n, 226n

Cyril of Jerusalem, St., 110, 117, 172, 207n

Damasus, Pope, 170n

David, Psalmist, Prophet and King, 46, 70, 194, 203, 205, 216–17, 228

deification (theosis), 16, 40, 58, 60, 62n, 75, 77–84, 99, 104, 109, 121–23, 129, 139, 143, 185, 189, 193, 197, 200–201, 225–26

Diadochus of Photiki, St., 61, 103, 128, 194

Dianius of Caesarea, 163

Diocletian, Emperor, 10

Dionysius of Alexandria, St., 162, 164–65, 174

Dionysius of Rome, 162

Dionysius the Areopagite, St., 33n, 38n, 66n, 88, 132, 139,151, 230n

Dostoyevsky, Fyodor, 44–45, 76, 149, 151, 153, 237–43

Dragutin, King of Serbia, 245

Eckhart, Meister, 76

ecological problems, ecology, 15n, 42, 66–68, 93

Economy, Divine, 14, 15n, 21, 55n, 67–68, 79, 87, 99–100, 104–6, 108–10, 113–14, 120, 171, 173, 184, 189–90, 195–97, 199, 202–4, 208, 210–11n, 211, 216, 220, 224n

Eden, see Paradise

Eliade, Mircea, 92, 151

Elijah, Prophet, 38, 150

Ephraim the Syrian, St., 29, 135

Epiphanius of Cyprus, St., 169n, 206n

eschatology, 14, 18, 26–37, 45, 48–49, 55, 58, 66, 70, 76, 82, 85–86, 88, 100, 115, 121, 131–55, 184, 190–91

Evagrius of Pontus, 124

Eve, Foremother, 204n, 217, 219, 223

Ezekiel, Prophet, 38

Florovsky, Fr. Georges, 25n, 28, 69n, 164, 165n, 166n, 169n, 174, 189, 208n

Germanus of Constantinople, St., 180–83, 186

Gouillard, J., 183n, 189n

Greek thought (Hellenistic thought), ancient/classical, 11n, 13, 45, 65, 77, 88, 94, 139, 148, 160, 200

Gregory of Cyprus, St., 186

255